Biblical Interpretation in the Early Church

Biblical Interpretation in the Early Church

Michael Graves

Fortress Press
Minneapolis

BIBLICAL INTERPRETATION IN THE EARLY CHURCH

Cover image: Photographer: Will Bergkamp

Cover design: Laurie Ingram

Print ISBN: 978-1-4514-9637-6

eBook ISBN: 978-1-5064-2560-3

The paper used in this publication meets the minimum requirements of American National Standard for Information Sciences — Permanence of Paper for Printed Library Materials, ANSI Z329.48-1984.

Manufactured in the U.S.A.

This book was produced using Pressbooks.com, and PDF rendering was done by PrinceXML.

Contents

Series Foreword

In his book *The Spirit of Early Christian Thought*, Robert Louis Wilken reminds us that "Christianity is more than a set of devotional practices and a moral code: it is also a way of thinking about God, about human beings, about the world and history" (xiii). From its earliest times, Wilken notes, Christianity has been inescapably ritualistic, uncompromisingly moral, and unapologetically intellectual.

Christianity is deeply rooted in history and continues to be nourished by the past. The ground of its being and the basis of its existence are the life of a historic person, Jesus of Nazareth, whom Christians identify as God's unique, historical act of self-communication. Jesus presented himself within the context of the history of the people of Israel and the earliest disciples understood him to be the culmination of that history, ushering in a new chapter in God's ongoing engagement with the world.

The crucial period of the first few centuries of Christianity is known as the Patristic era or the time of the Church Fathers. Beginning after the books of the New Testament were written and continuing until the dawn of the Middle Ages (ca. 100–700 CE), this period encompasses a large and diverse company of thinkers and personalities. Some came from Greece and Asia

Minor, others from Palestine and Egypt, and still others from Spain, Italy, North Africa, Syria, and present-day Iraq. Some wrote in Greek, others in Latin, and others in Syriac, Coptic, Armenian, and other languages.

This is the period during which options of belief and practice were accepted or rejected. Christian teachers and thinkers forged the language to express Christian belief clearly and precisely; they oversaw the life of the Christian people in worship and communal structure, and clarified and applied the worshiping community's moral norms.

Every generation of Christians that has reconsidered the adequacy of its practice and witness and has reflected seriously on what Christians confess and teach has come to recognize the church fathers as a precious inheritance and source for instruction and illumination. After the New Testament, no body of Christian literature has laid greater claim on Christians as a whole.

The purpose of this series is to invite readers "to return to the sources," to discover firsthand the riches of the common Christian tradition and to gain a deeper understanding of the faith and practices of early Christianity. When we recognize how Christian faith and practices developed through time we also appreciate how Christianity still reflects the events, thought, and social conditions of this earlier history.

Ad Fontes: Sources of Early Christian Thought makes foundational texts accessible through modern, readable English translations and brief introductions that lay out the context of these documents. Each volume brings together the best recent scholarship on the topic and gives voice to varying points of view to illustrate the diversity of early Christian thought. Entire writings or sections of writings are provided to allow the reader to see the context and flow of the argument.

Together, these texts not only chronicle how Christian faith and practice came to adopt its basic shape, but they also summon contemporary readers to consider how the events, insights, and social conditions of the early church continue to inform Christianity in the twenty-first century.

George Kalantzis
Series Editor

Introduction

The present volume offers English translations together with explanatory notes for fifteen important early Christian writings that deal with biblical interpretation. The purpose of this collection is to provide a useful survey of early Christian interpretation of Scripture through primary sources, giving enough annotation to help contemporary readers understand what they encounter and in some cases know where to go for further discussion. The study of early Christian biblical interpretation contributes to numerous fields of interest for today, including biblical hermeneutics, church history, early Christian theology, ancient literary criticism, and modern theological interpretation of Scripture.

Because of the foundational role of the Greek tradition and the significance of Latin authors for Western church history, and in view of space limitations, I have focused almost exclusively on Greek and Latin writers. Ephrem the Syrian is included as a representative of Christianity outside the Greek and Latin world. As for the choice of these specific sources: For the earlier period before biblical commentaries became common, I selected passages that illustrate major features of Christian exegesis, such as christological typology, proofs from prophecy, appeal to the Rule of Faith, salvation-historical paradigms, and use of Scripture to refute heresy. For the later period starting with Origen, I selected passages that articulate coherent ideas about how to interpret Scripture and also treat specific biblical texts with enough detail to show how the theoretical ideas work in practice.

All of the figures chosen for this volume were influential in their own day and were widely read in subsequent centuries by at least some significant segment of the Church. Some (for example, Origen, Eusebius, Diodore, Theodore, Cassian) came under suspicion or even outright condemnation in later times, but this does not take away from the insightfulness of their ideas, the carefulness of their work, or the lasting impact they had on the history of biblical interpretation. All were self-consciously orthodox as understood within their own context, and all (except John Chrysostom) died in fellowship with the churches they served. On a certain level, the same fresh engagement with Scripture and concern for coherent methodology that led these figures to say important things about biblical interpretation also sometimes led them to engage in theological discourse that aroused controversy.

One final comment on the selection of sources: I have chosen to emphasize texts that illustrate Christian interpretation of the Old Testament. It is not that early Christian writers failed to make insightful observations while expounding the New Testament. But I decided to focus on sources that take Old Testament passages as their starting point, partly because of the rich variety of Old Testament literature, partly due to the theological significance of motifs such as creation, law, and prophecy, and especially because the Old Testament provided a special hermeneutical challenge for early Christians who were committed to interpreting the whole Bible with Christ as the focal point. And as will be seen below, in the course of their exegesis these ancient interpreters typically cite a great many passages from the New Testament.

Contexts for Biblical Interpretation in the Early Church

In order to understand what these early Christians were doing with the biblical texts they were interpreting, it is important to take into account the intertwined contexts in which they lived. The following represent some of the most important contexts for appreciating early Christian biblical interpretation:

(1) The biblical text itself. Most of these writers knew the Old Testament in Greek translation, according to some recension of the Greek Old Testament that came to be known as the "Septuagint" (based on a legend whereby the text was translated by seventy-two translators). Latin authors generally used a Latin translation of the Greek text, with Jerome being the only figure to engage significantly with the Hebrew. The biblical text of early Christians was not exactly the same as what is commonly found in modern English Bibles (which are based on the Medieval Hebrew text), and sometimes their text differs slightly from modern critical editions of the "Septuagint," which aim to reconstruct a presumed original Greek text from pre-Christian times rather than the Greek text known to the early Church. Moreover, some Christian exegetes made use of the second-century CE Greek translations of Aquila, Symmachus, and Theodotion (see the Introduction to Origen).

(2) Jewish biblical interpretation. A key figure in showing Christians how to bring the biblical text to bear on Greco-Roman culture was Philo of Alexandria. Hellenistic Jewish writers, and Philo in particular, suggested multiple ways that

biblical teachings could be combined with Greek philosophy or else used to challenge it. In addition, some early Christian writers were familiar with Jewish traditions such as are known to us through intertestamental and Rabbinic writings.

(3) Ecclesiastical traditions. The biblical interpreters presented in this volume all approached the task of exegesis as committed Christians. Most were presbyters or bishops who preached regularly and fulfilled pastoral duties in their churches. Others were actively involved in Christian apologetics. Prominent among their concerns were explicating and defending Christian doctrine, encouraging proper worship, maintaining church order and discipline, and providing spiritual edification.

(4) Greco-Roman philosophy and literary criticism. Virtually all major early Christian writers were the beneficiaries of solid classical educations. Many continued to read philosophy and study classical literature into adulthood. Conceptual categories provided by philosophy, especially Platonism and Stoicism, helped early Christians express coherent and profound doctrines through biblical texts and also helped them address exegetical problems related to the content of Scripture. The practices of ancient classical "grammarians" (= literary scholars) provided Christians with the tools to interpret Scripture at the levels of textual criticism, grammar, language, rhetoric, and style.

(5) The political and social dynamics of late antiquity. In the second and third centuries, Christian networks were expanding but still marginal to society. During the fourth and fifth centuries Christians were navigating a shift to the center of social power. Most writers featured in this book came from relatively prominent families, and as Greek or Latin speakers they belonged to the prestige culture vis-à-vis local

populations (for example, Berber or Coptic). Moreover, all of these writers were male. These factors will sometimes be relevant for understanding how they approached their task or addressed certain issues.

Aspects of these contexts will be discussed where relevant in the Introductions and notes for each main selection given below. Within the notes I refer to many parallel passages from various ancient writers. The citation of a parallel in the notes in no way implies that the main source and the parallel source were saying precisely the same thing. On the contrary, each ancient writer usually brings his own unique insight to a common tradition or observation. As much as possible I try to offer a brief explanation for how the material in the notes relates to the main source. In general, I provide information about the ancient world that illuminates some dimension of meaning, for example, clarifying what the writer meant by a certain term, showing what information he was presupposing, or highlighting what alternative view he was trying to correct. In some cases, the note locates the early Christian interpreter's comment within a historically significant stream of thought. Such information is important. Although it would be a mistake to read Gregory of Nyssa strictly through the lens of Philo, as if the two were saying precisely the same thing, it would also be unsound to ignore Gregory's thought world and read him as if he were directly addressing medieval Europe, the Reformation era, or the contemporary Church. The notes seek to locate these early biblical interpreters within their proper intellectual and cultural contexts.

Historical Overview

The historical period treated in this volume stretches from the early second century CE to the fifth century. The earliest source, the *Epistle of Barnabas,* comes from the same era that saw the composition of the latest books to become part of the New Testament canon. Included among writings of this era are homilies, letters addressing doctrine and church order, narrative accounts of apostles and martyrs, and literature related to the Gospels. Much of this primitive Christian literature is direct and practical, while some texts relate stories and aphorisms, and some possess apocalyptic elements. Explicit interpretation of Scripture is not common among these writings. The *Epistle of Barnabas* with its extended discussion of the Old Testament is a notable exception and so serves as a useful starting point for this volume. As for the chronological ending point, the Greek and Latin churches from the third to the mid-fifth century produced numerous writers who engaged in direct, original exegesis of Scripture based on detailed study of the biblical text. This "golden age" of patristic exegesis is the period of focus for this volume. By the end of the fifth century, fresh, in-depth treatments of Scripture became less common. Christians in the Byzantine world began to create exegetical compilations based on extracts of earlier exegesis, such as one finds in the commentaries of Procopius of Gaza (d. 528) and the *Catenae* literature. Therefore, this volume concludes in the fifth century with a selection from John Cassian (d. ca. 435), who anticipates the medieval four senses of Scripture (see p. 248, n. 7).

New Testament documents and related writings set forth a salvation-historical paradigm culminating in Jesus, and they offered symbolic interpretations of Israel's Scriptures to show

how Jesus was prefigured through patterns ("types") and fulfilled prophecies. In early Christian sources up to the mid-second century, scriptural texts were often employed to support these christological aims. The Church's major concerns were teaching right doctrine and pastoral oversight.

By the middle of the second century, the attention of many Christian writers turned to defending the Christian faith against outsiders (apologetics), establishing right doctrine (anti-heresy), and resolving church conflicts. Important figures for this period include Justin Martyr (d. ca. 165), Tatian (d. ca. 185), Athenagoras (d. ca. 195), Irenaeus (d. ca. 200), Clement of Alexandria (d. ca. 220), and Hippolytus (d. ca. 240) in Greek; and Tertullian (d. ca. 220), Minucius Felix (d. ca. 250), and Cyprian (d. 258) in Latin. Certain passages of Scripture figure prominently in these authors, but their writings are not exegetical in nature. Rather, they utilize Scripture in the course of addressing whatever concerns were most pressing. The memory of apostolic traditions and the structure of Christian theology were determinative for their application of Scripture. It is not clear to what extent these writers were familiar with the Bible as a whole, especially the Old Testament. At least some of them may have had knowledge only of certain books and oft-quoted passages. In chapter five below I offer an excerpt from Cyprian, *To Quirinus: Testimonies against the Jews*, which is a collection of biblical prooftexts. This work illustrates the textual format in which many early Christians encountered Scripture.

Origen of Alexandria (ca. 185–253) was the first early Christian writer to work through a wide range of biblical books systematically. Admittedly, we learn from Origen about a treatise on the Gospel of John by the "gnostic" Heracleon, and there are also select commentaries preserved on Daniel and the Song of Songs ascribed to Hippolytus. But Origen was the first to compose verse-by-verse expositions for nearly all biblical books, applying literary and philosophical methods as employed in classical commentaries. In the realm of theological interpretation, Origen took traditional Christian symbolic readings of the Old Testament and applied them more extensively throughout Scripture, thereby creating a comprehensive system of Christian biblical allegory, that is, figural readings across a coherent narrative, not just disconnected typologies. In terms of scholarship, Origen showed how insights from the study of literature, linguistics, textual criticism, and other aspects of classical philology could be used to interpret the Bible. Origen's writings exerted enormous influence on later Christian commentators, who developed his scholarly methods and also imitated aspects of his allegorical interpretation. In this volume I have included an illuminating passage on the interpretation of Scripture from Origen's *First Principles*.

In the fourth century Christianity not only obtained recognition as a legal religion but also developed into a prominent cultural and political force in the Roman Empire. This new situation allowed Christians freedom to devote more of their efforts to matters such as spiritual reflection, speculative theology, and technical biblical studies. A significant figure in the Church's transition to cultural authority was Eusebius of Caesarea (d. 339), an advisor to the emperor Constantine and student of one of Origen's disciples. Eusebius continued Origen's scholarly endeavors and made selective use of his spiritual exegesis. Many writers of the fourth century followed Origen's approach to spiritual interpretation even more closely than Eusebius did. Important biblical interpreters who borrowed extensively from Origen include Didymus of Alexandria (d. ca. 398), Hilary of Poitiers (d. 368), and Ambrose of Milan (d. 397). Origen was also influential on the three "Cappadocian Fathers": Basil of Caesarea (d. 379), Gregory of Nazianzus (d. 390), and Gregory of Nyssa (d. ca. 395). Selections are given below from Gregory of Nyssa's *Life of Moses*, which combines exegesis, theology, and spirituality in a manner that reflects the new Christian culture. The fourth century also saw the beginnings of Syriac Christian literature in the east. Most important are the Persian Aphrahat (fl. 340), who composed the first Syriac apologetic treatise, and Ephrem the Syrian (d. 373), whose numerous works include commentaries and hymns on biblical themes, such as the *Hymns on Paradise* offered below.

Not everyone in Origen's time or afterward accepted all of his ideas about Scripture and theology. Even those who appreciated aspects of Origen's thought expressed concerns about some of his conclusions. For example, Basil of Caesarea and Gregory of Nazianzus compiled a collection of favorite passages from Origen's writings on Scripture called the *Philocalia,* but Basil also criticized some allegorical interpreters who took Origen's approach too far. A stream of thinking arose in the fourth century that emphasized the "literal" (*kata lexin*) and "historical" (*historia*) sense of Scripture and denounced Origen's interpretive methodology. Early figures that contributed to this stream include Paul of Samosata, bishop of Antioch (d. 269), Lucian of Antioch (d. 312), and Eustathius of Antioch (d. ca. 337). Because of its connection to the city of Antioch this school of thought is usually called "Antiochene" exegesis. This movement was not literalistic in the sense that they denied a Christian spiritual understanding of Scripture. Rather, writers of this school emphasized the coherent discourse of the text as construed with the original audience in mind, and they focused where possible on the surface level meaning of the words. Such an interpretation served as the foundation for the spiritual sense, which they called *theōria* ("contemplation"). Prominent representatives of this movement whose exegetical writings survive include Diodore of Tarsus (d. ca. 394) and his students, Theodore of Mopsuestia (d. 428) and the renowned preacher John Chrysostom (d. 407). Selections from each of these three figures are given below.

In biblical interpretation as in theology, Greek writers laid the literary and theoretical foundations. Latin Christian writers tended to adapt and build on the ideas and methods developed by the Greeks. It is not the case, however, that Latin interpreters made no special contributions. Three Latin figures whose insights are particularly noteworthy and whose influence on the Latin Middle Ages was extensive are Jerome (d. 419), Augustine (d. 430), and John Cassian (ca. 435). Jerome combined linguistic erudition, Antiochene historical sensibilities, Origenian allegory, and Jewish traditions to create his own unique style of scholarly commentary. Augustine synthesized earlier observations on biblical interpretation and recast this material through his own fresh reading of Scripture and vision for Christian culture. John Cassian brought his own practical wisdom to bear on eastern monastic spirituality, which he rearticulated for the Latin Church. Selections from these three authors will illustrate what Latin Christian writers of the late fourth and early fifth century contributed to the Church's understanding of biblical interpretation.

Of course, many important interpreters of Scripture from this period could not be included in this volume due to limitations of space. In addition to figures not included who were already mentioned in the preceding paragraphs numerous others could be added. For example, Athanasius of

Alexandria (d. 373) made extensive use of scriptural citations in the course of his apologetic, dogmatic, and pastoral writings. Moreover, a few important biblical interpreters lived at the tail end or shortly after the historical period addressed in this volume. Of prime importance among Greek writers due to their detailed exegetical works are Cyril of Alexandria (d. 444) and Theodoret of Cyrus (d. ca. 460). Among Latin writers Cassiodorus (d. ca. 580) and Gregory the Great (d. 604) wrote biblical commentaries and other works that consolidated and transmitted the insights of earlier Latin exegetes. As for biblical interpretation in Syriac, Ephrem was the starting point for a long tradition of translators and commentators, among whom Jacob of Edessa (d. 708) deserves special mention. The present volume cannot do full justice to the rich heritage of early Christian biblical interpretation, but I hope the sources presented here can offer a reliable introduction to this interesting and important subject.

The Literal Sense of Scripture

All early Christian interpreters of Scripture operated with the understanding that biblical texts generally have a literal sense and can also convey a higher or spiritual meaning. No great intellectual effort went into recognizing that Scripture has a literal sense. In most cases, some meaning presented itself to the interpreter as the obvious one, and this was taken to be the literal meaning. Unlike today, pride of place was not given to the literal sense. Consequently, there was little motivation to establish a precise definition of "literal." Expressions used to describe this basic sense include "according to the letter," "on the surface," "the obvious meaning," "the proper sense," "what is evident from the text," and "words used for what they were invented to signify." In reality, there is no clear concept of "literal" interpretation that is shared by all early Christian exegetes, and one cannot even assume that an individual author is entirely consistent in usage. Nevertheless, many writers offer helpful discussions of the literal sense in the course of describing their ideas about the spiritual or figurative sense. The primary sources presented in this volume can only give a taste for how the literal sense was handled by these writers.

A few examples will illustrate how the idea of a "literal" sense might be handled in different ways. (1) In speaking of the "nose" of a ship, one interpreter might call this a figurative and therefore nonliteral meaning, because the word "nose" properly describes a human nose. This figurative sense could then be interpreted in a spiritual way that connects theologically with the rest of Scripture. By way of contrast, another interpreter might regard this as a literary device and therefore part of the literal sense, rejecting a further spiritual interpretation. (2) With regard to the human biblical writer, one exegete might recognize that the human writers of the Old Testament expected actual animal sacrifices and a future blessing with physical abundance (= the literal sense), in contrast to the Christian interpretation that transcends what the human writer understood by pointing to Jesus's sacrifice and the harvest of the gospel (= the spiritual sense); conversely, another exegete might suggest that the human biblical writer actually meant to teach a fully Christian spiritual meaning, taking the Old Testament as a self-conscious allegory like George Orwell's *Animal Farm*. On this latter understanding, one could say that the Old Testament text has no literal sense. (3) Regarding history, some Christian interpreters may see the literal sense of an Old Testament text as the meaning that applies to ancient Israel, whereas the higher sense is the meaning that applies to Jesus. But how does this relate to Old Testament prophecies that are taken to speak directly about the coming of Jesus? Are these literal prophecies of Jesus? Or are these examples where the prophet spoke a nonliteral meaning? (4) When Jesus in the Gospels says, "If your right eye causes you to sin, tear it out and throw it away" (Matt 5:29), what is the literal sense? Is it hyperbole? Is it figurative? On issues and questions such as these, early Christian exegetes will construe the "literal" meaning of the text in a variety of ways. Even within a single author different categories can sometimes be blurred.

The Spiritual Sense of Scripture

The early Church adopted Israel's Scriptures primarily in Greek translation as its own Scriptures (= the "Old Testament"), and from the beginning Christians applied to these scriptural texts interpretations beyond the literal level. Pauline letters contain several passages that served as models for other Christian spiritual interpreters to follow (for example, Gal 4:21–31; 1 Cor 10:1–11; 2 Cor 3:6, 15–16; Col 2:16–17). Jesus is described in the Gospels as using scriptural texts in a non-literal fashion (for example, Mark 12:24–27), and Old Testament passages are applied directly to Jesus based on exegesis that transcends the original historical sense (for example Acts 2:24–31; 4:25–28; Gal 3:16; Rom 10:6–8; Eph 4:8–11). The New Testament interpreted Old Testament realities such as "Israel," "unclean food," "land," and "Sabbath" in nonliteral ways (for example, Rom 2:29; 9:6–9; Mark 7:14–22; Rom 7:12; 14:17; Eph 6:3; Heb 4:8–11; 1 Pet 3:21). Old Testament sanctuary worship was seen as the shadow or pattern of a heavenly reality (Heb 8:5; 9:11, 24;

10:1-4). The nonliteral interpretive practices of the New Testament encouraged Christians in post-apostolic times to apply spiritual interpretation more broadly throughout the Old Testament.

Drawing on the New Testament, Jewish interpreters such as Philo of Alexandria, and philosophical commentators on classical texts, early Christians employed a variety of terms to describe the spiritual sense of Scripture. Some important terms were *tropologia* ("figuration"), *allēgoria* ("allegory"), *anagōgē* ("elevated sense"), *dianoia* ("understanding"), *hyponoia* ("deeper sense"), *intelligentia spiritalis* ("spiritual understanding"), *typos* ("pattern"), *theōria* ("contemplation"), and *sacramenta* ("mysteries"). Any given source will typically use only a few expressions to describe Scripture's higher meaning. Generally speaking, in the earliest Christian centuries these terms were used interchangeably. It was not until the latter half of the fourth century that interpreters began to make clear distinctions between specific terms. Because Antiochene interpreters distinguished *theōria* from *allēgoria* and employed the term *typos* in their theological exegesis, some modern theologians have distinguished between "typology," which takes history as its starting point, and "allegory," which does not. This may be a fair conceptual distinction to make, and Diodore of Tarsus would be pleased to see modern readers making it. Yet, in the first three centuries there are no particular exegetical distinctions associated with these terms.

The spiritual or figurative approach to interpretation that one encounters in early Christian sources does not reflect a general theory of textual indeterminacy. There is no sense that they read all texts in this manner. Rather, for early Christian readers spiritual interpretation followed naturally from the belief that God inspired the writers of Scripture. According to 2 Timothy 3:16–17, all Scripture is divinely inspired and therefore profitable for teaching, correcting, training in righteousness, and equipping for good works. For all "Scripture" (in this case the "Old Testament") to function this way for the Church, it must contain or point to distinctively Christian meanings. It was normally granted that biblical texts could be approached as ancient documents written by human writers with context-specific goals in mind. Even Origen gave a "literal" exposition of the Song of Songs to accompany his "spiritual" interpretation. But if one believes that this collection of writings constitutes "sacred Scripture" or the "word of God," such categories imply another dimension of meaning, namely, what the Spirit of Christ is teaching through the text. This teaching could arise directly from the text's human discourse, but not necessarily. According to the standard early Christian view, because the biblical text is the word of God it must be interpreted not as a merely human document but in light of its spiritual meaning.

One way for today's readers to make sense of early Christian spiritual interpretation is to recognize that these ancient readers did not limit themselves to explaining the text itself but endeavored to explain the text's subject matter. Because divine inspiration stands behind all Scripture, it was assumed that each biblical text fits into a comprehensive statement of divine truth on whatever topic or topics it touches upon. There is a dimension of constructive theology woven into the exegesis. The topic for comment is not just the text in front of them, but the reality in the external world that they believe the text points to. Thus, if Genesis 1 talks about God creating the world, and they know from elsewhere in Scripture that all things were made through the Son (John 1:3; Col 1:16), they will talk about Jesus in their discussion of Genesis, and many will scrutinize the text of Genesis to see if there are details that can be freshly explained in light of Christian revelation, since the same God who inspired Genesis also sent Jesus and the Apostles. I would not claim that early Christian interpreters always operated with this distinction between text and subject matter clearly in mind, but it is a useful distinction for helping today's readers grasp what these ancient writers were actually doing.

Allegorical interpretation was not primarily a tactic for resolving interpretive difficulties but was above all a means to find the theological unity of Scripture. The Christian Bible is the product of a historical process that created, in the midst of diversity, a host of recurring themes, images, and symbols. Through figurative interpretation the early Church was able to tie these recurring elements together into a unified theological narrative with Christ as the central figure. The driving force behind allegorical reading was didactic, not defensive. It is of course true that problem passages were often handled by appealing to symbolic interpretations. For many early Christians the fact that a problem exists at the literal level suggests a figurative mode of expression. The principle behind this approach is not unreasonable. If I heard a friend say, "I was in line at the grocery store all day yesterday," I would know that he or she was speaking figuratively precisely because the literal meaning is absurd. Many early Christians applied this interpretive principle to the divine discourse in Scripture in order to find Scripture's underlying theological unity. For ancient readers such as Origen, the Bible is like a large city filled with helpful shops, parks, and so forth at street level, but also containing some closed roads and alleys that lead nowhere. But these "stumbling blocks" are meant to remind us to look around and find the sewer hole that leads down to a golden city beneath the surface where every good exists in ideal form and all the streets interconnect in perfect harmony. Unquestionably the Bible contains what may be regarded as "problem passages," some of which were seen as problems in antiquity (for example, the wars in Joshua). Because Origen, Gregory of Nyssa, Augustine, and others often interpret such passages figuratively, they are sometimes accused of simply avoiding the problems. But I think the approach of these early Christian writers has considerable merit. First, early interpreters were honest enough to acknowledge that biblical texts at the literal level present problems. They did not attempt to deny this solely by appealing to genre or cultural background, as if these factors fully resolve the issues. For early Christian interpreters, the full theological message and unity of Scripture does not reside in the literal sense of every passage. Second, early Christians identified and evaluated problem passages on the basis of other scriptural texts and their understanding of God's character. In other words, theological categories guided their treatment of problem passages. This is preferable to a situation where one passage (for example, "show no pity," Deut 13:6-11) is labeled "difficult" and another passage (for example, "gleaning," Deut 24:17-22) is commended, without any explicit theological explanation for why one passage is a problem and the other is not. This lack of theological engagement often stems from reticence to address problems directly, which stands in contrast to Origen, Augustine, and others who recognized multiple levels of meaning in Scripture. Third, through allegorical interpretation early Christians sought to find what each biblical text teaches (cf. 2 Tim 3:16-17) in keeping with the message of Scripture as a whole. For example, wars against Canaanites represent wars against sin: to obey God is to conquer sin (Jericho, Joshua 6), and to disobey God is to be defeated by sin (Ai, Joshua 7). Often Christians today are content merely to neutralize problem passages: either to show that these passages do not suggest anything negative, or else to label them as "problematic" and therefore tacitly agree not to learn anything from them. For interpreters like Origen and Augustine, the end goal was to understand the text's symbolic teaching in a positive sense, which in many cases takes its lead from the stylized manner in which biblical books were written in the first place.

To sum up, I hope that Christian readers of this volume will look with fresh eyes on ancient spiritual interpretation and consider what it might have to teach the Church today.

Reading Early Christian Biblical Interpretation

One often encounters generalizations about how the Church Fathers interpreted the Bible, for example, that they were thoroughly Hellenized, or that they were steeped in Scripture, or that they were guided by orthodox belief, or that some were literalists and others allegorists, to name just a few. On their own, such broad descriptions are of limited value. Some generalizations of this nature are not accurate. Other generalizations are plausible, but without some firsthand knowledge of the sources to appreciate in what sense the generalization is true, even a plausible generalization can be misleading. The best way to move beyond generalities is to read as much as possible in the primary sources. This volume is intended to help in that endeavor.

Each source presented in this volume represents a contextualization of the Bible within a specific cultural setting. It is natural that all these writers interpreted Scripture in a way that reflects their cultural environments. It is also reasonable that those today who wish to learn from these sources will need to recontextualize their ideas for the contemporary world, drawing on the present state of knowledge in relevant areas and employing today's idioms. I hope this volume will facilitate historically informed critical reflection on early Christian biblical interpretation and so provide a useful resource for contemporary theology.

The sources are presented below in chronological order, so that the reader can gain a sense of the historical flow from earlier to later periods. Each source is prefaced with a short introduction that provides basic biographical information, some indication of the author's interpretive approach, and a brief orientation to the specific selection given.

PART I

Texts and Translations

1

Epistle of Barnabas

The *Epistle of Barnabas* was likely written in the first few decades of the second century CE. Its author is unknown. Many scholars have suggested Alexandria as its place of origin, but others have proposed Syria-Palestine or Asia Minor. Indeed, the *Epistle of Barnabas* reflects a variety of influences, from Alexandrian allegory to legal traditions known from rabbinic texts. Although it is presented in the form of a letter, the *Epistle of Barnabas* is really a treatise on the interpretation of the Old Testament (chs. 1–17) followed by moral exhortations (chs. 18–21). This treatise was ascribed to the apostle Barnabas by Clement of Alexandria (*Stromateis* 2.31.2; 2.35.5), was regarded as a "catholic epistle" by Origen (*Against Celsus* 1.63), and is included after Revelation in codex Sinaiticus (fourth century), but it was not ultimately recognized as part of the New Testament (see Eusebius, *Ecclesiastical History* 3.25.4, although it is a "disputed" book in 6.14.1; Jerome, *On Illustrious Men* 6).

A central purpose of the *Epistle of Barnabas* is to argue that Jews have misunderstood the sacred Scriptures (= the Old Testament), and that these Scriptures point definitively to Jesus. The sustained and abrasive polemic against Jews found in *Barnabas* suggests a context where Judaism posed a viable ideological threat to the writer's Christian audience. The *Epistle of Barnabas* offers a unique window into early Christian figural interpretation and presents many christological typologies that would become commonplace among later Christian writers. Many of the biblical quotations in *Barnabas* are inexact, not even matching the Septuagint. Some of the Old Testament citations have clearly been modified to make them more suitable as proofs of Christian teaching. The writer of the *Epistle of Barnabas* may have known many of these prooftexts from Christian homilies or lists of *testimonia*.[1] The selection offered below deals with the Day of Atonement (ch. 7), the Red Heifer (ch. 8), circumcision (ch. 9), dietary laws (ch. 10), baptism (ch. 11), and the cross (ch. 12).

Epistle of Barnabas 7–12

7

1. Understand, therefore, children of joy, that the good Lord has revealed everything to us beforehand, so that we might know whom we ought to praise when giving thanks for all things. 2. If, therefore, the Son of God, who is Lord and is destined to judge the living and the dead,[2] suffered in order that his wounds might give us life, let us believe that the Son of God could not suffer except for our sake.

3. But he also was given vinegar and gall to drink when

---

1. On Christian *testimonia* ("testimonies") literature, see chapter five on Cyprian below.
2. See 2 Tim 4:1.

he was crucified.[3] Hear how the priests of the temple have revealed something about this: when the command that "Whoever does not keep the fast shall surely die" was written,[4] the Lord commanded it because he himself was planning to offer the vessel of his spirit as a sacrifice for our sins, in order that the type established by Isaac, who was offered upon the altar,[5] might be fulfilled. 4. What, therefore, does he say in the prophet? "And let them eat from the goat that is offered at the fast for all their sins"—pay careful attention!—"and let all the priests (but only them) eat the unwashed intestines with vinegar."[6] 5. Why? "Since you are going to give me, when I am about to offer my flesh for the sins of my new people, gall with vinegar to drink, you alone must eat, while the people fast and lament in sackcloth and ashes"—this was to show that he must suffer at their hands. 6. Pay attention to what he commanded: "Take two goats, fine and well matched, and offer them, and let the priest take one for a whole burnt offering for sins."[7] 7. But what shall they do with the other one? "The other one," he says, "is cursed."[8] Notice how the type of Jesus is revealed! 8. "And all of you shall spit upon it and jab it, and tie scarlet wool around its head, and then let it be driven out into the wilderness."[9] And when these things have been done,

---

3. Matt 27:34, 48; Mark 15:23, 36; Luke 23:36; John 19:29.
4. Cf. Lev 23:29. For the Day of Atonement as a fast, see Josephus, *Jewish Antiquities* 3.240; Philo, *On the Special Laws* 1.186–88; 2.193; Justin Martyr, *Dialogue with Trypho* 40.4–5; 46.2; m. Yoma 8:1.
5. Gen 22:1–18.
6. This appears to be a creative quotation from Leviticus 16 (see Lev 16:27; cf. Lev 9:8–22; Ezek 43:18–24) adapted to serve as a Christian prooftext. The word for "goat" is not the one used in the Septuagint of Leviticus 16 (*chimaros*), but rather the one used in Heb 9:12–13, 19; 10:4 (*tragos*). For the reference to vinegar, see Ps 69:21.
7. Cf. Lev 16:7, 9. For the idea that the goats should be well matched in appearance and value, see m. Yoma 6:1.
8. Cf. Lev 16:8, 10. The goat as "cursed" may reflect the influence of Deut 21:23 and Gal 3:13.
9. This creative quotation based on Lev 16:10, 21 was adapted to fit the narrative of Jesus's crucifixion (spitting and jabbing; Matt 26:67; Mark 10:34; 14:65; Luke 18:32; 19:37). The scarlet thread attached to the scapegoat is mentioned in m. Yoma 4:2. Here, the scarlet

the man in charge of the goat leads it into the wilderness, and he removes the wool and places it upon the bush commonly called *rachia* (the buds of which we are accustomed to eat when we find them in the countryside; only the fruit of the *rachia* is sweet). 9 What is the meaning of this? Note well: "the one is for the altar, and the other is cursed," and note that the one cursed is crowned.[10] For they will see him on that day, wearing a long scarlet robe about his body, and they will say, "Is this not the one whom we once crucified, insulting and piercing and spitting on him? Surely this was the man who said then that he was the Son of God!" 10. Now how is he like that goat? The goats are well matched, fine, and almost identical, for this reason: so that when they see him coming then, they may be amazed at the similarity of the goat. Observe, therefore, the type of Jesus, who was destined to suffer. 11. And what does it mean when they place the wool in the midst of the thorns? It is a type of Jesus, set forth for the church, because whoever desires to take away the scarlet wool must suffer greatly, since the thorns are so terrible, and can only gain possession of it through affliction. Likewise, he says, "those who desire to see me and to gain my kingdom must receive me through affliction and suffering."[11]

8

1. Now what type do you think was intended when he commanded Israel that men who are utterly sinful should offer

---

thread calls to mind the christological interpretation of Rahab's scarlet thread (Josh 2:18, 21).

10. The practice of crowning the goat is not found in the biblical text and may reflect an earlier christological explanation of Leviticus 16 (see Matt 27:28–29; Mark 15:17; John 19:2, 5). For other Christian readings of the scapegoat ritual, see Justin Martyr, *Dialogue with Trypho* 40.3–5; and Tertullian, *Against Marcion* 3.7.8.

11. The source of this quotation is unknown. Cf. Acts 14:22.

a heifer, and slaughter and burn it, and that then the children should take the ashes and place them in containers, and tie the scarlet wool around a piece of wood (observe again the type of the cross and the scarlet wool) and the hyssop, and that then the children should sprinkle the people one by one, in order that they may be purified from their sins?[12] 2. Grasp how plainly he is speaking to you: the calf is Jesus; the sinful men who offer it are those who brought him to the slaughter. Then the men are no more; no more is the glory of sinners. 3. The children who sprinkle are those who preached to us the good news about the forgiveness of sins and the purification of the heart, those to whom he gave the authority to proclaim the gospel (there were twelve of them as a witness to the tribes, because there are twelve tribes of Israel). 4. And why are there three children who sprinkle? As a witness to Abraham, Isaac, and Jacob, because these men were great in God's sight. 5. And then there is the matter of the wool on the piece of wood: this signifies that the kingdom of Jesus is based on the wooden cross, and that those who hope in him will live forever. 6. But why the wool and the hyssop together? Because in his kingdom there will be dark and evil days, in which we will be saved, because the one who suffers in body is healed by means of the dark juice of the hyssop. 7. So, therefore, the things that happened in this way are clear to us but to them are quite obscure, because they did not listen to the voice of the Lord.

9

1. Furthermore, with respect to the ears he describes how he circumcised our heart. The Lord says in the prophet: "As soon

---

12. See Num 19:1–10, 17–21. Cf. Heb 9:13, 19. For the involvement of children, see m. Parah 3:2, 4. A different philosophical interpretation of the red heifer ritual is found in Philo, *On the Special Laws* 1.262–66.

as they heard, they obeyed me."[13] And again he says: "Those who are far off will hear with their ears, and they shall understand what I have done."[14] Also, "Circumcise your hearts,"[15] says the Lord. 2. And again he says: "Hear, Israel, for this is what the Lord your God says."[16] And again the spirit of the Lord prophesies: "Who is the one who desires to live forever?[17] With the ear let him hear the voice of my servant."[18] 3. And again he says: "Hear, heaven, and give ear, earth, for the Lord has spoken these things as a testimony."[19] And again he says: "Hear the word of the Lord, you rulers of this people."[20] And again he says: "Hear, children, the voice of one crying in the wilderness."[21] 4. In short, he circumcised our ears in order that when we hear the word we might believe.

But the circumcision in which they have trusted has been abolished, for he declared that circumcision was not a matter of the flesh. But they disobeyed, because an evil angel "enlightened" them. 5. He says to them: "This is what the Lord your God says" (here I find a commandment): "Do not sow among thorns, be circumcised to your Lord." And what does he say? "Circumcise your hardheartedness, and stop being stiff-necked."[22] Take this again: "Behold, says the Lord, all the nations have uncircumcised foreskins, but this people has an uncircumcised heart!"[23]

13. Ps 18:44.
14. This is a paraphrase of Isa 33:13.
15. Cf. Lev 26:41; Deut 10:16; 30:6; Jer 4:4; 9:25–26.
16. Cf. Deut 6:4; Jer 7:2–3.
17. Cf. Ps 34:12. The quotation here adds "forever" (*eis ton aiōna*), which is not in the Septuagint.
18. Isa 50:10.
19. Cf. Isa 1:2. The quotation here adds "as a testimony," which is not in the Septuagint. Cf. Mic 1:2.
20. Cf. Isa 1:10; 28:14.
21. Cf. Isa 40:3.
22. Deut 10:16; Jer 4:3–4.
23. Jer 9:25.

6. But you will say: "But surely the people were circumcised as a seal!" But every Syrian and Arab and all the idol-worshipping priests are also circumcised; does this mean that they too belong to their covenant? Why, even the Egyptians practice circumcision!

7. Learn abundantly, therefore, children of love, about everything: Abraham, who first instituted circumcision, looked forward in the spirit to Jesus when he circumcised, having received the teaching of the three letters. 8. For it says: "And Abraham circumcised ten and eight and three hundred men of his household."[24] What, then, is the knowledge that was given to him? Observe that it mentions the "ten and eight" first, and then after an interval the "three hundred." As for the "ten and eight," the *I* is ten and the *H* is eight; thus you have "Jesus." And because the cross, which is shaped like the *T*, was destined to convey grace, it mentions also the "three hundred."[25] So he reveals Jesus in the two letters, and the cross in the other one. 9. The one who placed within us the implanted gift of his covenant understands. No one has ever learned from me a more reliable word, but I know that you are worthy of it.

10

1. Now when Moses said, "You shall not eat a pig, or an eagle or a hawk or a crow, or any fish that has no scales,"[26] he received, according to the correct understanding, three precepts.

---

24. The statement in Gen 14:14 regarding the 318 in Abram's household is being combined with the circumcision account in Gen 17:23, 27.

25. In Greek, the number eighteen can be written with the letters *IH*, which *Barnabas* interprets as signifying *IHSOYS*, "Jesus." The number three hundred is written with the letter *T*, which *Barnabas* likens to the shape of the cross. On *T* as the shape of the cross, see also Tertullian, *Against Marcion* 3.22.5.

26. See Lev 11:1–47; Deut 14:3–21. On the ethical interpretation of Old Testament dietary regulations, see Mark 7:14–23; *The Letter of Aristeas* 128–71; Philo, *On the Special Laws* 4.100–121; Irenaeus, *Against Heresies* 5.8.3–4; Clement of Alexandria, *Stromateis* 2.105.1–3.

2. Furthermore, he says to them in Deuteronomy, "I will set forth as a covenant to this people my righteous requirements."[27] Therefore it is not God's commandment that they should not eat; rather Moses spoke spiritually.[28] 3. Accordingly he mentioned the pig for this reason: you must not associate, he means, with such people, who are like pigs. That is, when they are well off, they forget the Lord, but when they are in need, they acknowledge the Lord, just as the pig ignores its owner when it is feeding, but when it is hungry it starts to squeal and falls silent only after being fed again. 4. "Neither shall you eat the eagle or the hawk or the kite or the crow." You must not, he means, associate with or even resemble such people, who do not know how to provide food for themselves by labor and sweat but lawlessly plunder other people's property; indeed, though they walk about with the appearance of innocence, they are carefully watching and looking around for someone to rob in their greed, just as these birds alone do not provide food for themselves but sit idle and look for ways to eat the flesh of others—they are nothing more than pests in their wickedness. 5. "And you shall not eat," he says, "sea eel or octopus or cuttlefish." You must not, he means, even resemble such people, who are utterly wicked and are already condemned to death, just as these fish alone are cursed and swim in the depths, not swimming about like the rest but living in the mud beneath the depths. 6. Furthermore, "You shall not eat the hare." Why? Do not become, he means, one who corrupts children, or even resemble such people, because the hare grows another opening every year, and thus

27. E.g., Deut 4:1, 5–6, 40. The fact that these are called "righteous requirements" (LXX: dikaiōmata) is taken to indicate that all of the rules apply directly to the moral sphere of human ethical behavior.
28. Barnabas is atypical of early Christian writers in asserting that Moses never intended these dietary rules to be followed literally, although it was common among early Christians to believe that these rules were meant to convey symbolic meaning.

has as many orifices as it is years old. 7. Again, "Neither shall you eat the hyena." Do not become, he means, an adulterer or a seducer, or even resemble such people. Why? Because this animal changes its nature from year to year, and becomes male one time and female another. 8. But he also hated the weasel, and with good reason. Do not become, he means, like those men who, we hear, with immoral intent do things with the mouth that are forbidden, and do not associate with those immoral women who do things with the mouth that are forbidden. For this animal conceives through its mouth.

9. Concerning food, then, Moses received three precepts to this effect and spoke in a spiritual sense, but because of their fleshly desires the people accepted them as though they referred to actual food. 10. David received knowledge of the same three precepts and says similarly: "Blessed is the man who has not followed the counsel of ungodly men" (like the fish that swim about in darkness in the depths), "and has not taken the path of sinners" (like those who pretend to fear the Lord but sin like pigs), "and has not sat in the seat of pestilent men" (like the birds that sit waiting for plunder).[29] You now have the full story concerning food.

11. Again Moses says: "Eat anything that has a divided hoof and chews the cud." Why does he say this? Because when it receives food it knows the one who is feeding it and, relying upon that person, appears to rejoice. He spoke well with regard to the commandment. What, then, does he mean? Associate with those who fear the Lord, with those who meditate in their heart on the special significance of the word that they have received, with those who proclaim and obey the Lord's righteous requirements, with those who know that meditation is a labor of joy and who ruminate on the word of the Lord.

29. Ps 1:1.

But why does he mention "the divided hoof"? Because the righteous person not only lives in this world but also looks forward to the holy age to come. Observe what a wise lawgiver Moses was! 12. But how could those people grasp or understand these things? But we, however, having rightly understood the commandments, explain them as the Lord intended. He circumcised our ears and hearts for this very purpose, so that we might understand these things.

11

1. But let us inquire whether the Lord took care to foreshadow the water and the cross. Now concerning the water, it is written with reference to Israel that they would never accept the baptism that brings forgiveness of sins, but would create a substitute for themselves. 2. For the prophet says: "Be astonished, heaven, and let the earth shudder greatly at this, because this people has done two evil things: they have abandoned me, the fountain of life, and they have dug for themselves a pit of death."[30] 3. "Is my holy mountain Sinai a desert rock? For you shall be as the fledglings of a bird that flutter about when they are taken away from the nest."[31] 4. And again the prophet says: "I will go before you and level mountains and shatter brass gates and break iron bars in pieces, and I will give you treasures that lie in darkness, hidden, unseen, in order that they may know that I am the Lord God."[32] 5. And: "You shall dwell in a lofty cave of solid rock."[33] And: "His water will never fail; you will see the King in glory, and your soul will meditate on the fear of the Lord."[34]

30. Cf. Jer 2:12–13.
31. Cf. Isa 16:1–2.
32. Cf. Isa 45:2–3.
33. Cf. Isa 33:16.
34. Cf. Isa 33:17–18.

6. And again in another prophet he says: "And the one who does these things will be like the tree that is planted by the streams of water, which will yield its fruit in its season and whose leaf will not wither; and whatever that person does will prosper. 7. Not so are the ungodly, not so; instead they are like the dust that the wind blows from the face of the earth. Therefore the ungodly will not stand in judgment, or sinners in the council of the righteous, because the Lord knows the way of the righteous, and the way of the ungodly will perish."[35] 8. Notice how he pointed out the water and the cross together. For this is what he means: blessed are those who, having set their hope on the cross, descended into the water, because he speaks of the reward "in its season"; "at that time," he means, "I will repay." But for now what does he say? "The leaves will not wither." By this he means that every word that comes forth from your mouth in faith and love will bring conversion and hope to many. 9. And again in a different prophet he says: "And the land of Jacob was praised more than any land."[36] This means he is glorifying the vessel of his spirit. 10. Then what does he say? "And there was a river flowing on the right hand, and beautiful trees were rising from it, and whoever eats from them will live forever."[37] 11. By this he means that while we descend into the water laden with sins and dirt, we rise up bearing fruit in our heart and with fear and hope in Jesus in our spirits. "And whoever eats from these will live forever" means this: whoever, he says, hears these things spoken and believes them will live forever.

---

35. Cf. Ps 1:3–6.
36. The source of this quotation is unknown (cf. Ezek 20:15; Zeph 3:19; 2 Baruch 61:7).
37. The source of this quotation is unknown (cf. Gen 2:10; 3:22; Ezek 47:1–12; John 6:51; Rev 22:1–2).

12

1. Similarly he once again gives an explanation about the cross in another prophet, who says: "And when shall these things be accomplished? The Lord says: 'When a tree falls over and rises again, and when blood drips from a tree.'"[38] Once again you have a reference about the cross and about the one who was destined to be crucified. 2. And again he speaks to Moses, when war was being waged against Israel by foreigners, and in order that he might remind those being attacked that they had been handed over to death because of their sins, the Spirit says to the heart of Moses that he should make a symbol of the cross and of the one who was destined to suffer because, he is saying, unless they place their hope in him, war shall be waged against them forever. Therefore Moses piled one shield upon another in the midst of the battle, and standing high above them all he stretched out his hands, and so Israel was again victorious. But whenever he lowered them, the men began to be killed.[39] 3. Why so? So that they might learn that they cannot be saved unless they place their hope in him. 4. And again in another prophet he says: "All day long I have stretched out my hands to a disobedient people who oppose my righteous way."[40] 5. Again Moses makes a symbol of Jesus—showing that he must suffer, and that the very one whom they will think they have

---

38. The source of this quotation is unknown. If it was taken from a Jewish source (cf. 4 Esdras 4:33; 5:5), it has presumably been rewritten to serve as a Christian prooftext. This quotation also occurs later in Pseudo-Gregory of Nyssa, *Testimonies against the Jews*, ch. 7 (perhaps fifth cent. CE).

39. See Exod 17:8–16. This was a standard typology among early Christian writers, e.g., *Sibylline Oracles* 8.251–54; Justin Martyr, *Dialogue with Trypho* 90.4–91.4; 97.1; 111.1; 131.4–5; Tertullian, *Against Marcion* 3.18; *Against the Jews* 10.10; Irenaeus, *Demonstration* 46; Origen, *Homily on Exodus* 11.4; Cyprian, *To Quirinus: Testimonies against the Jews* 2.21; *Exhortation to Martyrdom* 8; Ephrem the Syrian, *Explanation of Exodus* 17.2; Gregory of Nyssa, *Life of Moses* 2.148–49; and many other fourth- and fifth-century Christian writers.

40. Cf. Isa 65:2. The stretching out of the hands is taken to represent Jesus on the cross.

destroyed shall give life—in a sign given when Israel was falling. For the Lord caused all kinds of serpents to bite them, and they were perishing (since the fall happened through the serpent, with the help of Eve), in order that he might convince them that they were being handed over to death because of their transgression. 6. Indeed, even though the same Moses had commanded, "You shall not have a cast or a carved image for your God," nevertheless Moses himself made one in order to show them a symbol of Jesus. So Moses made a bronze serpent and displayed it prominently, and called the people together by a proclamation. 7. When they had gathered together they begged Moses to offer a prayer for them, so that they might be healed. But Moses said to them: "Whenever," he says, "one of you is bitten, let that person come to the serpent that is placed upon the wooden pole, and let that one hope and believe that though it is dead it can nonetheless give life, and that person shall be saved immediately."[41] And so they did. Once again you have in these things the glory of Jesus, because all things are in him and for him.

8. Again, what does Moses say to "Jesus" the son of Nun when he gave him this name, since he was a prophet, for the sole purpose that all the people might hear that the Father was revealing everything about his Son Jesus? 9. Moses said to "Jesus" the son of Nun, when he gave him this name as he sent him to spy out the land, "Take a book in your hands and write what the Lord says, that in the last days the Son of God will cut off by its roots all the house of Amalek."[42] 10. Observe again that it is Jesus, not a son of man but the Son of God, and revealed in the flesh by a symbol.

---

41. See Num 21:6–9; John 3:14–15.
42. *Barnabas* appears to be making use of a Christian homiletic retelling of Moses's commissioning of Joshua (see Exod 17:14, 16; Num 13:17; 27:18–23).

Since, however, they were going to say that the Messiah is the son of David, David himself, fearing and understanding the error of sinners, prophesied: "The Lord said to my Lord, 'Sit at my right hand until I make your enemies a footstool for your feet.'"[43] 11. And again, Isaiah says as follows: "The Lord said to the Messiah my Lord, whose right hand I held, that the nations would obey him, and I will shatter the strength of kings."[44] Observe how David calls him "Lord," and does not call him "son."

43. Ps 110:1; Matt 22:41–46; Mark 12:35–37; Luke 20:41–44.
44. Cf. Isa 45:1.

2

Justin Martyr

Justin Martyr was born of non-Jewish parents ca. 100 CE in Flavia Neapolis in Palestine. He spent considerable time in Rome, where he wrote two Christian apologies (*1-2 Apology*) ca. 146–160 CE. Shortly afterward Justin wrote his *Dialogue with Trypho*, the earliest preserved Christian apologetic work addressing Judaism. Justin was put to death under the Roman prefect Junius Rusticus ca. 163–167. Eusebius mentions other works by Justin, such as a disputation *On the Soul* (*Ecclesiastical History* 4.18.5), but these are not preserved. Throughout his two apologies and the dialogue Justin offers numerous arguments intended to show that the doctrines of the *Logos*-Christ are superior to pagan philosophy and that Christianity is the true fulfillment of the law and prophets.

Some have taken the *Dialogue with Trypho* to be the record of a real debate between Justin and a Jew from Ephesus (cf. Eusebius, *Ecclesiastical History* 4.18), which presumably took place ca. 135 CE at the time of the second Jewish War (see *Dialogue* 1.3). To be sure, the *Dialogue* shows Justin's awareness of basic Jewish objections to Christianity. But certain aspects of the dialogue, including Trypho's surprisingly compliant attitude as Justin systematically unfolds his case, suggest that the *Dialogue* as we have it is primarily Justin's own literary creation. Whether or not there was a historical Jewish intellectual named Trypho is uncertain.

Justin begins the *Dialogue* by telling the story of how he explored various philosophical schools: Stoic, peripatetic, Pythagorean, and Platonic, until he came to see the truth of Christianity (chs. 1-8). This search for truth by sampling different philosophies was a traditional literary theme by Justin's time, as seen in Lucian's satire *Philosophies for Sale*.[1] After this Justin tries to show that ancient Israel's law was valid only for a time, whereas the true and universal law for humankind came in the Christian spiritual understanding of the Old Testament (chs. 9-47). Next comes a long series of prophetic and typological proofs meant to demonstrate that Jesus is both the Messiah and Divine (chs. 48-108). Finally, Justin argues that those who believe in Jesus and follow his law are the true Israel and heirs to God's promises (chs. 109-42).

Dialogue with Trypho 86, 90-92

86

1. After saying this, I continued, "Understand now how he whom the Scriptures announce as about to return in glory

---

1. See Tessa Rajak, "Talking at Trypho: Christian Apologetic as Anti-Judaism in Justin's *Dialogue with Trypho the Jew*," in *Apologetics in the Roman Empire: Pagans, Jews, and Christians*, ed. M. J. Edwards, M. Edwards, S. Price, and C. Rowland (Oxford: Clarendon, 1999), 64-65.

after his crucifixion was symbolized both by the tree of life (which is said to have been planted in Paradise)[2] and by what was about to happen to all the just. When Moses was sent with a rod to deliver the people,[3] he held it in his hands at their head, and he divided the sea in two.[4] With this rod he touched the rock and saw water gush forth.[5] And, by throwing a tree into the bitter waters of Marah, he made them sweet.[6]

2. "By placing rods in their drinking-places, Jacob caused the sheep of his mother's brother to conceive, so that he might gain possession of their young.[7] The same Jacob boasts that he crossed the river with his rod.[8] He also claimed that he saw a ladder, and the Scripture has stated that God rested on it,[9] and we have shown from the Scriptures that this was not the Father.[10] And when Jacob had poured oil over a stone at the same place, God appeared to him and told him that he had anointed a pillar in honor of the God whom he had seen.[11]

3. "We likewise have proved that in many Scriptural passages Christ is symbolically called a 'Stone.'[12] We have likewise shown that every chrism, whether of oil, or myrrh,

2. Gen 2:9; 3:22, 24; Rev 2:7; 22:2, 14, 19. The Septuagint uses "paradise" for "garden" in Genesis 2:9; 3:24. In some cases, Justin's quotations do not even match the Septuagint, e.g., *Dial.* 73.1, where Justin quotes Ps 96:10 as "Say among the nations: 'The Lord reigns from the tree.'" Justin's Christian source added the words "from the tree," which are absent from both the Hebrew and the Septuagint, yet Justin accuses the Jews of having removed this clause from the text (see *Dial.* 71.1–73.1). See also *Dial.* 120.4–5, where Justin quotes Gen 49:10 in a Christianized version and charges the Jews with corrupting the Septuagint, when in fact the text he ascribes to the Jews was the Septuagint text of the day, as Justin himself shows in *Dial.* 52.2; see Oskar Skarsaune, *The Proof from Prophecy* (Leiden: Brill, 1987), 25–46, 90–91.
3. Exod 4:17.
4. Exod 14:16.
5. Exod 17:5–6; Num 20:8.
6. Exod 15:23–25.
7. Gen 30:37–43.
8. Gen 32:10.
9. Gen 28:12–13.
10. Cf. *Dial.* 60.2.
11. Gen 28:18–22.
12. Cf. *Dial.* 34.2; 76.1; see also 110.4; 113.6; 114.4; 126.1.

or any other balsam compound, was a figure of Christ;[13] for the Word says, 'Therefore God, your God, has anointed you with the oil of gladness above your fellow kings.'[14] All kings and other anointed persons are called kings and anointed by participation in him, just as he himself received from the Father the titles of 'King' and 'Christ' and 'Priest' and 'Angel' and all other titles of this kind which he has or had.

4. "Aaron's rod, by blossoming, proved him to be the high priest.[15] Isaiah, indeed, foretold that Christ 'would come forth as a rod from the root of Jesse.'[16] And David declared that 'the just man is like a tree which is planted near the running waters, which shall bring forth its fruit in due season, and his leaf shall not fall off.'[17] And, again, it is said that the righteous man shall 'flourish like a palm tree.'[18]

5. "From a tree God appeared to Abraham, as it is written, 'by the oak tree of Mamre.'[19] After crossing the river Jordan, the people found seventy willow trees and twelve springs.[20] David declares that God comforted him with a rod and staff.[21]

6. "Elisha, by throwing a piece of wood into the River Jordan, brought up to the surface the iron head of the axe with which the sons of the prophets had begun to cut wood for the construction of a building in which they proposed to read the precepts of God and study them;[22] just as our Christ, by being

---

13. Cf. *Dial.* 56.14; 63.4.
14. Ps 45:7. The word "kings" is absent from the Hebrew and Septuagint.
15. Num 17:8.
16. Isa 11:1.
17. Ps 1:3.
18. Ps 92:12.
19. Gen 18:1.
20. Cf. Exod 15:27; Num 33:9. He means the Red Sea, not the Jordan River, and palm trees rather than willow trees. On the twelve springs as the apostles and the seventy palm trees as those sent out by Jesus (Luke 10:1), see Tertullian, *Against Marcion* 4.13, 24; Irenaeus, *Demonstration* 46; Origen, *Homily on Exodus* 7.1–3; and many fourth- and fifth-century Christian writers.
21. Ps 23:4.
22. See 2 Kgs 6:1–7. Cf. Tertullian, *Against the Jews* 13; Irenaeus, *Against Heresies* 5.17.4.

crucified on the wood of the cross and by sanctifying us by water, raised up us who had been immersed in the mire of our mortal sins and made us a house of prayer and worship?[23] Finally, it was a rod which signified that Judah was the father of the twins who were born of Tamar by a great mystery."[24]

90

1. "Lead us forward, then, from the Scriptures," said Trypho, "that we too may believe you. We are indeed aware that 'he was to endure suffering, and to be led as a sheep to the slaughter.'[25] But what we want you to prove to us is that he was to be crucified and subjected to so disgraceful and shameful a death (which even in the Law is cursed).[26] We find it impossible to think that this could be so."

2. "You know," I said, "in fact, you already admitted to us that what the prophets said or did they often expressed in parables and types, thus concealing the truth they held. As a result, it is not easy for the multitude to understand most of what they taught, but only those who take the trouble to find out and learn."

"We never doubted it," they replied.

3. "Then, please listen," I said, "to what I am going to say. Moses was the first to make known this apparent curse of Christ by the symbolic acts which he performed."

"What acts do you mean?" asked Trypho.

4. "When your people," I answered, "waged war with Amalek, and the son of Nun, Jesus [Joshua], was leader of the battle, Moses himself, stretching out both hands, prayed to God

23. Cf. Isa 56:7; Jer 7:11; Matt 21:13; Mark 11:17.
24. Gen 38:25–26.
25. Isa 53:7.
26. Deut 21:23; Gal 3:13. See also *Dial.* 95.1–3; Tertullian, *Against Marcion* 3.18.

for help.[27] Now, Hur and Aaron held up his hands all day long, lest he should become tired and let them drop to his sides. For, if Moses relaxed from that figure which was a figure of the cross, the people were defeated (as Moses himself testifies); but as long as he remained in that position Amalek was defeated, and the people drew their strength from the cross.

5. "In truth, it was not because Moses prayed that his people were victorious, but because, while the name of Jesus was at the battle front, Moses formed the sign of the cross. Who among you does not know that that prayer is the most pleasing to God which is uttered with lamentation and tears, with prostrate body or bended knees? But on this occasion Moses, or any after him, did not pray in such a manner; he was seated on a stone. And I have shown that even the stone is symbolical of Christ.

91

1. "Furthermore, God indicated in yet another way the power of the mystery of the cross when he said through Moses, in the blessing pronounced over Joseph, 'From the blessing of the Lord is his land; for the seasons of heaven, and for the dews, and for the deep springs from beneath, and for the fruits brought forth by the course of the sun, and for the conjunctions of the months, and for the tops of the ancient mountains, and for the top of the hills, and for the ever flowing rivers, and for the abundance of the earth. And let those things which are pleasing to him who appeared in the bush come upon the head and crown of Joseph, who was glorified among his brethren. His beauty is as of a firstling of a bullock, and his

27. Exod 17:8–16.

horns are the horns of a unicorn; with them shall he push the nations even to the ends of the earth.'[28]

2. "Now, no one can assert or prove that the horns of a unicorn represent any other matter or figure than that of the cross.[29] The one beam of the cross stands upright, from which the upper part is lifted up like a horn when the crossbeam is fitted on, and the ends of the crosspiece resemble horns joined to that one horn. And the part that is fixed in the middle of the cross, on which the bodies of the crucified are supported, also projects like a horn, and it, too, looks like a horn when it is shaped and joined to the other horns.

3. "And the words 'With them shall he push the nations even to the ends of the earth'[30] clearly describe what is now taking place in all the nations. For, men of all nations have been pushed by the horns, that is, goaded to compunction, by means of this mystery, and have abandoned their vain idols and demons to turn to the worship of God. But to unbelievers, the same sign is shown to be the cause of their destruction and condemnation, as when the people had come out of Egypt, and Israel was victorious over conquered Amalek by the sign of Moses's outstretched hands and by the imposition of the name Jesus [Joshua] upon the son of Nun.

4. "Likewise, the figure and sign, erected to counteract the effects of the serpents that bit Israel, was clearly intended for the salvation of those who believe that this sign was to show that through the crucified one death was to come to the serpent, but salvation to those who had been bitten by the serpent and who had sought protection of him who sent his

---

28. Deut 33:13–17 according to the Septuagint, including the reference to the "unicorn" in v. 17.
29. Cf. Origen, *Homilies on Numbers* 16.6.2, who says that the unicorn in Num 23:22 (according to the Septuagint) signifies Christ with his single, universal kingdom.
30. Deut 33:17.

Son into the world to be crucified.[31] For the prophetic Spirit did not instruct us through Moses to believe in a serpent, since he announces that the serpent was cursed by God from the beginning,[32] and through Isaiah he informs us that it will be slain as an enemy by the great sword, which is Christ.[33]

92

1. "If, therefore, one were not endowed with God's great grace to understand the words and deeds of the prophets, it would be quite useless for him to relate their words and actions, when he can give no explanation of them.[34] Moreover, will not those words and deeds seem despicable to most people if they are told by those who do not understand them?

2. "For if anyone were to ask you why, when Enoch, and Noah with his children, and any others like them, were pleasing to God without being circumcised or without observing the Sabbath, God required by new leaders and another law, after the lapse of so many generations, that those who lived between the times of Abraham and Moses should be justified by circumcision, and that those who lived after Moses be justified by both circumcision and the other precepts, that is, the Sabbaths, sacrifices, burnt offerings, and oblations, [God would be unjustly criticized] unless you point out, as I have already said, that God in his foreknowledge was aware that your people would deserve to be expelled from Jerusalem and never be allowed to enter there.[35]

---

31. Num 21:6–9; John 3:14–15.
32. Gen 3:14.
33. Isa 27:1.
34. Justin expresses the idea that one needs special divine grace in order to understand the words of Scripture (see also *Dial.* 7.3; 119.1).
35. The Roman emperor Hadrian expelled the Jews from Jerusalem after the Second Jewish Revolt (132–135 CE).

3. "For, as I have said earlier, you are distinguishable by no other means than by the circumcision of the flesh.[36] Abraham, indeed, was considered just, not by reason of his circumcision, but because of his faith. For before his circumcision it was said of him, 'Abraham believed God, and it was reputed to him unto justice.'[37]

4. "We also, therefore, because of our belief in God through Christ, even though we are uncircumcised in the flesh, have the salutary circumcision, namely that of the heart, and we thereby hope to be just and pleasing to God, since we have already obtained this testimony from him through the words of the prophets. But you Jews were ordered to observe the Sabbaths, and make offerings; and you were allowed by God to erect a place in which he could be invoked, so that you might not worship idols and forget God, and thus become impious and godless, as, indeed, you always seem to have been.[38]

5. "Now it was precisely for this reason that God issued his ordinances about the Sabbaths and oblations, as I have already proved by my previous words, but for the sake of the new arrivals today I had better repeat most of my proofs. If this had not been the reason, God could be accused of not having foreknowledge and of not teaching all men to know and to observe the same just precepts (for there surely were many generations of men before the time of Moses), and the Scripture would be judged false that says, 'God is true and just,

---

36. Cf. *Dial.* 16.3.
37. Gen 15:6; Rom 4:3; Gal 3:6.
38. Justin's view is that God allowed ancient Israel to offer sacrifices as a concession to their weakness, to prevent them from worshiping idols (see also *Dial.* 19.5–6; cf. *Dial.* 20.1, 4, on dietary laws). Justin also states that God imposed on Israel certain elements of the Sinai law, such as sacrifice and Sabbath, because of their sin, especially the sin of the golden calf (*Dial.* 21.1; 22.1, 11; 67.8; see also Irenaeus, *Against Heresies* 4.15.1–2; 4.16.5, below).

and all his ways are judgments, and there is no iniquity in him.'[39]

6. "But since the Scripture is evidently true, God does not desire that you always remain foolish and conceited as you now are, but that you may be saved with Christ, who pleased God and was approved by him, as I have already shown from the writings of the holy prophets."

---

39. Cf. Deut 32:4; Ps 25:10; 92:16.

3

Irenaeus

Irenaeus was born ca. 135 CE in Asia Minor, spent considerable time in Rome ca. 155–165, and eventually served as bishop of Lyon in Gaul from at least 177. He died some time after 198. As a young man Irenaeus met Polycarp, who related to him various personal reminiscences about the apostle John (Eusebius, *Ecclesiastical History* 5.20.4–8). We possess two theological treatises by Irenaeus, both originally written in Greek: an apologetic work called *Demonstration of the Apostolic Preaching,* which is preserved in Armenian translation; and his major work in five books, *The Exposing and Refutation of Falsely-called Knowledge,* usually referred to as *Against Heresies,* which is preserved complete only in Latin translation, although many Greek fragments survive. The major task of *Against Heresies* is to expose and refute certain groups that existed in the second half of the second century CE who followed teachers claiming to offer secret "knowledge" (*gnosis*). Although each of these groups included Christian ideas and vocabulary in their doctrinal systems, the overall salvation narrative for each was significantly different from what is found in the New Testament.

In Book 1, Irenaeus describes the teaching of various "gnostic" teachers, starting with Valentinus (mid-second century CE), and touching on other teachers as well, such as Basilides, Cerinthus, and Marcion. For Valentinus, the material world is the result of decline, and only the spiritual aspect of people can achieve salvation. The physical world is governed by lesser divine powers; the deity of the Old Testament is not the highest god; and the body will not be resurrected. "Gnostic" teachers made use of a variety of idiosyncratic documents, and they claimed to have secret oral traditions handed down from the apostles to which only they and their followers had access. In "gnostic" thought, the transcendent God revealed himself through emanations that comprised a divine world called *plērōma*, "Fullness," out of which comes divine contact with the material world. Strictly speaking, the teacher Marcion of Rome did not belong to this "gnostic" way of thinking, but he likewise viewed the material world negatively and rejected the Old Testament.

Book 2 of *Against Heresies* offers rational arguments against "gnostic" teachers and Marcion. In Book 3 Irenaeus attempts to refute his opponents based on Scripture and ecclesiastical tradition, focusing especially on the person of Christ. Irenaeus devotes Book 4 to demonstrating the unity of the Old and New Testaments. While acknowledging differences between the old and new dispensations in God's dealing with humanity, Irenaeus argues that both Testaments together describe a single plan of salvation, with the Old prefiguring and preparing the way for the New. Book 5 contains various points intended to sum up Irenaeus's arguments, for example, that God plans to save our physical bodies, and that the Creator God is the same as the God and Father of Jesus Christ.

Selections are offered below from Book 1, in which Irenaeus explains how "gnostics" distort the Scriptures to prove their doctrines; Book 3, where Irenaeus lays out the charge that his opponents follow neither Scripture nor tradition; and Book 4, in which Irenaeus addresses the relationship between the Old and New Testaments.

Against Heresies 1.3.6

Such things, therefore, they assert about their "Fullness" and the formation of the universe. They do violence to the good words of Scripture in adapting them to their wicked fabrications. Not only from the words of the evangelists and apostles do they try to make proofs by perverting the interpretations and by falsifying the explanations, but also from the law and the prophets. Since many parables and allegories have been spoken and can be made to mean many things, what is ambiguous they cleverly and deceitfully adapt to their fabrication by an unusual explanation. Thus they lead away from the truth into captivity those who do not guard a firm faith in the one Father Almighty and in one Jesus Christ, the Son of God.

Against Heresies 1.8.1

Such is their system, which neither the prophets preached, nor the Lord taught, nor the apostles handed down. They boast rather loudly of knowing more about it than others do, citing it from non-scriptural works; and, as people would say, they attempt to braid ropes of sand. They try to adapt to their own sayings, in a manner worthy of credence, either the Lord's parables, or the prophets' sayings, or the apostles' words, so that their fabrication might not appear to be without witness. They disregard the order and the connection of the Scriptures and, as much as they are able, they disjoint the members of the truth. They transfer passages and rearrange them; and, making one thing out of another, they deceive many through the badly composed phantasy of the Lord's words that they adapt. By way of illustration, suppose someone would take the beautiful image of a king, carefully made out of precious stones by a skillful artist, and would destroy the features of the man on it and change around and rearrange the jewels, and make out of them the form of a dog or a fox, and a rather bad piece of work at that. Suppose he would then say with determination that this is the beautiful image of the king that the skillful artist had made, all the while pointing to the jewels which had been beautifully fitted together by the first artist into the image of the king, but which had been badly changed by the second into the form of a dog. And suppose he would through this fanciful arrangement of the jewels deceive the inexperienced, who had no idea of what the king's picture looked like,[1] and would persuade them that this base picture of a fox is that beautiful image of the king. In the same way these people patch together old women's fables,[2] and then pluck words and sayings and parables from here and there and wish to adapt these words of God to their fables. We have already

---

1. As an example of how this illustration plays out in Irenaeus's argument, in *Against Heresies* 3.4.2 Irenaeus says that there are many Christians who live in regions without a written language who nevertheless know better than to believe Valentinian or Marcionite deceptions, simply because they know the basic Christian message through apostolic tradition (see *Against Heresies* 1.9.4, below). In other words, because they know what the king's completed picture (= a summary of apostolic teaching) looks like, they will not be fooled by someone who creates a false picture by rearranging the jewels out of which the picture was made.

2. Cf. 1 Tim 4:7.

said how much of these words they adapt to the things within the "Fullness."

Against Heresies 1.9.4

After having entirely fabricated their own system, they gather together sayings and names from scattered places and transfer them, as we have already said, from their natural meaning to an unnatural one. They act like those who would propose themes which they chance upon and then try to put them to verse using lines from Homeric poems, so that the inexperienced think that Homer composed the poems with that theme, whereas in reality they are of recent composition.[3] Actually, many are so misled by the contrived sequence of the verses that they wonder whether Homer may have indeed composed them thus; for example, suppose if someone were to compose as follows the Homeric lines about Hercules, who was sent by Eurystheus to the dog in Hades. For the sake of illustration it is not forbidden to cite these verses, since in both cases the attempt is similar,[4] even identical:

3. Irenaeus likens his opponents' use of Scripture to the poetic form known as the *cento*. When writing a *cento*, the poet took various lines from here and there out of a famous poem (often Homer in Greek and Virgil in Latin), and pieced them together in a new order so that a whole new story was created out of the bits and pieces of the original poem. Irenaeus's point is that no one who knows the actual plot of the Homeric poems would be fooled into thinking that the *cento* is really saying the same thing as the original, even though the *cento* has been constructed out of "Homeric" language. See Robert L. Wilken, "The Homeric Cento in Irenaeus, 'Adversus haereses' 1.9.4," *Vigiliae Christianae* 21 (1967): 25–33; and M. D. Usher, *Homeric Stitchings: The Homeric Centos of the Empress Eudocia* (Lanham, MD: Rowman & Littlefield, 1998), 9–17. For a similar criticism of how heretics quote Scripture in a piecemeal fashion and without regard for context, see Clement of Alexandria, *Stromateis* 7.16.96.

4. In other words, both in the case of the "gnostic" use of Scripture and in the case of someone composing a *cento* out of Homer, the writer appropriates the language of a classic text and employs it to compose a new composition with a novel theme.

When thus it had been spoken, there was sent from his house
 deeply groaning
Hercules powerful hero, with brilliant deeds acquainted,
By Eurystheus, the son of Sthenelus, Perseus's offspring,
That from Erebus he might fetch the dog of dark Hades.
So, like a mountain-bred lion he went, confident of his prowess,
Rapidly through the city while all his friends followed after,
Unmarried maidens and youths, also much experienced old men,
Bitterly weeping for him as one going forward to death.
Therefore Hermes together with blue-eyed Athena did send him;
For she knew how the heart of her brother was suffering with
 grief.[5]

What simpleminded person would not be misled by these verses and believe that Homer composed them in this manner for that very theme? One who is well versed in Homeric themes will recognize the verses, but he will not recognize the theme, since he knows that some of them were spoken of Ulysses, others of Hercules himself, others of Priam, and others of Menelaus and Agamemnon. However, if he takes them and puts each one back into its own theme, he will make their fabricated theme disappear. In the same way, anyone who keeps within himself the unchangeable Rule of Truth[6] that was received through baptism will recognize the names, sayings, and parables from the Scriptures, but this blasphemous theme of

---

5. This *cento,* constructed out of various Homeric passages (*Odyssey* 10.76; *Odyssey* 21.26; *Iliad* 19.123; *Iliad* 8.368; *Odyssey* 6.130; *Iliad* 24.327; *Odyssey* 11.38; *Iliad* 24.328; *Odyssey* 11.626; *Iliad* 2.409), has been arranged to tell a new story about Hercules.

6. By "Rule of Truth" Irenaeus seems to mean the same thing as "Rule of Faith" (see *Demonstration* 3), which is a summary of Christian teaching (see *Demonstration* 1). Irenaeus invokes the "Rule of Faith" or "Rule of Truth" in connection with the teaching of Scripture (*Against Heresies* 2.28.1–2; 4.35.4) and also for his own summaries of the basic Christian message as transmitted in apostolic churches, perhaps through baptismal confessions (*Against Heresies* 1.10.1; 3.4.2). Statements similar in content to Irenaeus's Rule are found in other early Christian writers, for example: Tertullian, *Against Praxeas* 2; *Prescription against Heretics* 13.1–6; *Concerning the Veiling of Virgins* 1.3; Hippolytus, *Homily on the Heresy of Noetus* 17–18; Origen, *First Principles,* "Preface" 4–10; *Didascalia apostolorum* 15.26; Cyprian, *Letter* 73.5.2; and Novatian, *On the Trinity* 9. For further discussion, see Everett Ferguson, *The Rule of Faith: A Guide* (Eugene, OR: Cascade, 2015).

theirs he will not recognize. For even if he recognizes the jewels, he will not accept the fox for the image of the king. He will restore each one of the passages to its proper order and, having fit it into the body of the truth, he will expose their fabrication and show that it is without support.

Against Heresies 3.2.1-2

1. Indeed, when they are exposed by means of the Scriptures, they turn round and make accusations against the Scriptures themselves, as if these were not correct, or were not authentic and stated things variously, and that the truth cannot be found in them by those who are ignorant of tradition. They claim the truth was not handed down by writings, but by a living voice, about which Paul spoke when he said, "On these matters we do impart wisdom—although it is not the wisdom of this world."[7] And each one of them claims as this wisdom whatever he discovers on his own, which is really a fiction, so that their truth may fittingly be in Valentinus at one time, in Marcion at another, in Cerinthus at another, or finally in Basilides, or even in another who disputes against all of these and is incapable of saying anything pertaining to salvation.[8] For each one of them, being totally corrupt, is not ashamed to deprave the Rule of Truth and preach himself.[9]

2. When, however, we refer them again to the tradition that derives from the apostles and is guarded in the Churches by the succession of the presbyters,[10] they are opposed to tradition

7. Cf. 1 Cor 2:6.
8. See *Against Heresies* 1.11.3.
9. Cf. 2 Cor 4:5.
10. See *Against Heresies* 3.3.2–3, where Irenaeus gives a list of the bishops of Rome from Linus (see 2 Tim 4:21) to his own day. According to Irenaeus, it would be tedious to recite the succession of bishops for every city, so he gives only the list for Rome because of its "preeminent authority" (*propter potentiorem principalitatem*), in that the faithful from everywhere who have preserved the apostolic tradition are to be found

and claim that they are wiser not only than the presbyters but even than the apostles, and have found the unadulterated truth. In fact, they maintain that the apostles mixed with the Savior's words matter from the law, and that not only the apostles but also the Lord Himself gave discourses derived at times from the Demiurge, at other times from the Intermediate Region, and yet at others from the Highest Authority.[11] They, however, know the hidden mystery without doubt, admixture or adulteration.[12] That, indeed, is a most impudent blasphemy against their Creator. The result is that they no longer agree with either the Scriptures or tradition.

Against Heresies 4.15.1–2

1. The Jews had therefore a law, a course of discipline, and a prophecy of future things. For God, warning them at first by means of natural precepts that from the beginning He had implanted in humankind by means of the Decalogue (which, if any one does not observe, he has no salvation), did not then demand anything more from them. As Moses says in Deuteronomy, "These are all the words which the Lord spoke to the whole assembly of the sons of Israel on the Mountain, and He added no more; and He wrote them on two tables of stone, and gave them to me."[13] For this reason He did this,

---

throughout that city. In other words, the Roman Church of Irenaeus's day was something of a microcosm of the Church throughout the Mediterranean world. The Latin text of this passage contains some difficulties, and unfortunately the original Greek is lost. For discussion and bibliography, see *St. Irenaeus of Lyons: Against the Heresies, Book 3*, trans. Dominic J. Unger, rev. Matthew C. Steenberg (ACW 64; Mahwah, NJ: Newman, 2012), 126–27; and J. Quasten, *Patrology* (Allen, TX: Christian Classics, 1995), 1:302–4.

11. The Demiurge (adapted from Plato's *Timaeus*) in "gnostic" thought was the creator of the material world, an entity flawed in its creative purpose that produced flawed matter. The "Highest Authority" (*summitas*) may be the highest entity within the hierarchy of the *Plērōma* ("Fullness"), with the "Intermediate Region" (*Medietas*) being something in between. Cf. *Against Heresies* 4.35.1.

12. Cf. Eph 3:9; Col 1:26.

so that they who are willing to follow Him might keep these commandments. But when they turned themselves to make a calf, and went back in their minds to Egypt, desiring to be slaves instead of free people, they were consequently placed into a state of servitude suited to their wishes—a slavery that did not in fact cut them off from God, but subjected them to the yoke of bondage;[14] as Ezekiel the prophet, when stating the reasons for the giving of such a law, declares: "And their eyes were after the desire of their heart; and I gave them statutes that were not good, and judgments in which they shall not live."[15] Luke also recorded that Stephen, who was the first elected into the diaconate by the apostles, and who was the first slain for the testimony of Christ, spoke regarding Moses as follows: "This man did indeed receive the commandments of the living God to give to us, whom your fathers would not obey, but thrust Him away, and in their hearts they turned back again to Egypt, saying to Aaron, 'Make us gods to go before us; for we do not know what has happened to this Moses, who led us from the land of Egypt.' And they made a calf in those days, and offered sacrifices to the idol, and were rejoicing in the works of their own hands. But God turned, and gave them up to worship the hosts of heaven; as it is written in the book of the prophets: 'O you house of Israel, Did you offer to me sacrifices and oblations for forty years in the wilderness? But you took up the tabernacle of Molech and the star of the god Rephan, figures which you made in order to worship them'";[16] pointing out plainly that the law, being such, was not given to them by another God, but that, although adapted to their condition of servitude, it originated from the very same God as

---

13. Deut 5:22.
14. Cf. Justin Martyr, *Dialogue with Trypho* 92.4–5, above.
15. Ezek 20:24.
16. See Acts 7:38–43. The quotation of the "book of the prophets" is from Amos 5:25–26.

we worship. For which reason also He says to Moses in Exodus: "I will send forth my angel before you; for I will not go up with you, because you are a stiff-necked people."[17]

2. And not only so, but the Lord also showed that certain precepts were enacted for them by Moses on account of their hardness of heart and because of their unwillingness to be obedient; he showed this when, on their saying to him, "Why then did Moses command to give a certificate of divorce, and to send one's wife away?" He said to them, "Because of the hardness of your hearts he permitted these things to you; but from the beginning it was not so";[18] thus exonerating Moses as a faithful servant, but acknowledging the one God who from the beginning made them male and female, thereby reproving them as hard-hearted and disobedient. And so it was in this manner that they received from Moses this law of divorce, which was adapted to their hard nature. But why should I say these things concerning the Old Testament only? For in the New Testament also the apostles are found doing this very thing on the same ground as has been mentioned, with Paul plainly declaring, "But these things I say, not the Lord."[19] And again: "But this I speak by way of concession, not by way of commandment."[20] And again: "Now, as concerning virgins, I have no commandment from the Lord; yet I give my judgment, as one that has obtained mercy from the Lord to be faithful."[21] And again, in another passage he says: "so that Satan may not tempt you because of your lack of self-control."[22] If, therefore, even in the New Testament the apostles are found granting certain precepts in consideration of human weakness, on

17. Exod 33:2–3.
18. Matt 19:7–8.
19. 1 Cor 7:12.
20. 1 Cor 7:6.
21. 1 Cor 7:25.
22. 1 Cor 7:5.

account of some people's lack of self-control, so that such persons do not grow stubborn, despair altogether of salvation, and so become apostates from God—it should not be surprising that also in the Old Testament the same God permitted similar indulgences for the benefit of His people. His purpose was to guide them by means of the aforementioned ordinances, so that, obeying the Decalogue they might obtain the gift of salvation through them, and being restrained by God they might not revert to idolatry nor apostatize from God, but learn to love Him with their whole heart. And if certain persons, simply because of the disobedience and ruin of the Israelites, assert that the Teacher of the law is limited in power, they should recognize that in our era "many are called, but few chosen";[23] that there are some who inwardly are wolves, yet wear sheep's clothing on the outside;[24] and that God has always preserved human freedom and the power of human self-determination, while at the same time issuing His own exhortations, so that those who do not obey Him may be rightly judged because they have disobeyed, whereas those who obey and believe on Him may be honored with immortality.

Against Heresies 4.16.4–5

4. And this is why Scripture says, "These words the Lord spoke to all the assembly of the children of Israel on the Mountain, and He added no more";[25] for, as I have already observed, He stood in need of nothing from them. And again Moses says: "And now Israel, what does the Lord your God require of you, but to fear the Lord your God, to walk in all

---

23. Matt 20:16.
24. Matt 7:15.
25. Deut 5:22.

His ways, and to love Him, and to serve the Lord your God with all your heart, and with all your soul?"[26] Now these things did indeed make humanity glorious by supplying what was lacking in humans, namely, the friendship of God; but they profited God nothing, for God did not at all stand in need of human love. For the glory of God was lacking in humanity, and people could obtain this glory only by serving God. And therefore Moses says to them again: "Choose life, that you may live, you and your seed, to love the Lord your God, to hear His voice, and to cleave to Him; for this is your life, and the length of your days."[27] Preparing humanity for this life, the Lord Himself did speak in His own person to all alike the words of the Decalogue; and so they remain permanently with us, receiving by means of His advent in the flesh extension and increase, but not abrogation.

5. The laws of bondage, however, were one by one promulgated to the people by Moses, suited either for their instruction or for their punishment, as Moses himself declared: "And the Lord commanded me at that time to teach you statutes and judgments."[28] These things, therefore, which were given for bondage and as a sign to them, He cancelled by the New Covenant of freedom. But in the New Covenant, He increased and widened those laws that are natural, noble and common to all, generously and gladly allowing people to know God the Father by adoption, to love Him with their whole heart and to follow His word unswervingly, while they abstain not only from evil deeds, but even from the desire for them. Moreover, He also increased the feeling of reverence; for sons should have more veneration and greater love for their father

26. Deut 10:12.
27. Deut 30:19–20.
28. Deut 4:14.

than the slaves do. And therefore the Lord says, "As to every idle word that people have spoken, they shall render an account for it on the day of judgment."[29] And, "he who has looked upon a woman to lust after her, has committed adultery with her already in his heart";[30] and, "he that is angry with his brother without cause shall be in danger of the judgment."[31] All this is declared so that we may know that we shall give account to God not only for our deeds, as slaves do, but even for our words and thoughts, as those who have truly received the power of freedom, by which people are more severely tested as to whether they will reverence, fear, and love the Lord. And for this reason Peter says, "that we have freedom not as a cloak of wickedness,"[32] but as the means of testing and demonstrating faith.

Against Heresies 4.26.1

1. Anyone, therefore, who reads the Scriptures attentively will find in them an account of Christ and a foreshadowing of the new calling. For Christ is the treasure that was hid in the field,[33] that is, in this world (for "the field is the world");[34] but the treasure hid in the Scriptures is Christ, since He was pointed out by means of types and parables. Hence His human nature could not be understood prior to the consummation of those things that had been predicted, that is, the advent of

---

29. Matt 12:36.
30. Matt 5:28.
31. Matt 5:22. Irenaeus's text of Matt 5:22 contains "without cause" (Greek: *eikē*). This reading is found in other early witnesses including the Syriac Peshitta, the Old Latin Version, the Coptic Version, Codex Bezae (fifth cent.), and a seventh-century corrector of codex Sinaiticus. The word is omitted in early witnesses such as P-64 (early third cent.), and the fourth-century manuscripts Vaticanus and Sinaiticus. It is usually interpreted as an early explanatory addition.
32. 1 Pet 2:16.
33. Matt 13:44.
34. Matt 13:38.

Christ. And therefore it was said to Daniel the prophet: "Shut up the words, and seal the book even to the time of consummation, until many learn, and knowledge be completed. For at that time, when the dispersion shall be accomplished, they shall know all these things."[35] But Jeremiah also says, "In the last days they shall understand these things."[36] For every prophecy, before its fulfillment, is full of enigmas and ambiguities from a human standpoint. But when the time has arrived and the prediction has come to pass, then the prophecies have clear and certain explanations. For this reason, even now when the law is read to the Jews, it is like a fable; for they do not possess the explanations of all things pertaining to the advent of the Son of God, which took place in human nature; but when the law is read by Christians, it is indeed a treasure hidden in a field, which is brought to light by the cross of Christ. Once the law has been explained, it enriches human understanding, shows forth the wisdom of God, declares His dispensations with regard to humanity and the prior forming of Christ's kingdom, preaches by anticipation the inheritance of the holy Jerusalem, and proclaims beforehand that the one who loves God shall arrive at such excellency as even to see God and hear His word, and from hearing His discourse be glorified to such an extent that others cannot behold the glory of his countenance, as was said by Daniel: "Those who understand shall shine as the brightness of the sky, and many of the righteous shall shine as the stars for ever and ever."[37] So then, I have shown it to be this way, if anyone will simply read the Scriptures. For thus it was that the Lord discoursed with the disciples after His resurrection

35. Dan 12:4, 7.
36. Jer 23:20.
37. Dan 12:3.

from the dead, proving to them from the Scriptures themselves "that the Christ must suffer and enter into His glory, and that remission of sins should be preached in His name throughout all the world."[38] And each disciple will be perfected and rendered like the householder "who brings forth from his treasure things new and old."[39]

38. Luke 24:26, 47.
39. Matt 13:52.

4

Tertullian

Tertullian was born ca. 160 CE in the North African city of Carthage, and he lived until at least 220. He evidently received a solid education, especially in rhetoric and law; and although he was fully competent in Greek, Tertullian became the first Christian writer to compose his own theological works in Latin, bequeathing to the Latin-speaking church of later times many important ecclesiastical terms and phrases. Also significant is the fact that Tertullian is the earliest major author representing Christianity in Roman North Africa. Tertullian's literary output was extensive, including apologetic works, polemical treatises aimed at refuting false teachings, and moral and ascetic compositions. Perhaps his best-known work is his defense of Christianity titled *Apologeticum*, which was written in 197. Little is known of Tertullian's personal life, but his writings show him to be equipped with a sharp (yet inflexible) mind, a vigorous style of argumentation, and an inclination toward moral severity. In 207 Tertullian joined the Montanists, a Christian group that emphasized new prophetic revelations and moral rigor. Separating themselves from the mainstream church, the Montanists found adherents primarily in Asia Minor and North Africa.

The first excerpt below comes from Tertullian's *De praescriptione haereticorum*, "On the prescription of heretics" (usually *Prescription against Heretics*), probably written somewhere between 200 and 207. The term *praescriptio* is used in a technical, judicial sense: the advocate objects to the plaintiff's legal right to advance his suit as he has formulated it. As Tertullian argues, the heretics have advanced their claims on the basis of Scripture, but in fact they have no right to appeal to these Scriptures in the first place, because the Scriptures belong exclusively to Christians who maintain the apostolic tradition (see also *Prescription* 21). The second excerpt is from *On Baptism,* written in order to refute a certain "Cainite" sect (see ch. 1) that evidently had a negative view of water baptism. In his defense of baptism, Tertullian affirms that God uses everyday elements for spiritual purposes, explains the theological meaning of the baptismal ritual, shows the typological basis in Scripture for water baptism, and surveys the significant role of water in Scripture.

Prescription Against Heretics 15–19

15

1. We come, then, to our main point; for to this indeed we were steering, and for this we were laying the preparatory foundation in our preceding discourse. So that from this point onward we may contest the ground on which our opponents make their appeal.[1] 2. They make the Scriptures the ground of

their plea, and by this audacious stroke of theirs immediately influence a certain number of persons. Moreover, in the encounter itself, they weary even the strong, they capture the weak, and the undecided they send away anxious. 3. We therefore make our strongest stand in maintaining that they are not to be admitted to any discussion of the Scriptures at all. 4. If the Scriptures are to be their source of strength, then the question as to who are the rightful possessors of the Scriptures must be gone into first, so as to prevent their use by one who has no manner of right to them.

16

1. I might be bringing forward this objection from a want of confidence, or from a wish to enter upon the case in dispute in a different manner from the heretics, were not a reason to be found at the outset in that our Faith owes obedience to the Apostle who forbids us to enter into questionings, or to lend our ears to novel sayings, or to associate with a heretic after one admonition[2]—he does not say after discussion. 2. Indeed, he forbade discussion by fixing on admonition as the reason for meeting a heretic.[3] And he mentions this one admonition, because a heretic is not a Christian, and to prevent his

---

1. Insight into the Roman legal mindset underlying Tertullian's argument can found in ancient *stasis* ("stance") theory, which sought to identify the precise question at issue. For example, in a criminal trial, the question might be: "Did he do it?" Or, if it is clear that the defendant did the action, the question might be one of definition: "Is this really a crime?" Or, if it is acknowledged that the action was a crime, the question might be: "Was there a justifiable reason why the defendant needed to do this action?" Or one might even object to the legal process: "Does this court have the jurisdiction to rule in this case?" Cf. Cicero, *On Invention* 1.8.10; Quintilian, *Institutes of Oratory* 3.5.14; 3.6.55–57; see George A. Kennedy, *A New History of Classical Rhetoric* (Princeton: Princeton University Press, 1994), 97–101. Tertullian asserts that disputing with heretics about the interpretation of Scripture is not the proper stance; rather, the real question is: "Do heretics even have the right to appeal to our Scriptures in the first place?"
2. 1 Tim 6:4; Titus 3:10.
3. On the admonition not to speak with heretics, see also Ignatius, *Letter to the Smyrnaeans*

appearing worthy of being, like a Christian, censured once and again in the presence of two or three witnesses;[4] since he is to be censured for the same reason that he is not to be disputed with—because argumentative contests about the Scriptures profit nothing, save of course to upset the stomach or the brain.

17

1. This or that heresy rejects certain of the Scriptures, and those which it receives it perverts both by additions and excisions to agree with its own teaching.[5] For even when it receives them it does not receive them entire, and if it does in some cases receive them entire, it nonetheless perverts them by fabricating heterodox interpretations.[6] 2. A spurious interpretation injures the Truth quite as much as a tampered text. Baseless presumptions naturally refuse to acknowledge the means of their own refutation. 3. They rely on passages that they have fraudulently rearranged or received because of their obscurity. 4. What will you effect, though you are most skilled in the Scriptures, if what you maintain is rejected by the other side and what you reject is maintained? 5. You will indeed lose nothing—save your voice in the dispute; and gain nothing—save indignation at the blasphemy.

4.1; 7.2; *Didache* 11.2; Irenaeus, *Against Heresies* 3.3.4; Cyprian, *On the Unity of the Church* 17.

4. Matt 18:15–16.

5. For example, it was reported that Marcion established his own version of a Christian canon by editing the Gospel of Luke and certain letters of Paul, removing textual elements that connected the ministry of Jesus and the teaching of Paul back to the Old Testament; see Irenaeus, *Against Heresies* 1.27.2; 3.12.12; cf. Tertullian, *Against Marcion* 1.19.

6. On distorted interpretations of Scripture among heretics, see also Irenaeus, *Against Heresies* 1.9.4; and Clement of Alexandria, *Stromateis* 7.16.96.

18

1. But the man for whose sake you may have entered into an argument from the Scriptures in order to strengthen him when wavering, will he incline more to the Truth or to heresies? 2. Influenced by the very fact that he sees you have effected nothing, since each side possesses equal vantage-ground in denial and assertion, and is without doubt in a like position, he will go away rendered still more uncertain by the discussion, and not knowing which he is to adjudge the heresy. 3. For they themselves are naturally bound to retort these charges upon us. They must necessarily assert that the falsification of the Scriptures and lying interpretations have been introduced by us, because they equally maintain that the Truth is with them.

19

1. Appeal, therefore, must not be made to the Scriptures, nor must the contest be carried on concerning points where victory is impossible or uncertain or too little certain. 2. For even if the discussion from the Scriptures would not so result as to place each side in an equal position, the order of things would demand that this point should first be decided—the point which alone now calls for discussion, namely: Who holds the Faith to which the Scriptures belong? From whom and through whom, and when, and to whom was the doctrinal teaching delivered whereby people are made Christians? 3. For wherever it shall appear that the true Christian religion and faith exist, there will be found the true Scriptures and interpretations and all Christian traditions.[7]

---

7. On Tertullian's understanding of the basic "Rule of Faith" that summarized Christian belief, see *Prescription Against Heretics* 13.1–6; *Against Praxeas* 2; *Concerning the Veiling of Virgins* 1.3.

On Baptism 6–9

6

1. Not that the Holy Spirit is given to us in the water, but that in the water we are made clean by the action of the angel, and made ready for the Holy Spirit.[8] Here also a type had come first.[9] As John was our Lord's forerunner, preparing his ways,[10] so also the angel, the mediator of baptism, makes the ways straight for the Holy Spirit who is to come next.[11] He does so by that cancelling of sins which is granted in response to faith signed and sealed in the Father and the Son and the Holy Spirit.[12] 2. For if in three witnesses every word shall be established,[13] how much more shall the gift of God? By the benediction we have the same mediators of faith as we have sureties of salvation. That number of the divine names of itself suffices for the confidence of our hope. Yet because it is under the charge of three that profession of faith and promise of salvation are in pledge, there is a necessary addition, the mention of the Church; because where there are the three, the Father and the Son and the Holy Spirit, there is the Church, which is a body of three.[14]

---

8. See *On Baptism* 4. Tertullian is our earliest source for the practice of invoking the Holy Spirit over the water prior to baptism.
9. In Tertullian's thought, just as the Old Testament presented "types" of realities that came to clear expression in the New Testament, so also the Old and New Testaments present "types" of realities that find clear expression in Christian ritual.
10. Cf. Matt 3:3; Mark 1:2; Luke 3:4.
11. In *On Baptism* 4, Tertullian says that baptismal waters acquire healing power through the intervention of an angel. See also *On Baptism* 5 on the pool of Bethesda; cf. John 5:4: "For at times an angel would come down into the pool and stir up the water. So the first person to go down after the water had been stirred would be healed of whatever disease he had." This verse appears in various forms only in later New Testament manuscripts and is usually regarded as an interpolation. Tertullian is the earliest evidence for its existence.
12. On baptism in the name of the Father, Son, and Holy Spirit, see *Didache* 7 (late first or early second cent. CE); Justin Martyr, *1 Apology* 61; 65; and Tertullian, *Against Praxeas* 26.
13. Cf. Deut 19:15; Matt 18:16; 2 Cor 13:1.

7

1. After that we come up from the washing and are anointed with the blessed unction, following that ancient practice by which, ever since Aaron was anointed by Moses, there was a custom of anointing them for priesthood with oil out of a horn.[15] That is why the high priest is called "Christ,"[16] from *chrism*, which is the Greek for "anointing": and from this also our Lord obtained his title, though it had become a spiritual anointing, in that he was anointed with the Spirit by God the Father: and so it says in the Acts, "For in truth they were gathered together in this city against your holy son, whom you anointed."[17] 2. So also in our case, the unction flows upon the flesh, but turns to spiritual profit, just as in the baptism itself there is an act that touches the flesh, that we are immersed in water, but a spiritual effect, that we are set free from sins.

8

1. Next follows the imposition of the hand in benediction, inviting and welcoming the Holy Spirit. Human ingenuity has been permitted to summon spirit to combine with water, and by application of a man's hands over the result of their union to animate it with another spirit of excellent clarity;[18] and shall

14. See Matt 18:20. Cf. 1 John 5:7, 8, which in a few late manuscripts, at first as merely a marginal comment in the text, reads "in heaven, the Father, the Word and the Holy Spirit, and these three are one; and there are three who testify on earth." Tertullian may have been a key source for this later explanatory comment.
15. Exod 30:30; Lev 8:12. See also the church order *Didascalia Apostolorum* 3.12 and the apocryphal *Acts of Thomas*, chs. 27; 121; 132; 157 (both Syrian, third cent. CE), which describe a pre-baptismal anointing with oil, as opposed to Tertullian's post-baptismal anointing (cf. Tertullian's *On the Resurrection of the Flesh* 8). Justin Martyr, *1 Apology* 61; 65, does not mention anointing with oil in connection with baptism.
16. In the Septuagint, Lev 4:3 refers to the high priest as *o kechrismenos*, "the one who has been anointed," and then in Lev 4:5 it speaks of the priest as *o christos*, "the anointed one."
17. Cf. Acts 4:27.

not God be permitted, in an organ of his own, by the use of holy hands to play a tune of spiritual sublimity? 2. But this too is involved in that ancient sacred act in which Jacob blessed his grandsons, Joseph's sons, Ephraim and Manasseh, by placing his hands interchanged upon their heads,[19] turned transversely upon themselves in such a manner as to make the shape of Christ,[20] and at that early date to prefigure the blessing that was to be in Christ. 3. At this point, that most holy Spirit willingly comes down from the Father upon bodies cleansed and blessed, and comes to rest upon the waters of baptism as though revisiting his primal dwelling-place.[21] He came down upon our Lord in the form of a dove,[22] and thus the nature of the Holy Spirit was clearly revealed in a creature of simplicity and innocence, since even physically the dove is without gall, 4. which is why he says, "Be ye simple, like doves."[23] And this too has the support of a type which has preceded: for as, after those waters of the Flood by which the ancient iniquity was cleansed away, after the baptism (so to express it) of the world, a dove as herald announced to the earth peace from the wrath of heaven, having been sent forth of the ark and having returned with an olive-leaf[24]—and towards the heathen too this is held out as a sign of peace—by the same divine ordinance of spiritual effectiveness the dove who is the Holy Spirit is sent forth from heaven, where the Church is, of which the ark is a type,[25] and flies down bringing God's peace to the earth which

18. By "human ingenuity" Tertullian is alluding to the water organ devised by the third-century BCE Alexandrian inventor Ctesibius, who utilized water and compressed air to create a musical instrument similar to the modern pipe organ (cf. Pliny, *Natural History* 7.37).

19. Gen 48:14.

20. Either the crossing of the hands makes the shape of the Greek letter χ, which is the first letter of "Christ," or else the crossed hands physically depict the cross.

21. Cf. Gen 1:2.

22. Matt 3:16; Mark 1:10; Luke 3:22; John 1:32.

23. Matt 10:16.

24. See Gen 8:10, 11.

is our flesh, as it comes up from the washing after the removal of its ancient sins. 5. "But," you object, "the world sinned again, so that this equating of baptism with the flood is not valid." Indeed, the world sinned again and so is appointed for the fire; so also a man is when he renews his sins after baptism: so that this also needs to be accepted as a sign and a warning to us.

<h2 style="text-align:center">9</h2>

1. See how many then are the advocacies of nature, the special provisions of grace, the customary observances of conduct, the types, the preparations in act or word, which have laid down the rule for the sacred use of water. The first, that when the people of Israel are set free from bondage in Egypt and by passing through the water are escaping the violence of the Egyptian king, the king himself with all his forces is destroyed by water.[26] This is a type made abundantly clear in the sacred act of baptism: I mean that the gentiles are set free from this present world by means of water, and leave behind, drowned in the water, their ancient tyrant the Devil. 2. Secondly, water is healed of the blemish of bitterness, and restored to its own sweet usefulness, by the tree Moses throws in;[27] and that tree was Christ, who from within himself heals the springs of that nature which was previously poisoned and embittered, converting them into exceedingly healthful water, that of baptism. 3. This is the water which flowed forth for the people of Israel from the rock that followed them: and as that rock was Christ,[28] without doubt this shows us that baptism is made blessed in Christ by water. See how great is the grace that

25. Cf. 1 Pet 3:20–21.
26. Exod 14:28.
27. Exod 15:23–25.
28. Exod 17:6; 1 Cor 10:4.

water has in the presence of God and his Christ for the corroboration of baptism. 4. Wherever Christ is, there is water: he himself is baptized in water;[29] when called to a marriage he inaugurates with water the first rudiments of his power;[30] when engaged in conversation he invites those who are thirsty to come to his everlasting water;[31] when teaching of charity he approves of a cup of water offered to a little one as one of the works of affection;[32] at a well-side he restores his strength;[33] he walks upon the water;[34] by his own choice he crosses over the water;[35] with water he makes himself a servant to his disciples.[36] He continues his witness to baptism right on to his passion: when he is given up to the cross, water is in evidence, as Pilate's hands are aware;[37] when he receives a wound, water bursts forth from his side, as the soldier's spear can tell.[38]

29. Matt 3:16; Mark 1:10; Luke 3:21–22.
30. John 2:7–11.
31. John 4:14; 7:38.
32. Matt 10:42.
33. John 4:6.
34. Matt 14:25; Mark 6:48; John 6:19.
35. Matt 14:34; Mark 6:53; John 6:21.
36. John 13:5.
37. Matt 27:24.
38. John 19:34.

5

Cyprian

Born ca. 200–210 CE to a wealthy family in North Africa, Cyprian obtained renown as an orator prior to his conversion to Christianity ca. 246. Shortly thereafter in 249 he was elected bishop of Carthage, having demonstrated his pastoral disposition by employing his wealth to give generously to the poor. During the Decian persecution of 250–251, Cyprian retreated into exile from where he discharged his ecclesiastical duties, writing letters and receiving visitors. During his nine years in office he wrote numerous letters and pastoral treatises, such as *On the Lapsed,* dealing with Christians who had compromised their faith during persecution and later sought reconciliation to the Church, and *On the Unity of the Church,* the first work devoted specifically to ecclesiology. A new wave of persecution aimed at Church leadership broke out under the emperor Valerian in 257, resulting in Cyprian's execution on

September 14, 258. Immediately after his martyrdom Cyprian's tomb became an important location for Christian devotion.

The selection below is taken from one of Cyprian's earliest works, *To Quirinus: Testimonies against the Jews,* written between 247 and 249, after his conversion but before he became bishop. The work consists of three collections of biblical prooftexts listed under various subject headings. Book 1 contains biblical quotations aimed at showing that God had rejected the Jews and that in their place the Gentile Church received the Kingdom of God. Book 2 presents numerous prooftexts demonstrating various facets of the Christian understanding of Jesus as Christ and Lord. Book 3, which was written shortly afterward, offers a survey of biblical texts that describe Christian duties and virtues. Presented here are four subject headings, with their accompanying prooftexts, selected from book two.

Cyprian's *To Quirinus: Testimonies against the Jews* represents the earliest preserved Christian example of *testimonia* ("testimonies") literature. In antiquity, Greek and Roman authors made use of *florilegia* ("anthologies"), which consisted of quotations of famous authors organized by theme. Christian *testimonia* lists are *florilegia* devoted to biblical prooftexts. Because Cyprian compiled his "testimonies" so soon after his conversion, many have supposed that he must have borrowed from earlier Greek collections of *testimonia.* The discovery of *testimonia* texts at Qumran (4QFlorilegium; 4QTestimonia) strengthens the likelihood that collections of biblical prooftexts were available to Christians before the time of Cyprian. Indications that an author may have been utilizing a *testimonia* list include: (1) composite quotations without awareness that different sources have been combined; (2) quotations where the wording seems to have been adjusted to support a common theme; and (3) the use of a specific series of quotations in different places to prove the same point. It has been suggested, for example, that some of the biblical quotations in the *Epistle of Barnabas* and Justin Martyr were taken from Christian books of "testimonies." Not only is Cyprian's *To Quirinus: Testimonies against the Jews* important because later Christian writers used it extensively, but it may also provide a window into earlier Christian *testimonia* literature.[1]

To Quirinus: Testimonies against the Jews 2.1, 6, 27–28

2.1. That Christ is the first-born, and that he is the wisdom of God, by whom all things were made:

In Solomon, in the Proverbs: "The Lord established me in the beginning of his ways, into his works: before the world he founded me. In the beginning, before he made the earth and before he appointed the abysses, before the fountains of waters gushed forth, before the mountains were settled, before all the hills, the Lord begot me. He made the countries and the uninhabitable places, and the uninhabitable bounds under heaven. When he prepared the heaven, I was present with him; and when he set apart his seat. When he made the strong clouds above the winds, and when he placed the strengthened fountains under heaven, when he made the mighty foundations of the earth, I was by his side, ordering them: I was he in whom he delighted: moreover, I daily rejoiced before his face in all time, when he rejoiced in the perfected earth."[2] Also

---

1. On *testimonia* literature and early Christianity, see *Pseudo-Gregory of Nyssa: Testimonies Against the Jews*, trans. Martin C. Albl (Atlanta: SBL, 2004), xiii–xvii; and M. Kamptner, "Testimonies, Collections of," in *Dictionary of Early Christian Literature*, ed. S. Döpp and W. Geerlings (New York: Crossroad, 2000), 558–59.
2. Prov 8:22–31. Cyprian's scriptural quotations serve as important witnesses to the "Old

in the same, in Ecclesiasticus:[3] "I went forth out of the mouth of the Most High, first-born before every creature; I made the unwearying light to rise in the heavens, and I covered the whole earth with a cloud; I dwelt in the high places, and my throne in the pillar of the cloud; I compassed the circle of heaven, and I penetrated into the depth of the abyss, and I walked on the waves of the sea, and I stood in all the earth; and in every people and in every nation I had the preeminence, and by my own strength I have trodden the hearts of all the excellent and the humble; in me is all hope of life and virtue; pass over to me, all you who desire me."[4] Also in the eighty-eighth Psalm: "And I will establish him as my first-born, the highest among the kings of the earth. I will keep my mercy for him forever, and my faithful covenant for him; and I will establish his seed forever and ever. If his children forsake my law, and walk not in my judgments; if they profane my judgments, and do not observe my precepts, I will visit their wicked deeds with a rod, and their sins with scourges; but my mercy I will not scatter away from them."[5] Also in the Gospel according to John, the Lord says: "And this is life eternal, that they should know you, the only and true God, and Jesus Christ, whom you have sent. I have glorified you on the earth: I have finished the work that you gave me to do. And now, glorify me with yourself, with the glory which I had with you before the world was made."[6] Also Paul to the Colossians: "Who is

Latin" Bible, that is, the earliest translations of the Septuagint into Latin. The "Old Latin" (*Vetus Latina*) was the Bible used by Latin-speaking Christians before Jerome's translations became dominant. Moreover, the "Old Latin" text sometimes provides the best witness to the original (i.e., pre-hexaplaric) version of the Septuagint, that is, the form of the Septuagint text before it was interpolated with words and phrases from Origen's *Hexapla*, as one finds in the major manuscript witnesses to the Septuagint.

3. "In the same," that is, "in Solomon," who is taken to be the author of Ecclesiasticus (also known as Ben Sira or [the Wisdom of] Sirach).

4. Cf. Sir 24:3–6, 19 (Greek); 24:11 (Vulgate).

5. Ps 89:27–33 (Psalm 88 in the Septuagint).

6. John 17:3–5.

the image of the invisible God, and the first-born of every creature."[7] Also in the same place: "The first-born from the dead, that he might in all things become the holder of the preeminence."[8] In the Apocalypse, too: "I am Alpha and Omega, the beginning and the end. I will give to him that is thirsting from the fountain of the water of life freely."[9] That he also is both the wisdom and the power of God, Paul proves in his first Epistle to the Corinthians. "Because the Jews require a sign, and the Greeks seek after wisdom: but we preach Christ crucified, to the Jews indeed a stumbling-block, and to the Gentiles foolishness; but to them that are called, both Jews and Greeks, Christ the power of God and the wisdom of God."[10]

2.6. That Christ Is God:

In Genesis: "And God said to Jacob, 'Arise, and go up to the place of Bethel, and dwell there; and make there an altar to that God who appeared to you when you fled from the face of your brother Esau.'"[11] Also in Isaiah: "Thus says the Lord, the God of Sabaoth:[12] 'Egypt is wearied; moreover, the merchandise of the Ethiopians and the tall men of the Sabeans shall pass over to you, and they shall be your servants and shall walk after you bound with chains; and they shall worship you and shall pray to you, because God is in you, and there is no other God besides you. For you are God, and we did not know it, O God of Israel, our Savior. They who oppose you shall all

---

7. Col 1:15.
8. Col 1:18.
9. Rev 21:6.
10. 1 Cor 1:22–24.
11. Gen 35:1.
12. The Hebrew here simply has YHWH, "the LORD." The preserved Septuagint gives *kyrios sabaōth*, which reflects the Hebrew YHWH ṣeba'ōt, "the LORD of Hosts." Cyprian's text has two words for God ('the Lord, the God'), and passes on the Septuagint's transliteration of *sabaōth* ("Hosts").

be confounded and made afraid, and they shall fall into confusion.'"[13] Likewise in the same: "The voice of one crying in the wilderness, prepare the way of the Lord, make straight the paths of our God. Every channel shall be filled up, and every mountain and hill shall be made low, and all crooked places shall be made straight, and rough places plain; and the glory of the Lord shall be seen, and all flesh shall see the salvation of God, because the Lord has spoken it."[14] Moreover, in Jeremiah: "This is our God, and no other shall be esteemed beside him, who has found all the way of knowledge and has given it to Jacob his son, and to Israel his beloved. After this he was seen upon earth, and he conversed with people."[15] Also in Zechariah God says: "And they shall cross over through the narrow sea, and they shall smite the waves in the sea, and they shall dry up all the depths of the rivers; and all the haughtiness of the Assyrians shall be confounded, and the scepter of Egypt shall be taken away. And I will strengthen them in the Lord their God, and in his name they shall glory, says the Lord."[16] Moreover, in Hosea the Lord says: "I will not act in accordance with the anger of my indignation, I will not allow Ephraim to be destroyed; for I am God, and there is not a holy man in you: and I will not enter into the city; I will go after God."[17] Also in the forty-fourth Psalm: "Your throne, O God, is forever and ever; the scepter of righteousness is the scepter of your kingdom. You have loved righteousness and hated iniquity; therefore God, your God, has anointed you with the oil of gladness above your fellows."[18] So, too, in the forty-fifth Psalm: "Be still, and know that I am God. I will be exalted among the nations, and

---

13. Isa 45:14–16.
14. Isa 40:3–5. Note the "Old Latin" (and Septuagint) phrase "the salvation of God."
15. This is a quotation of the deuterocanonical book of Baruch 3:35–37.
16. Zech 10:11–12.
17. Hos 11:9–10 (see the Septuagint).
18. Ps 45:6–7 (Psalm 44 in the Septuagint).

I will be exalted in the earth."[19] Also in the eighty-first Psalm: "They have not known, neither have they understood; they will walk on in darkness."[20] Also in the sixty-seventh Psalm: "Sing to God, sing praises to his name; make a way for him who goes up into the west; God is His name."[21] Also in the Gospel according to John: "In the beginning was the Word, and the Word was with God, and God was the Word."[22] Also in the same: "The Lord said to Thomas, 'Reach here your finger, and behold my hands; and do not be faithless, but believing.' Thomas answered and said to him, 'My Lord and my God.' Jesus says to him, 'Because you have seen me, you have believed; blessed are they who have not seen, and yet have believed.'"[23] Also Paul to the Romans: "I would wish that I myself were accursed from Christ for my brethren and my kindred according to the flesh; who are Israelites, to whom belong the adoption, and the glory, and the covenant, and the appointment of the law, and the service of God, and the promises; whose are the fathers; of whom, according to the flesh, Christ came, who is God over all, blessed for evermore."[24] Also in the Apocalypse: "I am Alpha and Omega, the beginning and the end. I will give to him that is thirsting from the fountain of the water of life freely. He that overcomes shall possess these things, and their inheritance; and I will be his God, and he shall be my son."[25] Also in the eighty-first Psalm: "God stood in the congregation of gods, and judging gods in the midst."[26] And again in the same place: "I have said, 'You are

19. Ps 46:10 (Psalm 45 in the Septuagint).
20. Ps 82:5 (Psalm 81 in the Septuagint).
21. Ps 68:4 (Psalm 67 in the Septuagint).
22. John 1:1.
23. John 20:27–29.
24. Rom 9:3–5.
25. Rev 21:6–7.
26. Ps 82:1 (Psalm 81 in the Septuagint).

gods; and you are all the children of the Highest: but you shall die like mortals.'"[27] But if they who have been righteous and have obeyed the divine precepts may be called gods, how much more is Christ, the Son of God, God! Thus he himself says in the Gospel according to John: "Is it not written in the law that I said, 'You are gods'? If he called them 'gods' to whom the word of God was given, and the Scripture cannot be relaxed, do you say to him whom the Father has sanctified and sent into the world, 'you blaspheme,' because I said, 'I am the Son of God'? If I do not perform the works of my Father, do not believe me; but if I do, and yet you will not believe me, believe the works, and know that the Father is in me, and I in Him."[28] Also in the Gospel according to Matthew: "And you shall call his name 'Emmanuel,' which is, being interpreted, 'God with us.'"[29]

2.27 That it is impossible to attain to God the Father, except by his Son Jesus Christ:

In the Gospel: "I am the way, and the truth, and the life: no one comes to the Father but by me."[30] Also in the same place: "I am the door; by me if anyone shall enter in, he shall be saved."[31] Also in the same place: "Many prophets and righteous men have desired to see the things that you see, and have not seen them; and to hear those things that you hear, and have not heard them."[32] Also in the same place: "The one who believes on the Son has eternal life; the one who is not obedient in word to the Son does not have life; but the wrath of God shall abide upon him."[33] Also Paul to the Ephesians: "And when he

---

27. Ps 82:6–7 (Psalm 81 in the Septuagint).
28. John 10:34–38.
29. Matt 1:23.
30. John 14:6.
31. John 10:9.
32. Matt 13:17. Cf. John 8:56.

had come, he preached peace to you, to those who are far off, and peace to those who are near, because through him we both have access in one Spirit to the Father."[34] Also to the Romans: "For all have sinned and fail of the glory of God; but they are justified by his gift and grace, through the redemption which is in Christ Jesus."[35] Also in the Epistle of Peter the apostle: "Christ died once for our sins, the just for the unjust, that he might present us to God."[36] Also in the same place: "For in this also it was preached to them that are dead, that they might be raised again."[37] Also in the Epistle of John: "Whoever denies the Son, the same one also does not have the Father. The one who confesses the Son has both the Son and the Father."[38]

2.28. *That Jesus Christ shall come as a Judge:*

In Malachi: "Behold, the day of the Lord comes, burning as an oven; and all the foreigners and all the wicked shall be as stubble; and the day that comes shall burn them up, says the Lord."[39] Also in the forty-ninth Psalm: "God the Lord of gods has spoken, and he has called the earth. From the rising of the sun even to its setting, out of Zion is the beauty of his glory. God shall come manifestly; our God, and he shall not keep silent. A fire shall burn before him, and around him shall be a great storm. He has called the heaven above, and the earth, that he may separate his people. Gather together his saints to him, those who arrange his covenant with sacrifices. And the heavens shall announce his righteousness, for God is

33. John 3:36.
34. Eph 2:17–18.
35. Rom 3:23–24.
36. 1 Pet 3:18.
37. 1 Pet 4:6.
38. 1 John 2:23.
39. Mal 4:1.

the judge."[40] Also in Isaiah: "The Lord God of strength shall go forth, and he shall smash war; he shall stir up strife, and shall cry aloud over his enemies with strength. I have been silent; shall I always be silent?"[41] Also in the sixty-seventh Psalm: "Let God arise, and let his enemies be scattered; and let those who hate him flee from His face. As smoke vanishes, let them vanish; as wax melts from the face of fire, thus let the sinners perish from the face of God. And let the righteous be glad and rejoice in the sight of God; and let them be glad with joyfulness. Sing to God, sing praises to His name; make a way for Him who goes up into the west. God is his name. They shall be cast into confusion before the face of Him who is the Father of orphans and the Judge of widows. God is in his holy place: God, who makes people to dwell with one mind in a house, bringing forth them that are bound in strength, and similarly those who provoke to anger, who dwell in the tombs. God, when you went forth in the sight of your people, in passing through the desert."[42] Also in the eighty-first Psalm: "Arise, O God, judge the earth; for You will drive them out, among all nations."[43] Also in the Gospel according to Matthew: "What have we to do with you, O Son of David? Why have you come here to punish us before the time?"[44] Likewise according to John: "The Father judges nothing, but he has given all judgment to the Son, that all may honor the Son as they honor the Father. He who does not honor the Son honors not the Father who sent him."[45] So, too, in the second Epistle of Paul to the Corinthians: "We must all appear before the judgment seat of Christ, so that every

---

40. Ps 50:1–6 (Psalm 49 in the Septuagint).
41. Isa 42:13–14.
42. Ps 68:1–7 (Psalm 67 in the Septuagint).
43. Ps 82:8 (Psalm 81 in the Septuagint).
44. Matt 8:29.
45. John 5:22–23.

one may bear the things proper to his body, according to those things which he has done, whether they be good or evil."[46]

46. 2 Cor 5:10.

6

Origen

Origen was born ca. 185 CE to Christian parents living in Alexandria, Egypt. He received a thorough education in classical literature and philosophy, and his writings also reflect his intimate familiarity with the Bible and with theological authors such as Philo and Clement of Alexandria. Origen's father died as a martyr ca. 202 and his family's property was seized, so Origen supported his mother and brothers by teaching literature. Later, Origen turned over the teaching of secular studies to others and focused his attention exclusively on catechetical instruction and more advanced lectures in theology. Origen's immense literary output was made possible by the financial support of a wealthy patron in Alexandria named Ambrose, whom Origen had led out of "gnostic" beliefs into mainstream Christian faith.

Throughout his career, Origen would travel around—for example, to Rome, Athens, Arabia, Syria, and Jerusalem—

defending Christianity against pagan critics and disputing with those whom the mainstream church regarded as heretics. In ca. 231 Origen was ordained as a presbyter by bishops in Palestine, which caused such a rift between Origen and the bishop of Alexandria that Origen had to leave Alexandria and relocate to Caesarea, where he died and left his library. During the Decian persecution of 250, Origen was placed under torture in order to force him to renounce his beliefs, since he was a prominent spokesperson for Christianity. Nevertheless, he held firm to his Christian faith and refused to apostatize. Origen was still alive when the Emperor Decius died in 251, but his health was apparently weakened as a result of his ordeals and he died shortly afterward, ca. 253. Among Origen's many compositions are *An Exhortation to Martyrdom, On Prayer,* and the apologetic treatise *Against Celsus,* which is a defense of Christianity in the face of learned pagan criticism. Origen also composed numerous homilies, commentaries, and exegetical notes on Scripture. He was the first early Christian scholar to work through biblical books systematically and to provide Christian exegesis for the whole biblical canon. Origen's knowledge of Scripture clearly went beyond select prooftexts; throughout his writings he cites a wide range of parallel biblical passages from all over the canon. Of Origen's exegetical output only a small portion survives; for example: parts of commentaries on Matthew, John, Romans, and the Song of Songs, and homilies on Genesis, Exodus, Leviticus, Numbers, Joshua, Judges, Isaiah, Jeremiah, and Ezekiel. Origen's writings on Scripture had an enormous influence on later Christian biblical interpretation, both in their original Greek versions and through Latin translations. Interpreters such as Eusebius of Caesarea, Gregory of Nyssa, Didymus of Alexandria, Hilary of Poitiers, Ambrose of Milan, and Jerome of Stridon borrowed extensively from Origen, and virtually every biblical exegete of the fourth century in Greek and Latin came under Origen's influence in some way.

One of Origen's major contributions to biblical studies was the *Hexapla,* a six-column version of the Old Testament prepared under Origen's supervision. In its original form the *Hexapla* presented (I) the Hebrew text in one column, (II) a transliteration of the Hebrew into Greek characters in the next, and then four Greek translations: (III) Aquila, (IV) Symmachus, (V) the Septuagint, and (VI) Theodotion. Aquila, Symmachus, and Theodotion were Greek translations produced in the second century CE, although Theodotion at least was based on earlier revisions to the Septuagint. Aquila was regarded as the most literalistic in comparison with the Hebrew original, Symmachus was generally thought to be the clearest translation, and Theodotion was the closest to the Septuagint. In the Septuagint column, Origen added words and clauses (mostly from Theodotion) where these were present in the Hebrew but lacking in the Septuagint, marking these with an *asterisk*; and he signaled with an *obelus* wherever the Septuagint contained something that was absent from the Hebrew. Origen adapted these critical signs from classical literary scholars. Later Christian writers made extensive use of Origen's *Hexapla* as an exegetical tool, as will be seen below (e.g., Eusebius of Caesarea and Jerome).

Origen's legacy in the church is complicated.[1] On the one hand, his writings were foundational for the development of mainstream Christian theology and exegesis. On the other hand, some of Origen's ideas sparked considerable

---

1. On Origen's both favorable and negative reception in later church history, see Mario Baghos, "The Conflicting Portrayals of Origen in the Byzantine Tradition," *Phronema* 30 (2015): 69–104; and H. Crouzel and E. Prinzivalli, "Origen," in *Encyclopedia of Ancient Christianity*, ed. A. Di Berardino (Downers Grove, IL: InterVarsity, 2014): 2:977–83.

controversy, especially when later admirers took certain of his ideas to extremes. This eventually led to an official condemnation of Origen at Constantinople in the sixth century. The formal status of this ecclesiastical pronouncement against Origen is debated today, but the controversies attached to Origen's name after his death certainly account for the loss of so many of his writings. In evaluating Origen, however, it is important to remember his time and place in history. Origen taught and defended the faith within a Greco-Roman world that was highly critical of Christianity. He addressed a great many complex theological questions for the first time without the aid of any major church council or previous Christian commentaries. In the preface to his theological treatise *First Principles*, Origen states that he accepts as authoritative the teaching of the church as handed down from the apostles; his goal is simply to explore the foundational principles for doctrines that had not been fully explained (*First Principles*, "Preface" 2–10), proposing solutions to difficult problems, but not claiming to have the final answer (see *First Principles* 1.6.4; 2.3.7; 3.4.5). Origen saw himself as obedient to the Church's received tradition as he knew it in his own context. It is understandable that he does not always conform to doctrinal standards of later times.

The selection below is from book 4 of *First Principles*, which was written ca. 229, shortly before Origen's move to Caesarea. This work is preserved in its entirety only in the Latin translation made by Rufinus of Aquileia, who made slight alterations in the translation in order to soften some of Origen's more controversial suggestions. However, numerous fragments of the original Greek survive, including the selection given here, which is preserved in the *Philocalia* of Origen, a collection of passages from Origen's writings dealing with

Scripture compiled in the fourth century by Basil of Caesarea and Gregory of Nazianzus. The first three books of *First Principles* address topics such as the nature of God, free will, and the final consummation of the world. Book 4, chs. 1-3, discuss the interpretation of Scripture. Origen begins book 4, ch. 1, with reasons why he regards the Old and New Testaments as divine writings, such as the fact that Moses alone succeeded in enacting a law that people beyond his own nation accepted, and the fact that many people from diverse places have adopted the religion of Jesus despite persecutions. Origen then attempts to demonstrate the divine nature of Jesus, and on this basis to show that the writings that prophesy about Jesus are divinely inspired (*First Principles* 4.1.6).

First Principles 4.2.1-9; 4.3.1-5

Book 4, ch. 2: *How Divine Scripture should be read and interpreted.*

1. Now that we have spoken cursorily about the inspiration of the divine Scriptures it is necessary to discuss the manner in which they are to be read and understood, since many mistakes have been made in consequence of the method by which the holy documents ought to be interpreted not having been discovered by the multitude. For the hard-hearted and ignorant members of the circumcision have refused to believe in our Savior because they think that they are keeping closely to the language of the prophecies that relate to him, and they see that he did not literally "proclaim release to captives," or build what they consider to be a real "city of God," or "cut off the chariots from Ephraim and the horse from Jerusalem," or "eat butter and honey, and choose the good before he knew or preferred the evil."[2]

Further, they think that it is the wolf, the four-footed animal, which is said in prophecy to be going to "feed with the lamb, and the leopard to lie down with the kid, and the calf and bull and lion to feed together, led by a little child, and the ox and the bear to pasture together, their young ones growing up with each other, and the lion to eat straw like the ox";[3] and having seen none of these events literally happening during the advent of him whom we believe to be Christ they did not accept our Lord Jesus, but crucified him on the ground that he had wrongly called himself Christ.

And the members of the heretical sects, reading the passage "A fire has been kindled in my anger"; and "I am a jealous God, visiting the sins of the fathers upon the children to the third and fourth generation"; and "It repents me that I have anointed Saul to be king"; and "I, God, make peace and create evil"; and elsewhere "There is no evil in a city, which the Lord did not do"; and further "Evils came down from the Lord upon the gates of Jerusalem"; and "An evil spirit from the Lord troubled Saul";[4] and ten thousand other passages like these, have not dared to disbelieve that they are the writings of God, but believe them to belong to the Creator, whom the Jews worship. Consequently, they think that since the Creator is imperfect and not good, the Savior came here to proclaim a more perfect God who they say is not the Creator, and about whom they entertain diverse opinions.[5] Then having once fallen away from the Creator, who is the sole unbegotten God, they have given themselves up to fictions, fashioning mythical

---

2. See, respectively, Isa 61:1 (cf. Luke 4:19); Ps 46:4; 87:3; Ezek 48 (cf. Rev 21); Zech 9:10 (cf. Matt 21:4–5; John 12:14–16); Isa 7:15 (cf. Matt 1:23).

3. Isa 11:6–7.

4. See Deut 32:22; Jer 15:14; Exod 20:5; 1 Sam 15:11; Isa 45:7; Amos 3:6; Mic 1:12; 1 Sam 18:10.

5. Cf. *First Principles* 2.5.1, where Origen offers his refutation against those who assert that the Creator God is not the God and Father of Jesus Christ.

hypotheses according to which they suppose that there are some things that are seen and others that are not seen, all of which are the fancies of their own minds.

Moreover, even the simpler of those who claim to belong to the Church, while believing indeed that there is none greater than the Creator, in which they are right, yet believe such things about Him as would not be believed of the most savage and unjust of men.[6]

2. Now the reason why all those we have mentioned hold false opinions and make impious or ignorant assertions about God appears to be nothing else but this, that Scripture is not understood in its spiritual sense, but is interpreted according to the bare letter.[7] On this account we must explain to those who believe that the sacred books are not the works of men, but that they were composed and have come down to us as a result of the inspiration of the Holy Spirit by the will of the Father of the universe through Jesus Christ, what are the methods of interpretation that appear right to us, who keep to the rule of the heavenly Church of Jesus Christ through the succession from the Apostles.[8] That there are certain mystical revelations made known through the divine Scriptures is

---

6. A similar thought was expressed, independently of Origen, by Maimonides (d. 1204 CE), *Guide for the Perplexed* 1.59: "We cannot approve of what those foolish persons do who are extravagant in praise, fluent and prolix in the prayers they compose, and in the hymns they make in the desire to approach the Creator. They describe God in attributes which would be an offence if applied to a human being. . . . If they find some phrase suited to their object in the words of the Prophets they are still more inclined to consider that they are free to make use of such texts—which should at least be explained—to employ them in their literal sense, to derive new expressions from them, to form from them numerous variations, and to found whole compositions on them"; see *Moses Maimonides: The Guide for the Perplexed*, trans. M. Friedländer (2nd ed.; London: Routledge, 1904), 86.

7. Origen directs criticism against three groups: Jews ("members of the circumcision"), heretics (such as Marcionites and "gnostic" teachers), and simpler Christians, each of whom is censured for excessive literalism, although the error is theologically fatal only for the first two groups.

8. Origen here expresses his commitment to interpret Scripture within the context of the Church's apostolic tradition.

believed by all, even by the simplest of those who are adherents of the word; but what these revelations are, fair-minded and humble men confess that they do not know. If, for instance, an inquirer were to be in a difficulty about the intercourse of Lot with his daughters,[9] or the two wives of Abraham,[10] or the two sisters married to Jacob,[11] or the two handmaids who bore children by him,[12] they can say nothing except that these things are mysteries not understood by us.

But when the passage about the equipment of the tabernacle is read,[13] believing that the things described therein are types, they seek for ideas which they can attach to each detail that is mentioned in connection with the tabernacle. Now so far as concerns their belief that the tabernacle is a type of something they are not wrong; but in rightly attaching the word of Scripture to the particular idea of which the tabernacle is a type, here they sometimes fall into error. And they declare that all narratives that are supposed to speak about marriage or the begetting of children or wars or any other stories whatever that may be accepted among the multitude are types; but when we ask, of what, then sometimes owing to the lack of thorough training, sometimes owing to rashness, and occasionally, even when one is well trained and of sound judgment, owing to humanity's exceedingly great difficulty in discovering these things, the interpretation of every detail is not altogether clear.

3. And what must we say about the prophecies, which we all know are filled with riddles and dark sayings?[14] Or if we come to the Gospels, the accurate interpretation even of these,

9. Gen 19:30–38.
10. Gen 16:1–4.
11. Gen 29:21–30.
12. Gen 30:3–13.
13. Exodus 25–30; 35–40.
14. Prov 1:6; cf. *Against Celsus* 3.45; 7.10.

since it is an interpretation of the mind of Christ, demands that grace that was given to him who said, "We have the mind of Christ, that we may know the things that were freely given to us by God. Which things also we speak, not in words which human wisdom teaches, but which the Spirit teaches."[15] And who, on reading the revelations made to John, could fail to be amazed at the deep obscurity of the unspeakable mysteries contained therein, which are evident even to him who does not understand what is written? And as for the apostolic epistles, what man who is skilled in literary interpretation would think them to be plain and easily understood, when even in them there are thousands of passages that provide, as if through a window, a narrow opening leading to multitudes of the deepest thoughts?

Seeing, therefore, that these things are so, and that thousands of people make mistakes, it is dangerous for us when we read to declare lightly that we understand things for which the "key of knowledge" is necessary, which the Savior says is with "the lawyers."[16] And as for those who are unwilling to admit that these men held the truth before the coming of Christ, let them explain to us how it is that our Lord Jesus Christ says that the "key to knowledge" was with them, that is, with men who as these objectors say, had no books containing the secrets of knowledge and the all-perfect mysteries. For the passage runs as follows: "Woe unto you lawyers, for you have taken away the key of knowledge. You entered not in yourselves, and them that were entering in you hindered."[17]

4. The right way, therefore, as it appears to us, of approaching the Scriptures and gathering their meaning, is the

15. 1 Cor 2:16, 12–13.
16. Luke 11:52; cf. Matt 23:1–3.
17. Luke 11:52.

following, which is extracted from the writings themselves. We find some such rule as this laid down by Solomon in the Proverbs concerning the divine doctrines written therein: "And you, register them for yourself threefold in counsel and knowledge, that you may answer words of truth to those who question you."[18]

One must therefore register the meaning of the sacred writings in a threefold way upon one's own soul, so that the simple person may be edified by what we may call the flesh of the scripture, this name being given to the obvious interpretation; while the one who has made some progress may be edified by its soul, as it were; and the one who is perfect and like those mentioned by the apostle: "We speak wisdom among the perfect; yet a wisdom not of this world, nor of the rulers of this world, which are coming to nothing; but we speak God's wisdom in a mystery, even the wisdom that has been hidden, which God foreordained before the worlds unto our glory"[19]—this person may be edified by the spiritual law,[20] which has "a shadow of the good things to come."[21] For just as a human being consists of body, soul and spirit, so in the same way does the Scripture, which has been prepared by God to be given for the salvation of human beings.[22]

We therefore read in this light the passage in the *Shepherd*, a book which is despised by some, where Hermas is bidden to "write two books," and after this to "announce to the presbyters of the Church" what he has learned from the Spirit.

18. Prov 22:20–21 (Septuagint).
19. 1 Cor 2:6–7.
20. See Rom 7:14.
21. Heb 10:1.
22. Origen speaks here of three levels of meaning in the Scriptures. In the course of his exegesis Origen does not regularly identify two different spiritual senses beyond the literal, but occasionally he does; see Elizabeth Ann Dively Lauro, *The Soul and Spirit of Scripture within Origen's Exegesis* (Leiden: Brill, 2005).

This is the wording: "You shall write two books, and shall give one to Clement and one to Grapte. And Grapte shall admonish the widows and the orphans. But Clement shall send to the cities without, and you shall announce to the presbyters of the Church."[23]

Now Grapte, who admonishes the widows and orphans, is the bare letter, which admonishes those child souls that are not yet able to enroll God as their Father and are on this account called orphans, and which also admonishes those who while no longer associating with the unlawful bridegroom are in widowhood because they have not yet become worthy of the true one. But Clement, who has already gone beyond the letter, is said to send the sayings "to the cities without," as if to say, to the souls that are outside all bodily and lower thoughts; while the disciple of the Spirit is bidden to announce the message in person, no longer through letters but through living words, to the presbyters or elders of the whole Church of God, to men who have grown grey through wisdom.

5. But since there are certain passages of Scripture that, as we shall show in what follows, have no bodily sense at all, there are occasions when we must seek only for the soul and the spirit, as it were, of the passage. And possibly this is the reason why the water pots which, as we read in the Gospel according to John, are said to be set there "for the purifying of the Jews," contain two or three firkins apiece.[24] The language alludes to

---

23. This quotation comes from the *Shepherd of Hermas,* Vision II, 4.3. The *Shepherd of Hermas* is a composite work made up of "Visions," "Mandates," and "Similitudes," which were compiled together in the second century CE. Visions I–IV appear to be among the oldest parts. The *Shepherd* is found in codex Sinaiticus (fourth cent.) after the *Epistle of Barnabas.* The *Muratorian Canon* 73–80 (ca. second cent.) says that the *Shepherd* should be read by Christians, but not publicly in church among the Prophets or Apostles. The high status ascribed to the *Shepherd* in segments of early Christianity is attested not only by Origen, but also by Clement of Alexandria (*Stromateis* 6.131.2–4) and Irenaeus (*Against Heresies* 4.20.2). Tertullian (*On Prayer* 16; *On Modesty* 10) regarded the *Shepherd* as non-canonical, as did Jerome (*On Illustrious Men* 10) and most Christians by the fourth century.

those who are said by the apostle to be Jews "inwardly,"[25] and it means that these are purified through the word of the Scriptures, which contain in some cases "two firkins," that is, so to speak, the soul meaning and the spiritual meaning, and in other cases three, since some passages possess, in addition to those before-mentioned, a bodily sense as well, which is capable of edifying the hearers. And six water pots may reasonably allude to those who are being purified in the world, which was made in six days, a perfect number.[26]

6. That it is possible to derive benefit from the first, and to this extent helpful meaning, is witnessed by the multitudes of sincere and simple believers. But of the kind of explanation which penetrates as it were to the soul an illustration is found in Paul's first Epistle to the Corinthians. "For," he says, "it is written; you shall not muzzle the ox that treads out the corn." Then in explanation of this law he adds, "Is it for the oxen that God cares? Or does he say it altogether for our sake? Yes, for our sake it was written, because he that plows ought to plow in hope, and he that threshes, to thresh in hope of partaking."[27] And most of the interpretations adapted to the multitude which are in circulation and which edify those who cannot understand the higher meanings have something of the same character.

But it is a spiritual explanation when one is able to show of what kind of "heavenly things" the Jews "after the flesh" served a copy and a shadow, and of what "good things to come" the law has a "shadow."[28] And, speaking generally, we have,

24. John 2:6.
25. Rom 2:29.
26. On six as a perfect number, see Philo, *On the Creation of the World* 13–14; *Allegorical Interpretation* 1.3. As Philo explains, six is the first perfect number, in that 3 is half of 6, 2 is a third of 6, and 1 is a sixth of 6. Moreover, 2 is the first female number, 3 is the first male number, and $2 \times 3 = 6$.
27. 1 Cor 9:9–10; Deut 25:4. Cf. *First Principles* 2.4.2.

in accordance with the apostolic promise, to seek after "the wisdom in a mystery, even the wisdom that has been hidden, which God foreordained before the worlds unto the glory" of the righteous, "which none of the rulers of this world knew."[29] The same apostle also says somewhere, after mentioning certain narratives from Exodus and Numbers, that "these things happened unto them figuratively, and they were written for our sake, upon whom the ends of the ages are come."[30] He also gives hints to show what these things were figures of, when he says: "For they drank of that spiritual rock that followed them, and that rock was Christ."[31]

In another epistle, when outlining the arrangements of the tabernacle he quotes the words: "You shall make all things according to the figure that was shown you on the mountain."[32] Further, in the Epistle to the Galatians, speaking in terms of reproach to those who believe that they are reading the law and yet do not understand it, and laying it down that they who do not believe that there are allegories in the writings do not understand the law, he says: "Tell me, you that desire to be under the law, do you not hear the law? For it is written, that Abraham had two sons, one by the handmaid and one by the free woman. The son by the handmaid is born after the flesh; but the son by the free woman is born through promise. Which things contain an allegory; for these women are two covenants,"[33] and what follows. Now we must carefully mark each of the words spoken by him. He says, "You that desire to be under the law" (not "you that are under the law")

28. See Heb 8:5; Rom 2:28; 8:5; 9:8; Heb 10:1.
29. 1 Cor 2:7–8.
30. 1 Cor 10:11.
31. 1 Cor 10:4.
32. Heb 8:5; Exod 25:40.
33. Gal 4:21–24.

"do you not hear the law?" hearing being taken to mean understanding and knowing.

And in the Epistle to the Colossians, briefly epitomizing the meaning of the entire system of the law, he says: "Let no man therefore judge you in meat or in drink or in respect of a feast day or a new moon or a Sabbath, which are a shadow of the things to come."[34] Further, in the Epistle to the Hebrews, when discoursing about those who are of the circumcision, he writes: "They who serve that which is a copy and shadow of the heavenly things."[35] Now it is probable that those who have once admitted that the apostle is a divinely inspired man will feel no difficulty in regard to the five books ascribed to Moses; but in regard to the rest of the history they desire to learn whether those events also "happened figuratively."[36] We must note the quotation in the Epistle to the Romans: "I have left for myself seven thousand men, who have not bowed the knee to Baal,"[37] found in the third book of the Kings. Here Paul has taken it to stand for those who are Israelites "according to election,"[38] for not only are the gentiles benefited by the coming of Christ, but also some who belong to the divine race.

7. This being so, we must outline what seems to us to be the marks of a true understanding of the Scriptures. And in the first place we must point out that the aim of the Spirit who, by the providence of God through the Word who was "in the beginning with God,"[39] enlightened the servants of the truth, that is, the prophets and apostles, was pre-eminently concerned with the unspeakable mysteries connected with the affairs of people—and by people I mean at the present moment

34. Col 2:16–17.
35. Heb 8:5.
36. 1 Cor 10:11.
37. Rom 11:4; 1 Kgs 19:18.
38. See Rom 11:5.
39. John 1:1.

souls that make use of bodies—his purpose being that the one who is capable of being taught might, by "searching out" and devoting himself to the "deep things"[40] revealed in the spiritual meaning of the words, become partaker of all the doctrines of the Spirit's counsel.

And when we speak of the needs of souls, who cannot otherwise reach perfection except through the rich and wise truth about God, we attach of necessity pre-eminent importance to the doctrines concerning God and His only-begotten Son; of what nature the Son is, and in what manner he can be the Son of God, and what are the causes of his descending to the level of human flesh and completely assuming humanity; and what, also, is the nature of his activity, and towards whom and at what times it is exercised. It was necessary, too, that the doctrines concerning beings akin to humanity and the rest of the rational creatures, both those that are nearer the divine and those that have fallen from blessedness, and the causes of the fall of these latter, should be included in the accounts of the divine teaching; and the question of the differences between souls and how these differences arose, and what the world is and why it exists, and further, how it comes about that evil is so widespread and so terrible on earth, and whether it is not only to be found on earth but also in other places—all this it was necessary that we should learn.

8. Now while these and similar subjects were in the mind of the Spirit who enlightened the souls of the holy servants of the truth, there was a second aim, pursued for the sake of those who were unable to endure the burden of investigating matters of such importance. This was to conceal the doctrine relating to the before-mentioned subjects in words forming

40. 1 Cor 2:10.

a narrative that contained a record dealing with the visible creation, the formation of humanity and the successive descendants of the first human beings until the time when they became many; and also in other stories that recorded the acts of righteous people and the sins that these same people occasionally committed, seeing they were but human, and the deeds of wickedness, licentiousness and greed done by lawless and impious people.

But the most wonderful thing is, that by means of stories of wars and the conquerors and the conquered certain secret truths are revealed to those who are capable of examining these narratives; and, even more marvelous, through a written system of law the laws of truth are prophetically indicated, all these having been recorded in a series with a power which is truly appropriate to the wisdom of God. For the intention was to make even the outer covering of the spiritual truths, I mean the bodily part of the Scriptures, in many respects not unprofitable but capable of improving the multitude insofar as they receive it.[41]

9. But if the usefulness of the law and the sequence and ease of the narrative were at first sight clearly discernible throughout, we should be unaware that there was anything beyond the obvious meaning for us to understand in the Scriptures. Consequently the Word of God has arranged for certain stumbling-blocks, as it were, and hindrances and impossibilities to be inserted in the midst of the law and the history, in order that we may not be completely drawn away by the sheer attractiveness of the language,[42] and so either reject

---

41. In other words, through Scripture the Word reveals deeper truths to those ready to receive them, and at the same time conceals these harder doctrines from those not yet ready. Meanwhile, even the bodily sense of Scripture, underneath which the deeper truths are concealed, is intended by the Spirit to provide benefit for the novice reader.

42. According to Origen, God ordained that Scripture be written in a humble style in order to give prominence to the message, to highlight the power of God rather than

the true doctrines absolutely, on the ground that we learn from the Scriptures nothing worthy of God,[43] or else by never moving away from the letter fail to learn anything of the more divine element.

And we must also know this, that because the principal aim was to announce the connection that exists among spiritual events, those that have already happened and those that are yet to come to pass, whenever the Word found that things which had happened in history could be harmonized with these mystical events He used them, concealing from the multitude their deeper meaning. But wherever in the narrative the accomplishment of some particular deeds, which had been previously recorded for the sake of their more mystical meanings, did not correspond with the sequence of the intellectual truths, the Scripture wove into the story something which did not happen, occasionally something which could not happen, and occasionally something which might have happened but in fact did not.[44] Sometimes a few

human rhetorical skill, and to communicate with the masses; see Michael Graves, "The Literary Quality of Scripture as Seen by the Early Church," *Tyndale Bulletin* 61 (2010): 166–68.

43. On the principle that any proper interpretation of Scripture must present theological teaching that is "worthy of God," see (for example) Clement of Alexandria, *Stromateis* 6.15.124; 7.16.96; Origen, *Homilies on Joshua* 8.1, 6–7; *Homilies on Numbers* 27.12.12; *Homilies on Leviticus* 7.5.7; *Homilies on Jeremiah* 20.1; *Philocalia* 21.1–23; 27.1–13; Eusebius of Caesarea, *Preparation for the Gospel* 8.10; Didymus of Alexandria, *Commentary on Genesis* 1:4; Gregory of Nyssa, *Life of Moses* 2.91. Cf. John Chrysostom, *Homilies on Genesis* 15.8 ("let us understand everything in a manner proper to God because applied to God"); and Augustine, *On Christian Teaching* 3.11.17; 3.16.24. See Michael Graves, *The Inspiration and Interpretation of Scripture* (Grand Rapids: Eerdmans, 2014), 123–30; and Mark Sheridan, *Language for God in Patristic Tradition: Wrestling with Biblical Anthropomorphism* (Downers Grove, IL: InterVarsity, 2015), 224–26.

44. In Aristotle's *Poetics*, ch. 9, the distinction is made between the historian, who describes things that have happened, and the poet, whose task is to describe not what has happened but a kind of thing that might happen. Because of this distinction, poetry is sometimes more philosophical and of graver import than history, since poetry's statements are universal by nature, whereas history deals strictly with particulars. Sextus Empiricus divided narration into three categories: *historia*, a narration of things that happened, *plasma*, a narration of things that are not historically true but are similar to real events (= realistic fiction), and *mythos*, a narration of things that did

words are inserted which in the bodily sense are not true, and at other times a greater number.[45]

A similar method can be discerned also in the law, where it is often possible to find a precept that is useful for its own sake, and suitable to the time when the law was given. Sometimes, however, the precept does not appear to be useful. At other times even impossibilities are recorded in the law for the sake of the more skillful and inquiring readers, in order that these, by giving themselves to the toil of examining what is written, may gain a sound conviction of the necessity of seeking in such instances a meaning worthy of God.

And not only did the Spirit supervise the writings which were previous to the coming of Christ, but because he is the same Spirit and proceeds from the one God he has dealt in like manner with the Gospels and the writings of the apostles. For the history even of these is not everywhere pure, events being

---

not happen and are unrealistic (*Against the Mathematicians* 1.263–65). Isidore of Seville, *Etymologies* 1.40–44, passed this basic system on to the Latin West as *historia* (history), *argumentum* (realistic fiction), and *fabula* (unrealistic fiction), with *fabula* serving either to entertain, to describe the nature of things, or to teach morals. Within this stream of thought, Origen is suggesting that biblical writers sometimes blended these categories together into a kind of literature that is both history and poetry.

45. Origen here may be contrasted with the first-century CE Stoic philosopher Cornutus, who perceived a mixture of falsehood and truth in Homer and Hesiod and so censured the poets for their errors. Cornutus calls a passage in the Iliad a "fragment of an ancient myth" and warns his readers: "There are situations where fictional accretions have been added to the genealogies which were passed on according to these myths by people who do not understand the message they cryptically contain, but use them as they do mere fictions. In these situations, one ought not to give them a place contrary to reason" (*Epidromē* 17.1, 3). Later, Cornutus says of Hesiod: "I think he has transmitted some things from the ancients, but has added other things of a more mythical nature from his own imagination. In this fashion he corrupted a great deal of the true primitive theology" (*Epidromē* 17.11); see R. S. Hays, "Lucius Annaeus Cornutus' *Epidromē* (Introduction to the Traditions of Greek Theology): Introduction, Translation, and Notes" (PhD diss., University of Texas at Austin, 1983), 77–78, 82. Origen's view of Scripture is significantly different. According to Origen, biblical writers incorporated fictional elements into Scripture under divine inspiration in order to teach the true theology which God intended. Whereas Cornutus instructs his Stoic readers to bracket out the fictional accretions in order to learn correct theology from the original myths, Origen teaches his Christian readers to accept the whole message of the biblical text as the inspired writer composed it.

woven together in the bodily sense without having actually happened; nor do the law and the commandments contained therein entirely declare what is reasonable.

Book 4, ch. 3: *The Principle underlying the obscurities in divine Scripture and its impossible or unreasonable character in places, if taken literally.*

1. Now what person of intelligence will believe that the first and the second and the third day, and the evening and the morning existed without the sun and moon and stars? And that the first day, if we may so call it, was even without a heaven?[46] And who is so silly as to believe that God, after the manner of a farmer, "planted a paradise eastward in Eden," and set in it a visible and palpable "tree of life," of such a sort that anyone who tasted its fruit with his bodily teeth would gain life; and again that one could partake of "good and evil" by masticating the fruit taken from the tree of that name?[47] And when God is said to "walk in the paradise in the cool of the day" and Adam to hide himself behind a tree, I do not think anyone will doubt that these are figurative expressions which indicate certain mysteries through a semblance of history and not through actual events.[48]

Further, when Cain "goes out from the face of God" it seems clear to thoughtful people that this statement impels the reader to inquire what the "face of God" is and how anyone can "go out" from it.[49] And what more need I say, when those

---

46. See Gen 1:3–13.
47. Gen 2:8–9, 15–17. Cf. Philo, *Allegorical Interpretation* 1.43: "Far be it from man's reasoning to be the victim of so great impiety as to suppose that God tills the soil and plants pleasures. We should at once be at a loss to tell from what motive He could do so. Not to provide Himself with pleasant refreshment and comfort. Let not such fables even enter our minds" (*Philo: Allegorical Interpretation*, trans. F. H. Colson and G. H. Whitaker [LCL 226; Cambridge, MA: Harvard University Press, 1929], 175).
48. Gen 3:8.

who are not altogether blind can collect thousands of such instances, recorded as actual events, but which did not happen literally?

Even the Gospels are full of passages of this kind, as when the Devil takes Jesus up into a "high mountain" in order to show him from there "the kingdoms of the whole world and the glory of them."[50] For what man who does not read such passages carelessly would fail to condemn those who believe that with the eye of the flesh, which requires a great height to enable us to perceive what is below and at our feet, the kingdoms of the Persians, Scythians, Indians, and Parthians were seen, and the manner in which their rulers are glorified by people? And the careful reader will detect thousands of other passages like this in the Gospels, which will convince him that events which did not take place at all are woven into the records of what literally did happen.

2. And to come to the Mosaic legislation, many of the laws, so far as their literal observance is concerned, are clearly irrational, while others are impossible.[51] An example of irrationality is the prohibition to eat vultures,[52] seeing that nobody even in the worst famine was ever driven by want to the extremity of eating these creatures. And in regard to the command that children of eight days old who are uncircumcised shall be destroyed from among their people,[53]

---

49. Gen 4:16. Cf. Philo, *On the Posterity of Cain* 1–9.
50. Matt 4:8.
51. Aristotle's *Poetics*, ch. 25, contains a discussion of literary "Problems and Their Solutions." Aristotle describes several kinds of problems that could be raised with traditional poetry and offers possible solutions. Potential criticisms against poets mentioned by Aristotle are that they have said things that are impossible (*adynata*), irrational (*aloga*), harmful (*blabera*), contradictory (*hypenantia*), or contrary to artistic standards (*para tēn orthotēta tēn kata technēn*). Origen invokes the categories of "impossible" and "irrational" here, not to condemn Scripture, but to argue that the intended sense of the text at these points is beyond the literal one.
52. Lev 11:13.
53. Gen 17:14.

if the law relating to these children were really meant to be carried out according to the letter, the proper course would be to order the death of their fathers or those by whom they were being brought up. But as it is the Scripture says: "Every male that is uncircumcised, who shall not be circumcised on the eighth day, shall be destroyed from among his people."[54]

And if you would like to see some impossibilities that are enacted in the law, let us observe that the goat-stag,[55] which Moses commands us to offer in sacrifice as a clean animal, is a creature that cannot possibly exist; while as to the griffin,[56] which the lawgiver forbids to be eaten, there is no record that it has ever fallen into human hands. Moreover in regard to the celebrated Sabbath, a careful reader will see that the command, "You shall sit each one in your dwellings; let none of you go out from his place on the Sabbath day,"[57] is an impossible one to observe literally, for no living creature could sit for a whole day and not move from his seat.

Consequently the members of the circumcision and all those who maintain that nothing more than the actual wording is signified make no inquiry whatever into some matters, such as the goat-stag, the griffin and the vulture, while on others they babble copiously, bringing forward lifeless traditions, as for instance when they say, in reference to the Sabbath, that each person's "place" is two thousand cubits.[58] Others, however, among whom is Dositheus the Samaritan, condemn such an

---

54. Gen 17:14; "on the eighth day" is present in the Septuagint.
55. The Hebrew text of Deut 14:5 permits eating the *'aqqō*, "wild goat." The Septuagint translated this as *tragelaphos*, "goat-stag," which was the name of a legendary creature.
56. See Lev 11:13; Deut 14:12. The Hebrew has *peres*, "vulture." The Septuagint translated this as *gryps*, "griffin," i.e., the mythological beast.
57. Exod 16:29.
58. In the Mishnah, movement on the Sabbath is restricted to no more than 2,000 cubits beyond the boundaries of one's town, or beyond some specific location that has been properly defined as one's temporary abode (m. Eruvin 4:3, 5, 7, 8; 5:7, 9; cf. m. Sotah 5:3; Num 35:5).

interpretation, and believe that in whatever position a man is found on the Sabbath day he should remain there until evening.[59]

Further, the command "not to carry a burden on the Sabbath day" is impossible;[60] and on this account the teachers of the Jews have indulged in endless chatter, asserting that one kind of shoe is a burden, but another is not, and that a sandal with nails is a burden, but one without nails is not, and that what is carried on one shoulder is a burden, but not what is carried on both.[61]

3. If now we approach the Gospel in search of similar instances, what can be more irrational than the command: "Salute no one by the way,"[62] which simple people believe that the Savior enjoined upon the apostles? Again, to speak of the right cheek being struck is most incredible,[63] for every striker, unless he suffers from some unnatural defect, strikes the left cheek with his right hand. And it is impossible to accept the precept from the Gospel about the "right eye that offends"; for granting the possibility of a person being "offended" through his sense of sight, how can the blame be attributed to the right eye, when there are two eyes that see? And what man, even supposing he accuses himself of "looking on a woman to

59. Dositheus of Samaria is a figure known from several early Christian sources as a teacher of heresy (Origen, *Against Celsus* 1.57; 6.11; Pseudo-Clementine, *Homilies* 2.24.1–7; Pseudo-Tertullian, *Against All Heresies* 1; Eusebius, *Ecclesiastical History* 4.22.5). The precise nature of Dositheus's views is not clear, but he appears to have insisted on strict observance of at least some aspects of Mosaic law.

60. Jer 17:21.

61. The Mishnah forbids a person from going out on the Sabbath wearing sandals shod with nails (m. Shabbat 6:2). Early rabbinic sources do not state that what is carried on both shoulders does not legally constitute a "burden," but as pointed out by N. de Lange, *Origen and the Jews* (Cambridge: Cambridge University Press, 1976), 40, such an argument could have been made on the basis of the singular noun "shoulder" in Num 7:9. Origen clearly knows something about rabbinic Jewish teaching, but his representations of Jewish views may sometimes reflect misunderstanding and are certainly skewed due to his polemical aims.

62. Luke 10:4.

63. See Matt 5:39.

lust after her" and attributes the blame to his right eye alone, would act rationally if he were to cast this eye away?[64]

Further, the apostle lays down this precept: "Was any called being circumcised? Let him not become uncircumcised."[65] Now in the first place anyone who wishes can see that these words have no relation to the subject at hand; and how can we help thinking that they have been inserted at random, when we remember that the apostle is here laying down precepts about marriage and purity? In the second place who will maintain that it is wrong for a man to put himself into a condition of uncircumcision, if that were possible, in view of the disgrace which is felt by most people to attach to circumcision?

4. We have mentioned all these instances with the object of showing that the aim of the divine power which bestowed on us the holy Scriptures is not that we should accept only what is found in the letter; for occasionally the records taken in a literal sense are not true, but actually absurd and impossible, and even with the history that actually happened and the legislation that is in its literal sense useful there are other matters interwoven.

But someone may suppose that the former statement refers to all the Scriptures, and may suspect us of saying that because some of the history did not happen, therefore none of it happened; and because a certain law is irrational or impossible when taken literally, therefore no laws ought to be kept to the letter; or that the records of the Savior's life are not true in a physical sense; or that no law or commandment of his ought to be obeyed. We must assert, therefore, that in regard to some things we are clearly aware that the historical fact is true; as that Abraham was buried in the double cave at Hebron,

64. Matt 5:28–29; 18:9.
65. 1 Cor 7:18.

together with Isaac and Jacob and one wife of each of them;[66] and that Shechem was given as a portion to Joseph;[67] and that Jerusalem is the chief city of Judaea, in which a temple of God was built by Solomon; and thousands of other facts. For the passages which are historically true are far more numerous than those which are composed with purely spiritual meanings.

And again, who would deny that the command which says "Honor your father and your mother, that it may be well with you"[68] is useful quite apart from any spiritual interpretation, and that it ought certainly to be observed, especially when we remember that the apostle Paul has quoted it in the self-same words?[69] And what are we to say of the following: "You shall not murder; you shall not commit adultery; you shalt not steal; you shall not bear false witness"?[70]

Once again, in the Gospel there are commandments written which need no inquiry whether they are to be kept literally or not, as that which says, "I say to you, if anyone is angry with his brother,"[71] and what follows; and, "I say to you, do not swear at all."[72] Here, too, is an injunction of the apostle of which the literal meaning must be retained: "Admonish the disorderly, encourage the faint-hearted, support the weak, be longsuffering toward all";[73] though in the case of the more earnest readers it is possible to preserve each of the meanings, that is, while not setting aside the commandment in its literal sense, to preserve the depths of the wisdom of God.[74]

66. See Gen 23:19; 25:9–10; 49:29–32; 50:13–14.
67. See Gen 48:22; Josh 24:32.
68. Cf. Deut 5:16; Exod 20:12.
69. Eph 6:2–3.
70. Exod 20:13–16; Deut 5:17–20.
71. Matt 5:22.
72. Matt 5:34.
73. 1 Thess 5:14.
74. See Rom 11:33; 1 Cor 2:10.

5. Nevertheless the exact reader will hesitate in regard to some passages, finding himself unable to decide without considerable investigation whether a particular incident, believed to be history, actually happened or not, and whether the literal meaning of a particular law is to be observed or not. Accordingly he who reads in an exact manner must, in obedience to the Savior's precept which says, "Search the scriptures,"[75] carefully investigate how far the literal meaning is true and how far it is impossible, and to the utmost of his power must trace out from the use of similar expressions the meaning scattered everywhere through the Scriptures of that which when taken literally is impossible.

When, therefore, as will be clear to those who read, the passage as a connected whole is literally impossible, whereas the outstanding part of it is not impossible but even true, the reader must endeavor to grasp the entire meaning, connecting by an intellectual process the account of what is literally impossible with the parts that are not impossible but are historically true, these being interpreted allegorically in common with the parts which, so far as the letter goes, did not happen at all. For our contention with regard to the whole of divine Scripture is, that it all has a spiritual meaning, but not all a bodily meaning; for the bodily meaning is often proved to be an impossibility. Consequently the one who reads the divine books reverently, believing them to be divine writings, must exercise great care.

---

75. John 5:39.

7

———

Eusebius of Caesarea

Eusebius was born in Palestine ca. 265 CE and was educated in
Caesarea under the tutelage of the Presbyter Pamphilus, who
was martyred in 310 during Diocletian's persecution. Caesarea
was the location of Origen's library, and Pamphilus had been
Origen's student. Eusebius inherited from Pamphilus a deep
respect for Origen. In fact, after Pamphilus's death Eusebius
completed the six-book *Defense of Origen* that his teacher had
started. In keeping with Origen, Eusebius exhibited scholarly
interest in the biblical text, concern for the spiritual meaning
of Scripture, and readiness to defend the Christian faith.
Eusebius became bishop of Caesarea ca. 313 and for many years
worked in close cooperation with the emperor Constantine in
forging a Christian-imperial identity for the Church. Eusebius
died in 339, leaving a vast literary heritage, including a *Life of
Constantine* and an address entitled *Praise of Constantine.*

As a student, Eusebius seems to have worked with Pamphilus

on revisions to the text of Scripture in the tradition of Origen's *Hexapla*. Other Eusebian works of biblical scholarship include a handbook on biblical geography (the *Onomasticon*), a harmony of the Gospels (*Gospel Sections*), a treatise on *Gospel Questions and Their Solutions*, and extensive commentaries on the Psalms and Isaiah. In the sphere of apologetics, Eusebius produced a Christian defense against the classical pagan tradition (*Preparation for the Gospel*), a defense of Christianity aimed at the Jews (*Proof of the Gospel*), and a refutation of the third-century critic of Christianity, Porphyry (*Against Porphyry*, which is not preserved). Above all, Eusebius is known as the founder of church history. In addition to his multi-columned tables of history covering such cultures as the Assyrians, Hebrews, Egyptians, Greeks, and Romans (*Chronicon*), Eusebius composed an *Ecclesiastical History* spanning the whole of Christian history from the origins of the Church down to Eusebius's own time, preserving many otherwise lost primary sources.

Presented below is the preface to Eusebius's *Commentary on Isaiah,* and also the section of the commentary dealing with Isa 55:1-5. This work comes from the last decade of Eusebius's life, ca. 330 CE. Based on what remains of Origen's exegesis of Isaiah, it appears that Eusebius made use of Origen's commentary but did not follow it slavishly. Like Origen, Eusebius often employs the hexaplaric translators Aquila, Symmachus, and Theodotion to explain or supplement the Septuagint, even expounding the Septuagint and another translation side by side without choosing one or the other. Anti-Jewish polemic is a persistent theme in the *Commentary on Isaiah,* and it appears in the selection below. Eusebius had a deep appreciation for history, and his commentary devotes significant attention to the "literal sense" (*kata lexin*), perhaps more so than Origen. At the same time, Eusebius believed that biblical texts often contain a spiritual sense (*dianoia*), and he also saw many direct prophecies about Christ in the straightforward wording of Isaiah.

Commentary on Isaiah, "Preface"

At times the Spirit delivered his revelation to the prophet plainly, so that there was no need of allegory to explain the message, but only an understanding of the actual words themselves. But at other times, the Spirit communicated through symbols and circumstances, placing other meanings in certain key words and even in names. For example, in Joseph's dreams, the number of the "eleven stars" that appeared to bow down represents his brothers.[1] At another time, he saw his brothers gathering ears of corn, thus foreshadowing the famine.[2] And so it is for the prophet Isaiah. Many of the things that he prophesied he saw through symbols, and many of the things that he prophesied he spoke in a complicated fashion, weaving together a literal and a metaphorical sense. Such things are also found in the teachings of the Savior, in which it is recorded that he said: "Do you not say, 'There are four months, then comes the harvest'? Lift up your eyes, and see how the fields are already white for harvest."[3] It is clear what this verse is about, and yet one could find countless meanings.[4] The same is true concerning the writings of the prophet at hand. You find phrases that should

---

1. Gen 37:9–11.
2. In Gen 37:6–8, Joseph has a dream where his brothers are binding sheaves of grain, and their sheaves bow down to Joseph's sheaf. In Gen 41:5–7, 22–31, Pharaoh has a dream in which seven parched heads of grain swallow seven healthy heads of grain, foreshadowing seven years of famine. Eusebius has conflated the two accounts.
3. John 4:35.
4. This sentence might also be translated: "Of these words, part is literal, but you would find much else that is spiritual [*dianoiai*]." See M. J. Hollerich, *Eusebius of Caesarea's Commentary on Isaiah* (Oxford: Clarendon, 1999), 69. Hollerich's understanding of the sentence fits the flow of thought well.

be understood precisely as stated, such as: "What to me is the multitude of your sacrifices? says the Lord; I am full of whole burnt offerings,"[5] and so on. But there are also verses that concern only the allegorical sense, such as: "The beloved had a vineyard on a hill, on a fertile place,"[6] and so forth.

Commentary on Isaiah 55:1–5

55:1. The prophecy at hand refers to the very Christ of God when it says: "You who thirst, go to water." Then he alludes to the grace that was freely given through the Savior to people when he says: "And as many of you as have no money, come, buy and drink without money." But instead of: "and wine and fat without price, in order that you should set a price with money," Symmachus writes: "And wine and milk with nothing in exchange." Aquila likewise translates this phrase "wine and milk,"[7] so that this verse promises not only water but also wine and milk to those who thirst. On the one hand, water "from the springs of salvation" clearly refers to the evangelical preaching,[8] and "wine and milk," on the other hand, allude to the mystery of regeneration in Christ. For those who are born again of water and the Spirit[9] like newborn babies are nursed with spiritual milk[10] and partake of the wine of the new covenant.[11] You should not be ignorant of the fact that, in former times, mystical milk was administered to those who were born again in Christ along with the body and blood of the new covenant. And they say that this custom is preserved

5. Isa 1:11.
6. Isa 5:1.
7. For the Hebrew word ḥlb, the Septuagint translated "fat" (ḥēleb), whereas Aquila and Symmachus translated "milk" (ḥalab), as in the Masoretic Text.
8. See Isa 12:3.
9. John 3:5.
10. 1 Pet 2:2.
11. Luke 22:20; 1 Cor 11:25.

in certain churches still even now. But if this text is not interpreted according to the literal sense, the mystical blood of Christ is administered to those who are deemed worthy of regeneration in Christ instead of wine and instead of milk. It could be said that the word "fat," which one finds in the Septuagint, alludes to the abundance, richness and nourishment of spiritual food in Christ, which again the Savior made clear when he said: "Unless you eat my flesh and drink my blood, you have no life in you."[12] What Isaiah called "fat," Jesus here calls "flesh," and what Jesus calls "blood," Isaiah called "wine"; the words "fat" and "flesh" clearly refer to his incarnate physical existence, and the words "wine" and "blood" signify the mystery of his suffering. Therefore, he promises to supply without reimbursement and to give freely these things to those who thirst for salvation in God.

55:2. Why do you dedicate your labor and occupy yourselves with things that do not nourish your soul? Why do you attempt to take pleasure in food that does not satisfy?[13] Therefore, according to Symmachus, the text reads: "Why do you spend your money on what is not bread and work for what does not satisfy?"[14] And you will perceive who they are who purchase with money the "bread" of the soul, and you will understand who they are who charge fees for spiritual teaching, promising to be the wise of this age,[15] or those who sell for payment the tradition of Jewish readings to those who would become their disciples. Next, after this, he exhorts them to incline their ears [v. 3] in order that they may understand and may apply the

---

12. John 6:53.
13. The Septuagint of this verse reads: "Why do you value with money, and your labor is for that which does not satisfy? Hear me, and you will eat good things, and your soul will revel in good things."
14. Symmachus offers a more accurate translation of the Hebrew phrase, "what is not bread."
15. 1 Cor 1:20.

obedient attention of their souls to the things that are being said. Therefore, he says: "Listen, and you shall eat good things, and your soul shall revel in good things." After this verse, he speaks of the hope of other "good things" and says that an inspired delight has been stored up for the souls of those who listen. For the gift of the good things to come is not presented to their bodies but expressly to their souls.[16]

55:3. After this, he adds: "Pay attention with your ears, and follow my ways." But according to Symmachus, the text reads: "Incline your ears and come to me, and obey me, and your soul will live among good things,"[17] and all these he promises to their souls. Then, after persuading them to listen and awakening their hearing, he begins to teach them: "I will make with you an everlasting covenant, the sacred things of David that are sure." For, indeed, because the old covenant was temporary, it passed away and came to an end. In many places in the Scriptures, promises are made to David that the Christ of God would come from his offspring,[18] and so discipline your ears and hear the Word concerning these things. For you know well that if you devote your ears to my words, I will produce in you the fruit of obedience. And the promise that I have made to David, I graciously give to you; therefore I will make with you a new covenant,[19] which will not only be for the time of Moses, but will be enduring and everlasting and will remain until the consummation of everything. And "the sacred things of David" which I promised to him, I will make "sure," for I will substantiate my promise.

---

16. Heb 10:1.
17. The Septuagint reads: "Pay attention with your ears, and follow my ways; listen to me, and your soul will live in good things." Symmachus gives a more precise translation of the Hebrew *haṭṭū*, "incline" (your ears), and *lekū ʾēlay*, "come to me" (rather than the Septuagint's "follow my ways").
18. For example: 2 Sam 7:12; Ps 132:11; Isa 11:10; Jer 23:5; 33:15.
19. Jer 31:31; 2 Cor 3:6; Heb 8:8, 13; 9:15; 12:24.

55:4–5. Then, because the prophetic Spirit is prescient and can predict the future, he was not unaware of the fact that the Jews would suppress these voices among themselves, and their souls will certainly not profit further. Therefore, he turns to the foreigners and the nations of other races, and he professes that he will give these promises to them when he says these words: "See, I have given him as a testimony among the nations, a ruler and a commander for the nations. Nations that do not know you shall call on you, and peoples that do not understand you shall flee to you for refuge, for the sake of the Lord your God, the Holy One of Israel, because he has glorified you." Therefore, in these verses he refers to what happened to the one who is signified in the verse above, where one reads: "Because those who were not informed about him shall see, and those who did not hear shall understand,"[20] and: "We saw him, and he had no form or beauty."[21] Therefore, he calls that one "him" about whom all these things have been spoken: "I have given him as a testimony among the nations." For this reason, I preached and exhorted the barren one who formerly did not bear and who had no husband to stretch out and enlarge her tent.[22] Because of what has been proclaimed concerning the sins of my people, he had to suffer these things. It has been said rightly, then: "I have given him as a testimony" not to the Jewish people, but "among all the nations" and as "a ruler and commander for the nations." For it is clear to my God that all the "nations" will listen to him before the people of the circumcision. And his "testimony" was what was preached about him, just as he taught when he said: "It is necessary for this gospel to be preached throughout the whole world, as a

---

20. Isa 52:15.
21. Isa 53:2.
22. See Isa 54:1–2.

testimony to all nations."[23] Then the Spirit addresses directly the one who is prophesied above and says: "Nations that do not know you shall call on you, and peoples that do not understand you shall flee to you for refuge." He says that all these things will happen "for the sake of the Lord your God, the Holy One of Israel, because he has glorified you."

23. Matt 24:14.

8

Ephrem the Syrian

Ephrem is the only figure included in this volume who did not write in Greek or Latin. Ephrem composed his works in Syriac, a dialect of Aramaic used by many Christians in the eastern parts of the Roman Empire and in regions under Persian rule. A comprehensive survey of biblical interpretation in the early church would include sources written not only in Greek and Latin, but also in Syriac, Armenian, Coptic, Ethiopic, and Arabic. The Syriac-speaking Church of late antiquity produced a number of important interpreters of Scripture, including Aphrahat (fl. 340), a Persian Christian who authored a Syriac apologetic work called *Demonstrations;* Ephrem the Syrian (ca. 306–373); Jacob of Serugh (ca. 450–521), who composed numerous metrical homilies on biblical themes; and Jacob of Edessa (d. 708), a prolific biblical translator and commentator. For this volume, Ephrem will serve as our representative example of early Christian biblical interpretation from the

Syriac tradition, and also as our only figure from outside the Greek and Latin world.

Christianity reached Antioch early (Acts 11:19), and from there it spread eastward into Syria and Mesopotamia (cf. also Acts 2:9). As elsewhere, the earliest Christian communities in these regions employed Greek, but by the end of the second century Christian literature was being composed in Syriac, as witnessed by Tatian's *Diatessaron,* a harmony of the Gospels. By the late second century Christianity was well established in the city of Edessa in northwestern Mesopotamia, which became a major center of learning. The city of Nisibis, located about one hundred miles east of Edessa, also gained a significant Christian population by the end of the third century. Both Edessa and Nisibis came under Roman control in 298.

Ephrem was born in Nisibis ca. 306 into a Christian home. As an adult, Ephrem served as a deacon and catechetical teacher in the church of Nisibis. He also composed numerous hymns and metrical homilies for church use. When the Persians took control of Nisibis in 363 and the Christian population left the city, Ephrem moved to Edessa where he continued to teach and write until his death in 373. Ephrem's writings played a foundational role in the development of Syriac literature, somewhat comparable to Homer in Greek or Cicero in Latin. Ephrem's many compositions gained him such a reputation in the Syriac Church that his liturgical poems were sometimes read after the scriptural lection in public worship, and a number of his works were translated into Greek (Jerome, *On Illustrious Men* 115). Prominent among Ephrem's prose works are his commentaries on Genesis, Exodus, and the *Diatessaron.* Examples of his liturgical poems include series of compositions *On the Nativity, On the Paschal Feast, On Faith, On Virginity, On the Church,* and *Against Heresies.* In appreciation of the beauty of his poetry, Ephrem's contemporaries referred to him as "the Harp of the Holy Spirit."

Offered below are four of Ephrem's *Hymns on Paradise,* probably composed when Ephrem was still in Nisibis. Ephrem knew traditional Christian theology as transmitted in the Greek-speaking churches of his day; but as a native speaker of Syriac—an Aramaic dialect akin to Hebrew—he also shows knowledge of Jewish traditions, which he probably learned through contact with the sizeable Jewish community of Nisibis. Both traditional Christian and also Jewish influences are present in the *Hymns on Paradise.* These hymns do not quote and comment on Scripture; rather, they retell the biblical narrative (in this case, Genesis 2–3) in a theological manner, developing points of doctrine, alluding to other parts of Scripture, and marveling at the text's profundity. Ephrem delights in paradoxes and typological parallels. He sees in all of Scripture symbols (*rāzē,* "mysteries") that reveal truth and ultimately point to Christ. In Ephrem's poetic account, Paradise is a holy mountain (cf. Ezek 28:13–14), surrounded by foothills where a fence protects the mountain and a Cherub stands guard (Gen 3:24).[1] Halfway up the mountain is the Tree of Knowledge, beyond which Adam and Eve were forbidden to ascend. Above this is the Tree of Life, and at the top of the mountain resides the Divine Presence.

---

1. The concept of Paradise as a mountain was likely adopted by Ephrem or earlier Syriac Christians from Jewish tradition (e.g., 1 Enoch 17; 24–25).

Hymn 1

1. Moses, who instructs all men
with his celestial writings,
He, the master of the Hebrews,[2]
has instructed us in his teaching—
the Law, which constitutes
a very treasure house of revelations,
wherein is revealed
the tale of the Garden—
described by things visible,
but glorious for what lies hidden,
spoken of in few words,
yet wondrous with its many plants.
Response: Praise to Your righteousness
which exalts those who prove victorious.

2. I took my stand halfway
between awe and love;
a yearning for Paradise
invited me to explore it,
but awe at its majesty
restrained me from my search.
With wisdom, however,
I reconciled the two;
I revered what lay hidden
and meditated on what was revealed.
The aim of my search was to gain profit,
the aim of my silence was to find succor.

---

2. The phrase, "master [Syriac: *rabbā*] of the Hebrews" is reminiscent of the Rabbinic Jewish title for Moses, *mōsheh rabbēnū*, "Moses our Master" (or: "Moses our Teacher").

3. Joyfully did I embark
on the tale of Paradise—
a tale that is short to read
but rich to explore.
My tongue read the story's
outward narrative,
while my intellect took wing
and soared upward in awe
as it perceived the splendor of Paradise—
not indeed as it really is,
but insofar as humanity
is granted to comprehend it.

4. With the eye of my mind
I gazed upon Paradise;
the summit of every mountain
is lower than its summit,
the crest of the Flood
reached only its foothills;[3]
these it kissed with reverence
before turning back
to rise above and subdue the peak
of every hill and mountain.
The foothills of Paradise it kisses,
while every summit it buffets.

5. Not that the ascent to Paradise
is arduous because of its height,
for those who inherit it
experience no toil there.
With its beauty it joyfully

3. Gen 7:19.

urges on those who ascend.
Amidst glorious rays
it lies resplendent,
all fragrant with its scents;
magnificent clouds
fashion the abodes
of those who are worthy of it.

6. From their abodes
the children of light descend,[4]
they rejoice in the midst of the world
where they had been persecuted;
they dance on the sea's surface
and do not sink,
for Simon, although a "Rock,"
did not sink.[5]
Blessed is he who has seen,
together with them, his beloved ones,
below in their bands of disciples,
and on high in their bridal chambers.

7. The clouds, their chariots
fly through the air;[6]
each of them has become the leader
of those he has taught;[7]
his chariot corresponds to his labors,
his glory corresponds to his followers.
Blessed the person who has seen
as they fly

4. 1 Thess 5:5.
5. Matt 14:29–31; 16:16–19.
6. See Dan 7:13, 25–27; 1 Thess 3:13; 4:16–17.
7. Dan 12:3.

the Prophets with their bands,
the Apostles with their multitudes;
for whoever has both acted and taught
is great in the kingdom.[8]

8. But because the sight of Paradise
is far removed,
and the eye's range
cannot attain to it,
I have described it over simply,
making bold a little.
Resembling that halo
which surrounds the moon
we should look upon Paradise
as being circular too,
having both sea and dry land
encompassed within it.

9. And because my tongue overflows
as one who has sucked
the sweetness of Paradise,
I will portray it in diverse forms.
Moses made a crown
for that resplendent altar;[9]
with a wreath entirely of gold
did he crown
the altar in its beauty.
Thus gloriously entwined
is the wreath of Paradise
that encircles the whole of creation.

8. Matt 5:19.
9. Exod 30:3.

10. When Adam sinned
God cast him forth from Paradise,
but in His grace He granted him
the low ground beyond it,
settling him in the valley
below the foothills of Paradise;
but when humankind even there continued to sin
they were blotted out,
and because they were unworthy
to be neighbors of Paradise,
God commanded the Ark
to cast them out on Mount Qardu.[10]

11. There the families
of the two brothers had separated:
Cain went off by himself
and lived in the land of Nod,[11]
a place lower still
than that of Seth and Enosh;[12]
but those who lived on higher ground,
who were called
"the sons of God,"[13]
left their own region and came down
to take wives

---

10. In Gen 8:4 the ark comes to rest on the mountains of "Ararat." The Syriac Peshitta version of Gen 8:4 identifies this as Mount Qardu in Armenia, as do a number of Jewish sources, including Josephus, *Jewish Antiquities* 1.3.5–6; Targum Onkelos (cf. *qadrun* in Targums Neofiti and Pseudo-Jonathan), and *Genesis Rabbah* 33.4. See also Ephrem's *Commentary on Genesis* 6.12.

11. Gen 4:16.

12. Gen 4:25–26; 5:4–7.

13. Gen 6:1–2. In his *Commentary on Genesis* 6.3, Ephrem explains that the "sons of God" are the sons of Seth, because in the days of Seth and Enosh people began to call on the name of the Lord (Gen 4:26; cf. *Comm. Gen.* 5.1). Thus, in Gen 6:2 the beautiful daughters of Cain became a snare to the sons of Seth, who came down and took the daughters of Cain as wives.

from the daughters of Cain below.

12. The children of light
dwell on the heights of Paradise,
and beyond the Abyss
they espy the rich man;[14]
he too, as he raises his eyes,
beholds Lazarus,
and calls out to Abraham
to have pity on him.
But Abraham, that man so full of pity,
who even had pity on Sodom,[15]
has no pity yonder
for him who showed no pity.

13. The Abyss severs any love
which might act as a mediary,
thus preventing the love of the just
from being bound to the wicked,
so that the good should not be tortured
by the sight, in Gehenna,
of their children or brothers
or family—
a mother, who had denied Christ,
imploring mercy from her son
or her maid or her daughter,
who all had suffered affliction for the sake of
Christ's teaching.

14. Luke 16:19–31.
15. Gen 18:16–33.

14. There the persecuted laugh
at their persecutors,
the afflicted at those who had caused them affliction,
the slain at those who had put them to death,
the prophets at those who had stoned them,
the apostles at those who had crucified them.
The children of light reside
in their lofty abode
and, as they gaze on the wicked
and count their evil actions,
they are amazed to what extent these people
have cut off all hope by committing such iniquity.

15. Woe to him who tries to hide
his shameful deeds in the dark,
who does wrong and then tries to deceive
those who have seen;
having gone in and committed some wrong
he lies so as to deceive those who have heard.
May the wings of Your grace[16]
protect me,
for there the accusing finger
points out
and daily proclaims
the sinner's shame and hidden dealings.

16. What I have told
must suffice my boldness;
but if there is anyone
who dares to go on and say
"As for the dull-witted and simple people,

16. Pss 17:8; 36:7; 51:7; 61:4; 63:7; 91:4.

who have done wrong out of ignorance,
once they have been punished
and paid their debt,
He who is good allows them to dwell
in some remote corner of Paradise
where they can gaze on
that blessed food of 'the crumbs' ..."[17]

17. This place, despised and spurned
by the denizens of Paradise,
those who burn in Gehenna
hungrily desire;
their torment doubles
at the sight of its fountains,
they quiver violently
as they stand on the opposite side;
the rich man, too, begs for succor,
but there is no one to wet his tongue,[18]
for fire is within them,
while the water is opposite them.

Hymn 3

1. As for that part of the Garden, my beloved,
which is situated so gloriously
at the summit of that height
where dwells the Glory,
not even its symbol
can be depicted in man's thought;

---

17. By not finishing the sentence ("If there is anyone who dares to go on and say . . ."),
Ephrem seems to leave the possibility open. On the "crumbs," see Matt 15:27; Mark
7:28; cf. Luke 16:21. On this same theme, see Ephrem, *Hymns on Paradise* 7.26–27.
18. Luke 16:24–26.

for what mind
has the sensitivity
to gaze upon it,
or the faculties to explore it,
or the capacity to attain to that Garden
whose riches are beyond comprehension.
Response: Praise to Your Justice that crowns the victorious.

2. Perhaps that blessed tree,
the Tree of Life,
is, by its rays,
the sun of Paradise;
its leaves glisten,
and on them are impressed
the spiritual graces
of that Garden.
In the breezes the other trees
bow down as if in worship
before that sovereign
and leader of the trees.

3. In the very midst He planted
the Tree of Knowledge,[19]
endowing it with awe,
hedging it in with dread,
so that it might straightway serve
as a boundary to the inner region of Paradise.
Two things did Adam hear
in that single decree:
that they should not eat of it[20]

19. Gen 2:9.
20. Gen 2:17.

and that, by shrinking from it,
they should perceive that it was not lawful
to penetrate further, beyond that Tree.

4. The serpent could not
enter Paradise,
for neither animal
nor bird
was permitted to approach
the outer region of Paradise,
and Adam had to go out
to meet them;
so the serpent cunningly learned,
through questioning Eve,
the character of Paradise,
what it was and how it was ordered.

5. When the accursed one learned
how the glory of that inner Tabernacle,
as if in a sanctuary,
was hidden from them,
and that the Tree of Knowledge,
clothed with an injunction,
served as the veil
for the sanctuary,
he realized that its fruit
was the key of justice
that would open the eyes of the bold
—and cause them great remorse.

6. Their eyes were open—
though at the same time they were still closed[21]

so as not to see the Glory
or their own low estate,
so as not to see the Glory
of that inner Tabernacle,
nor to see the nakedness
of their own bodies.
These two kinds of knowledge
God hid in the Tree,
placing it as a judge
between the two parties.

7. But when Adam boldly ran
and ate of its fruit
this double knowledge
straightway flew toward him,
tore away and removed
both veils from his eyes:
he beheld the Glory of the Holy of Holies
and trembled;
he beheld, too, his own shame and blushed,
groaning and lamenting
because the twofold knowledge he had gained
had proved for him a torment.

8. Whoever has eaten
of that fruit
either sees and is filled with delight,
or he sees and groans out.
The serpent incited them to eat in sin

---

21. As Ephrem explains in his *Commentary on Genesis* 2.21–22, their eyes were not opened in such a way that they became like God as the serpent said, but such that they could see their own nakedness. The opening of their eyes did not take them to Paradise, nor did it allow them to see the Tree of Life.

so that they might lament;
having seen the blessed state,
they could not taste of it—
like that hero of old
whose torment was doubled
because in his hunger he could not taste
the delights which he beheld.[22]

9. For God had not allowed him
to see his naked state,
so that, should he spurn the commandment,
his ignominy might be shown him.
Nor did He show him the Holy of Holies,
in order that, if he kept the command,
he might set eyes upon it
and rejoice.
These two things did God conceal,
as the two recompenses,
so that Adam might receive, by means of his contest,
a crown that befitted his actions.

10. God established the Tree as judge,
so that if Adam should eat from it,
it might show him that rank
which he had lost through his pride,
and show him, as well, that low estate
he had acquired, to his torment.
Whereas, if he should overcome and conquer,
it would robe him in glory

22. This is an allusion to the Greek mythological figure Tantalus, whom the gods punished
for his misdeeds by placing him in a pool of water with fruit hanging from a tree just
above him. Whenever he bent down to drink, the water would recede; and whenever
he tried to grasp the fruit, the branches of the tree would rise up beyond his reach.

and reveal to him also
the nature of shame,
so that he might acquire, in his good health,
an understanding of sickness.

11. A man, indeed, who has acquired
good health in himself,
and is aware in his mind
of what sickness is,
has gained something beneficial
and he knows something profitable;
but a man who lies
in sickness,
and knows in his mind
what is good health
is vexed by his sickness
and tormented in his mind.

12. Had Adam conquered,
he would have acquired
glory upon his limbs,
and discernment of what suffering is,
so that he might be radiant in his limbs
and grow in his discernment.[23]
But the serpent reversed all this
and made him taste
abasement in reality,
and glory in recollection only,

---

23. In the *Commentary on Genesis* 2.23, Ephrem explains that, if Adam had resisted the serpent and rejected sin, he would have been permitted to eat from the Tree of Life and the Tree of Knowledge, thereby gaining both immortal life and infallible knowledge.

so that he might feel shame at what he had found
and weep at what he had lost.

13. The Tree was to him
like a gate;
its fruit was the veil
covering that hidden Tabernacle.
Adam snatched the fruit,
casting aside the commandment.
When he beheld that Glory
within,
shining forth with its rays,
he fled outside;
he ran off and took refuge
among the modest fig trees.

14. In the midst of Paradise God had planted
the Tree of Knowledge
to separate off, above and below,
sanctuary from Holy of Holies.
Adam made bold to touch,
and was smitten like Uzziah:[24]
the king became leprous,
Adam was stripped.
Being struck like Uzziah,
he hastened to leave:
both kings fled and hid,[25]
in shame of their bodies.

---

24. 2 Chron 26:16–21.
25. On Adam as king, see 2 Enoch 30:11–12; 3:2–3; 5:3; Philo, *On the Creation of the World*
    148; *Testament of Abraham* 11.8–12; *Avot of Rabbi Nathan* 1; cf. Ephrem, *Hymns on Paradise*
    13.3–4; and the sixth-cent. CE Syriac text known as the *Cave of Treasures.*

15. Even though all the trees
of Paradise
are clothed each in its own glory,
yet each veils itself at the Glory;
the Seraphs with their wings,
the trees with their branches,
all cover their faces so as not to behold
their Lord.
They all blushed at Adam
who was suddenly found naked;
the serpent had stolen his garments,
for which it was deprived of its feet.[26]

16. God did not permit
Adam to enter
that innermost Tabernacle;
this was withheld,
so that first he might prove pleasing
in his service of that outer Tabernacle;
like a priest
with fragrant incense,
Adam's keeping of the commandment
was to be his censer;[27]
then he might enter before the Hidden One
into that hidden Tabernacle.

17. The symbol of Paradise
was depicted by Moses
who made the two sanctuaries,

26. Gen 3:14.
27. On Adam as priest, see Jubilees 3:26–27; *Life of Adam and Eve* 29.1–6; Tanḥuma (Buber) Toledot 12; cf. the *Cave of Treasures*.

the sanctuary and the Holy of Holies;
into the outer one
entrance was permitted,
but into the inner,
only once a year.[28]
So too with Paradise,
God closed off the inner part,
but He opened up the outer,
wherein Adam might graze.

Hymn 4

1. The Just One saw how Adam had become audacious
because He had been lenient,
and He knew that he would overstep again
if He continued thus;
Adam had trampled down
that gentle and pleasant boundary,
so instead God made for him
a boundary guarded by force.
The mere words of the commandment
had been the boundary to the Tree,
but now the cherub and the sharp sword
provided the fence to Paradise.[29]
Response: Deem me worthy that through Your grace
we may enter Your Paradise.

2. Adam in all his filth
sought to enter
that Holy of Holies

---

28. Lev 16:2–3, 29–30; Heb 9:7.
29. Gen 3:24.

which loves only those who resemble it;
and because he made bold to enter
that inner tabernacle,
God did not allow him to enter
the outer one either.
When that sea full of life
saw a corpse in its midst,
it did not leave it there
but cast it forth.

3. Moses depicted the type
among the people of the Hebrews:
when a man becomes leprous
within the encampment
he is driven from its midst
and cast outside;[30]
while if he sloughs off his leprosy
and makes supplication,
the priest purifies him
with hyssop, blood, and water,
and he returns to his former abode
and enters into his inheritance.[31]

4. Adam had been most pure
in that fair Garden,
but he became leprous and repulsive
because the serpent had breathed on him.
The Garden cast him from its midst;
all shining, it thrust him forth.
The High Priest,[32] the Exalted One,

---

30. Lev 13:45–46.
31. Lev 14:1–7.

beheld him
cast out from Himself:
He stooped down and came to him,
He cleansed him with hyssop,
and led him back to Paradise.

5. Adam had been naked and fair,
but his diligent wife
labored and made for him
a garment covered with stains.
The Garden, seeing him thus vile,
drove him forth.
Through Mary Adam had
another robe
which adorned the thief;[33]
and when he became resplendent at Christ's
promise,
the Garden, looking on,
embraced him in Adam's place.

6. Moses who doubted
saw but did not enter
the land of God's promise;[34]
the Jordan served as a boundary.
Adam went astray and left
the Garden of Life;
the cherub became a fence.

---

32. Heb 2:17; 3:1; 4:14–15; 5:5, 10; 6:20; 7:26; 8:1; 9:11.
33. Luke 23:39–43. Sebastian Brock explains: "The thought is densely packed here: the robe is the 'robe of glory' which Christ has once again made available for humanity (Adam), and the penitent thief is taken here as the first representative of the human race to re-enter Paradise in this robe" (S. Brock, *St. Ephrem the Syrian: Hymns on Paradise* [Crestwood, NY: St. Vladimir's Seminary Press, 1990], 191).
34. Num 20:12; Deut 32:48–52; 34:1–4.

Both boundaries were set
by the hand of our Lord,
but at the Resurrection they both entered:
Moses, into that land,
and Adam, into Paradise.

7. The tongue cannot relate
the description of innermost Paradise,
nor indeed does it suffice
for the beauties of the outer part;
for even the simple adornments
by the Garden's fence
cannot be related
in an adequate way.
For the colors of Paradise are full of joy,
its scents most wonderful,
its beauties most desirable,
and its delicacies glorious.

8. Even though the treasure
that adjoins the fence is lowly,
yet it surpasses all other treasures
in the world entire;
and by as much as the slopes, too,
are lowly in comparison
with that treasury
of the summit on high,
so the blessed state by the fence
is more glorious and exalted
than all that we experience as blessed,
who live in the valley below.

9. Be not angry that my tongue
has presumed to describe a theme
too great for it,
and so, through its own inadequacy, has
diminished that greatness.
As there is no mirror adequate
to reflect its beauty,
nor paints
which may portray it,
then may my attempt not be rejected,
for I have labored to compose
in my description of Paradise
a means whereby we may gain profit.

10. The mourner can find comfort therein,
the child be educated thereby,
the chaste become radiant through it,
the needy find provision from it.
And so let each one of them throw me
his little coin,[35]
and may they all make supplication for me
in Eden,
so that I may enter that place
whereof I have spoken in so far as I am able;
and so that the downcast may become desirous
of the riches that it promises.

11. May my purpose not be judged
by You, O Knower of all things;
may my search not be held blameworthy
by You, concealed from all;

35. Mark 12:42; Luke 21:2.

for I have not made bold to speak
of Your generation, hidden from all;
in silence
I have bounded the Word.
Yet because I have honored Your birth,
allow me to dwell in Your Paradise.
From all who love You
be praise to Your hiddenness!

Hymn 5

1. I considered the Word of the Creator,
and likened it
to the rock that marched
with the people of Israel in the wilderness;[36]
it was not from the reservoir
of water contained within it
that it poured forth for them
glorious streams:
there was no water in the rock,
yet oceans sprang forth from it;
just so did the Word
fashion created things out of nothing.[37]
Response: Blessed is that person accounted worthy
to inherit Your Paradise.

2. In his book Moses
described the creation of the natural world,
so that both Nature and Scripture

---

36. Exod 17:6; 1 Cor 10:4.
37. Heb 11:3. The manuscripts offer two different readings for these two lines (Brock, *St. Ephrem the Syrian: Hymns on Paradise*, 191). The other reading is: "Like the Word, it led the Hebrews out of nothingness" (see Sebastian Brock, *The Harp of the Spirit: Eighteen Poems of Saint Ephrem* [2nd ed.; San Bernardino, CA: Borgo, 1984], 21).

might bear witness to the Creator:
Nature, through humanity's use of it,
Scripture, through our reading of it.
These are the witnesses
which reach everywhere,[38]
they are to be found at all times,
present at every hour,
confuting the unbeliever
who defames the Creator.

3. I read the opening of this book
and was filled with joy,
for its verses and lines
spread out their arms to welcome me;
the first rushed out and kissed me,
and led me on to its companion;
and when I reached that verse
wherein is written
the story of Paradise,
it lifted me up and transported me
from the bosom of the book
to the very bosom of Paradise.

4. The eye and the mind
traveled over the lines
as over a bridge, and entered together
the story of Paradise.
The eye as it read
transported the mind;
in return the mind, too,
gave the eye rest

38. Ps 19:1–6; Rom 1:20.

from its reading,
for when the book had been read
the eye had rest,
but the mind was engaged.

5. Both the bridge and the gate
of Paradise
did I find in this book.
I crossed over and entered;
my eye indeed remained outside
but my mind entered within.
I began to wander
amid things not described.
This is a luminous height,
clear, lofty and fair:
Scripture named it Eden,[39]
the summit of all blessings.

6. There too did I see
the bowers of the just
dripping with unguents
and fragrant with scents,
garlanded with fruits,
crowned with blossoms.
In accord with a person's deeds
such was his bower;
thus one had few adornments,
while another was resplendent in its beauty;
one was but dim in its coloring,
while another dazzled in its glory.

39. Gen 2:8.

7. I enquired into this too,
whether Paradise
was sufficient in size
for all the righteous to live there.
I asked about what is not written in Scripture,
but my instruction came from what is written
there:
"Consider the man
in whom there dwelt
a legion of all kinds of demons;[40]
they were there although not apparent,
for their army is of a stuff finer and more subtle
than the soul itself.

8. That whole army
dwelt in a single body.
A hundred times finer
and more subtle
are the bodies of the righteous
when they are risen, at the Resurrection:
they resemble the mind
which is able,
if it so wills, to stretch out and expand,
or, should it wish, to contract and shrink;
if it shrinks, it is in some place,
if it expands, it is in every place.

9. Listen further
and learn
how lamps with thousands of rays
can exist in a single house,

40. Mark 5:9; Luke 8:30.

how ten thousand scents
can exist in a single blossom;
though they exist within a small space,
they have ample room
to disport themselves.
So it is with Paradise:
though it is full of spiritual beings,
it is amply spacious for their disportment.

10. Again, thoughts,
infinite in number, dwell
even in the small space of the heart,
yet they have ample room;
they neither constrict each other,
nor are they constricted there.
How much more will Paradise
the glorious
suffice for the spiritual beings
that are so refined in substance
that even thoughts
cannot touch them!"

11. I gave praise as far as I was able
and was on the point of departing
when, from the midst of Paradise,
there came a sudden thunderous sound,
and, like the blare of trumpets
in some camp,
a voice crying "holy"
thrice over.[41]
Thus I knew that the divinity

41. Isa 6:3.

received praise in Paradise;
I had supposed it was empty,
but I learn otherwise from the thunderous sound.

12. Paradise delighted me
as much by its peacefulness as by its beauty:
in it there resides a beauty
that has no spot;
in it exists a peacefulness
that knows no fear.
How blessed is that person
accounted worthy to receive it,
if not by right,
yet at least by grace;
if not because of good works,
yet at least through mercy.

13. I was in wonder as I crossed
the borders of Paradise
at how well-being, as though a companion,
turned round and remained behind.
And when I reached the shore of earth,
the mother of thorns,[42]
I encountered all kinds
of pain and suffering.
I learned how, compared to Paradise,
our abode is but a dungeon;
yet the prisoners within it
weep when they leave it!

42. Gen 3:17–19.

14. I was amazed at how even infants
weep as they leave the womb—
weeping because they come out
from darkness into light
and from suffocation they issue forth
into this world!
Likewise death, too,
is for the world
a symbol of birth,
and yet people weep because they are born
out of this world, the mother of suffering,
into the Garden of splendors.

15. Have pity on me,
O Lord of Paradise,
and if it is not possible for me
to enter Your Paradise,
grant that I may graze
outside, by its enclosure;
within, let there be spread
the table for the diligent,
but may the fruits within its enclosure
drop outside like the crumbs
for sinners, so that, through Your grace,
they may live!

9

Diodore of Tarsus

Diodore was born in Antioch ca. 330 CE and received a first-rate classical education. In the church of Antioch Diodore was ordained a priest and became the teacher of a group of ascetically minded students, including Theodore of Mopsuestia and John Chrysostom. Diodore left Antioch ca. 378 to become bishop of Tarsus, where he served until his death ca. 394. In matters of doctrine Diodore supported the full divinity of Jesus in opposition to Arianism, and he also insisted that Jesus possessed not only a human body but also a full human mind, in opposition to Apollinarism. Because of his support of Nicene Christianity Diodore was exiled in 372 by the Emperor Valens, and at the Council of Constantinople (381) Diodore played a prominent role. After his death, however, Diodore came to be seen as a predecessor of Nestorius (386–450), who fell under condemnation within Byzantine Christianity for his views on the relationship between Jesus's human and divine identities.

In the sixth century the Byzantine Church formally censured Diodore, primarily because it interpreted his Christology as equivalent to Nestorianism. This resulted in the loss of most of Diodore's writings. Later authors mention the titles of many of Diodore's works, including apologetic volumes such as *Against Plato: On God and the Gods*, and *Against Aristotle: On the Heavenly Bodies*; theological treatises such as *On the Holy Spirit*, and *On the Resurrection of the Dead*; and works devoted to biblical interpretation such as *On the Difference Between Theōria and Allēgoria, Questions on the Octateuch*, and his *Commentary on the Psalms*.

In the area of biblical interpretation Diodore is a key representative of the "Antiochene" school of thought, which also includes Theodore of Mopsuestia, John Chrysostom, and Theodoret of Cyrus. This group defined itself in contrast to an "Alexandrian" stream of interpretation whose model was Origen. In general terms the Alexandrian interpreters focused less on history and more on the spiritual sense, whereas the Antiochene interpreters placed more emphasis on the literal sense. The basis for this contrast is sometimes explained as the result of differences in Christology, that is, the Alexandrians focused on the divinity of Jesus and the divine sense of Scripture, whereas the Antiochenes focused on the humanity of Jesus and the human sense of Scripture; or, the difference is traced to contrasting literary paradigms applied to Scripture, that is, the Alexandrians read Scripture like philosophers read literature (i.e., looking for doctrine), whereas the Antiochenes read Scripture like rhetoricians read literature (i.e., looking for the flow of thought addressed to an audience). In any case, it is clear that writers such as Diodore and Theodore saw themselves as correcting problems in the interpretive methods of Origen and his followers.

Major ideas in Diodore's exegetical theory include: (1) the interpreter should seek to follow the logical coherence of the text, that is, the "flow of thought" (*akolouthia*); (2) each text has a main "theme" (*hypothesis*) that should be kept in mind; (3) the foundation of proper interpretation is the historical substance (*historia*) and literal sense (*lexis*) of the text, upon which the spiritual sense, "vision" or "contemplation" (*theōria*) should be built; (4) Christians should not read Scripture in the same way that pagans read their myths—this would be "allegory," which is illegitimate.

The text offered here is the preface to Diodore's *Commentary on Psalm 118* (Psalm 119 in English Bibles). Some specific points of interest in this selection are (a) Diodore's attention to what the text meant for its original audience; (b) his belief that the original meaning was often stated using hyperbole, allowing application to greater experiences in the future; and (c) his appeal to literary tropes and figures rather than allegory as a way to account for Scripture's figurative modes of expression.

Commentary on Psalm 118, "Preface"

In any approach to holy Scripture, the literal reading of the text reveals some truths while the discovery of other truths requires the application of theōria. Now, given the vast difference between historia and theōria, allegory and figuration [tropologia] or parable [parabolē], the interpreter must classify and determine each figurative expression with care and precision so that the reader can see what is history and what is theōria, and draw his conclusions accordingly.

Above all, one must keep in mind one point which I have stated very clearly in my prologue to the Psalter: Holy Scripture knows the term "allegory" but not its application.

Even the blessed Paul uses the term: "This is said by way of allegory, for they are two covenants."[1] But his use of the word and his application is different from that of the Greeks.

The Greeks speak of allegory when something is understood in one way but said in another. Since one or two examples must be mentioned for the sake of clarity, let me give an example. The Greeks say that Zeus, changing himself into a bull, seized Europa and carried her across the sea to foreign places. This story is not understood as it reads but is taken to mean that Europa was carried across the sea having boarded a ship with a bull as figurehead. A real bull could not possibly swim such a distance across the ocean.[2] This is allegory. Or another example: Zeus called Hera his sister and his wife. The plain text implies that Zeus had intercourse with his sister Hera so that the same person was both his wife and his sister. This is what the letter suggests; but the Greeks allegorize it to mean that, when ether, a fiery element, mingles with air, it produces a certain mixture which influences events on earth. Now, since air adjoins ether, the text calls these elements brother and sister because of their vicinity, but husband and wife because of their mixture.[3] Of such kind are the allegories of the Greeks.

1. Gal 4:21–31 was an important prooftext for early Christian proponents of allegory. Theodore of Mopsuestia, *Commentary on Galatians* 4:24, offers a lengthy explanation for why Paul's exegesis in this passage should not be considered "allegory."
2. This example is found in the fourth-century BCE writer Palaephatus, in his work *On Unbelievable Tales* 15: "They say that Europa, the daughter of Phoenix, was carried across the sea on the back of a bull from Tyre to Crete. But in my opinion neither a bull nor a horse would traverse so great an expanse of open water, nor would a girl climb on the back of a wild bull. As for Zeus—if he wanted Europa to go to Crete, he would have found a better way for her to travel. Here is the truth. There was a man from Cnossus by the name of Taurus ('bull') who was making war on the territory of Tyre. He ended up by carrying off from Tyre quite a number of girls, including the king's daughter, Europa. So people said: 'Bull has gone off with Europa, the king's daughter.' It was from this that the myth was fashioned" (*Palaephatus: On Unbelievable Tales*, trans. Jacob Stern [Wauconda, IL: Bolchazy-Carducci, 1996], 46). This is an example of euhemeristic allegory, according to which fantastic myths are thought to have evolved out of genuine historical events.
3. This illustration is similar to an allegory based on proper name etymologies related

The above examples should suffice lest, with all this allegory, I as an interpreter fall into foolishness myself as I mentioned earlier.

Holy Scripture does not speak of allegory in this way. In what way then does it speak? Let me explain briefly. Scripture does not repudiate in any way the underlying prior history but "theorizes," that is, it develops a higher vision [theōria] of other but similar events in addition, without abrogating history. As a test case, let us consider the very text of the apostle quoted above. This will be the most effective demonstration of our affirmation that the apostle means this theōria when he speaks of allegory. Based on the historical account of Isaac and Ishmael and their mothers, I mean Sarah and Hagar, Paul develops the higher theōria in the following way: He understands Hagar as Mount Sinai but Isaac's mother as the free Jerusalem, the future mother of all believers. The fact that the apostle "theorizes" in this way does not mean that he repudiates the historical account. For who could persuade him to say that the story of Hagar and Sarah was untrue? With the historical account as his firm foundation, he develops his theōria on top of it; he understands the underlying facts as events on a higher level. It is this developed theōria which the apostle calls allegory. As we said, he is aware of the term "allegory" but does not at all accept its application. I have

---

by the first-century CE Stoic philosopher Cornutus, *Epidromē* 3.1: "Tradition holds that Hera [*hēra*], who is the 'air' [*aēr*], is his [Zeus's] wife as well as his sister. She is fitted directly to him and joined to him, for she is rising from the earth, and he has come down to her. They have come into being from their flowing together: for substance, when it has 'flowed' [*rhyeisa*] toward fineness, gives rise to both fire [sc. Zeus] and air. On this basis it was told in myth that Rhea [*rhea*] was their mother" (Robert Stephen Hays, "Lucius Annaeus Cornutus' *Epidromē* [Introduction to the Traditions of Greek Theology]: Introduction, Translation, and Notes" [PhD diss., University of Texas at Austin, 1983], 58). This is an example of physical allegory, where myth is seen as depicting natural elements and forces (ancient "physics").

expressed this conviction in my prologue to the Psalter already, but for the sake of clarity it bears repetition here.

Figuration [tropologia] is present when, in describing an event, the prophet turns words with an obvious meaning into an expanded illustration of what he is saying. The figurative expression is then clarified by the continuation of the text. For instance, David says of the people: "You brought a vine out of Egypt";[4] then, having identified the people with the vine and leaving no doubt by adding, "you drove out the nations and planted it,"[5] he continues describing the people as if he were speaking of a vine. He mentions that the vine grew and unfolded its shoots;[6] he asks: "Why have you broken down its hedge so that all who pass along the way pluck its fruits?"[7] And then adds: "A wild boar from the forest has ravaged it."[8] Now it is quite clear that this is a covert allusion to Antiochus Epiphanes who brought great harm upon the Maccabees,[9] yet at the same time the prophet continues his figure; speaking of the people as a vine, he calls Antiochus a wild boar who tramples down the vine. Isaiah also uses this figure of the people, calling them a vineyard and saying: "My beloved had a vineyard on the hillside on fertile ground. I surrounded it with a wall and fenced it in,"[10] and so on. At the very end, clarifying the figurative character of the account, or rather of

---

4. Ps 80:8a.

5. Ps 80:8b.

6. Ps 80:9–11.

7. Ps 80:12.

8. Ps 80:13.

9. The Seleucid king Antiochus IV inflicted severe harm on the Jews of Judea in 167–164 BCE, as described in 1 Maccabees 1:10–64 and 2 Maccabees 5:11–26. See also Theodoret of Cyrus, *Commentary on Daniel* 8:23–25; 11:23–35. Even though Diodore believes that David prophesied this Psalm much earlier, he thinks it addresses a situation in the second century BCE. In basic agreement with Diodore's identification of the text's historical subject matter, Charles Briggs, *A Critical and Exegetical Commentary on the Book of Psalms* (New York: Scribner's, 1907), 2:203, dates Ps 80:16–17 to the Maccabean era.

10. Isa 5:1–2.

his prophecy, he adds: "For the vineyard of the Lord of hosts is the house of Israel, and the man of Judah is his beloved planting. I waited for him to perform justice but he acted lawlessly; instead of righteousness there was an outcry."[11] This is figuration [tropologia].

A parabolic expression [parabolē] is easy to recognize when it follows upon an introductory "like" or "as." To give some examples: "Like water I am poured out and all my bones are scattered";[12] or "I have become to them like a dead abomination."[13] There are many instances which follow this pattern. Often, however, Scripture speaks parabolically even without this introduction. It says, for instance: "You made my arms a bronze bow,"[14] instead of "like a brazen bow"; or: "And when Abraham looked up with his eyes, he saw three men,"[15] instead of "something resembling three men." In these cases, Scripture formulates parables by way of ellipsis, omitting the word "like." Frequently, Scripture also calls a narrative or a teaching "parable," for instance, when we read: "I will open my mouth in a parable, I will utter problems from the beginning."[16] Here the author's teaching, or at least the narrative, is called a parable. Actually, the parable itself may sometimes be called a "problem." Thus, it is even possible to speak of a problem as an "enigma": Samson proposed such a "problem" to the Philistines, or rather to the Palestinians—the Philistines are in fact the Palestinians—by saying: "Out of the eater came something to eat, and out of the strong came something sweet."[17] He would have defeated the Palestinians had he not

---

11. Isa 5:7.
12. Ps 22:14.
13. Cf. Ps 88:8 (LXX 87:9). This appears to be an inexact quotation.
14. Ps 18:34 according to the Septuagint (LXX Ps 17:35).
15. Gen 18:2.
16. Ps 78:2. Where the Hebrew has ḥîdōt, "riddles" or "dark sayings," the Septuagint has problēmata, "problems."

been betrayed, being unable to resist his lust for women, so that his sophisticated problem ended up being foolishness. This is the language of parable and problem, sometimes introduced by "like" or "as," sometimes not.

One would probably classify much of the material in the books of Moses as enigmas [ainigmata] rather than allegories. When the author writes: "The serpent said to the woman"; "the woman said to the serpent"; "God said to the serpent,"[18] we have enigmas. Not that there was no serpent; indeed there was a serpent, but the Devil acted through it. Moses speaks of the serpent as the visible animal but under this cover hints at the Devil in a hidden way. If this was allegory, only the word "serpent" should be there as we explained earlier. The truth is that there was both a reality and an enigma. The reality was the serpent, but since a serpent is by nature irrational and yet was speaking, it is obvious that it spoke empowered by the Devil. He who has the authority to reveal mysteries and enigmas points this out in the Gospels when he says of the Devil: "He was a murderer from the beginning and has not stood in the truth . . . for he is a liar and the father of lies."[19] This phrase, "and the father of lies," is very apt, for the Devil was the first one to lie as well as the one who begot lying. Therefore Christ adds: "and the father of lies," instead of saying, "lying personified." Now the Lord was able to clarify enigmas; the prophets and apostles could only report realities. Therefore, both Moses and the Apostle Paul said "serpent." The latter puts it this way: "I am afraid that as the serpent deceived Eve by its cunning, your thoughts will be corrupted";[20] here he also hints at the Devil by mentioning the serpent. The serpent

17. Judg 14:14.
18. Gen 3:2, 4, 14.
19. John 8:44.
20. 2 Cor 11:3.

is not a rational animal for him but points enigmatically to the Devil acting through it. Scheming is not the action of an irrational animal but of a rational being. Our brief remarks here must suffice on the topic of these figurative expressions. We have mentioned only a few points among many, leaving room for industrious scholars to make further points on the basis of similar examples.

In contrast, history [historia] is the pure account of an actual event of the past. It is authentic if it is not interwoven with the speaker's reflections, extraneous episodes, characterizations or fictitious speeches, as is, for example, the story of Job.[21] A plain, clear, and concise historical account does not weary the reader with reflections of the author and long characterizations.

Let this be enough on the modes of expression. But since, by the grace of God, I intend to interpret the 118th psalm,[22] I had to discuss in detail the above-mentioned modes of expression, as this psalm contains many of them. Therefore, I had to give my readers a clear statement about them in the preface in order to alert them to the fact that some parts of the Psalms are meant to be taken literally while others are figurative expressions, parables, or enigmas. What is emphatically not present is allegory. Of course, some interpreters have fancied that it is. They brush aside any historical understanding, introduce foolish fables of their own making in place of the text, and burden their readers' ears, leaving their minds devoid of pious thoughts. If they said that, being an utterance of God, this Psalm accompanies generations of human beings, conforming itself to events both actual and on a higher plane,

---

21. Theodore of Mopsuestia also held that the book of Job contains fictitious elaborations; see John Behr, *The Case against Diodore and Theodore: Texts and Their Contexts* (Oxford: Oxford University Press, 2011), 411–13.
22. Psalm 119 (118 in the Septuagint).

their interpretation would be quite correct. I am attempting to say something like this: In predicting future events, the prophets adapted their words both to the time in which they were speaking and to later times. Their words sounded hyperbolic in their contemporary setting but were entirely fitting and consistent at the time when the prophecies were fulfilled. For the sake of clarity there is nothing wrong with stressing this point more than once.

Historically, Psalm 29 was spoken by Hezekiah at the occasion of his deliverance from an illness and from the threat of war with the Assyrians.[23] These are his words after he was delivered from those ills: "I will extol you, O Lord, for you have protected me and have not let my foes rejoice over me. O Lord, my God, I cried to you and you have healed me. O Lord, you have brought up my soul from Hades, you have rescued me from those who go down to the pit."[24] Now these words did fit Hezekiah when he was delivered from his ills; but they also fit all human beings when they obtain the promised resurrection. For at that moment it will be timely for everyone to say to God what Hezekiah said: "I will extol you, O Lord, for you have protected me and have not let my foes rejoice over me." In Hezekiah's case, the foes were the Assyrians and those who rejoiced over his illness; the primary foes of all human beings are physical sufferings, death itself, and the Devil, the whole range of experiences connected with mortality. Again, when the Psalm continues: "O Lord, my God, I cried to you and you have healed me; Lord, you have brought up my soul from Hades," Hezekiah seems to have used hyperbole to describe his own situation; he was not actually rescued from Hades but from circumstances comparable to Hades on account of

23. Psalm 30 (29 in the Septuagint). See Isaiah 37–38 and 2 Kings 19–20.
24. Ps 30:1–3.

his very serious illness. But what sounded hyperbolical at that time, "you have brought up my soul from Hades," will fit his situation much more precisely when he rises from the dead. The same applies to the following verse: "You have rescued me from those who go down to the pit." It is quite clear that by the "pit" the author means death, but when he first uttered these words, they were used hyperbolically. When he actually rises from the dead, the former hyperbole will come true; the events themselves will have moved in the direction of the formerly hyperbolic expression. One will find more or less all utterances of the saints to be of this kind when one observes how they are made to fit the events of their own time but are also adapted to the events of the future. For this is the grace of the Spirit who gives eternal and imperishable gifts to human beings; I am speaking of the divine words which are capable of being adapted to every moment in time, down to the final perfection of human beings.

In the same way, Psalm 84 was pronounced in the person of those Israelites who had returned from Babylon.[25] It says: "Lord, you were favorable to your land, you have brought back the captivity of Jacob; you forgave your people their iniquity,"[26] and so on. These words were certainly fitting at the time of Israel's return; but they will be even more suitable at the resurrection when, freed from our mortality, we shall be liberated from all sins even more truly. Now if one understands Psalm 118 in this way, namely, as fitting the circumstances of those who first uttered it as well as those who come after them, one is entirely correct. But this is not a case of allegory; rather, it is a statement adaptable to many situations according to the grace of Him who gives it power. This great, rich, and beautiful

25. Psalm 85 (84 in the Septuagint).
26. Ps 85:1–2.

Psalm was pronounced in the person of the saints in Babylon who were longing to return to Jerusalem on account of the divine laws and the holy mysteries celebrated there, and who were emboldened to make such petitions by their pious lives. A man caught up in sin cannot pray for all his wishes except perhaps for deliverance from his ills; his conscience does not allow him to pray for greater gifts because it means sufficient grace for him if he is set free from his present ills. Therefore, the prayer of great and more saintly people is supported by lives accompanied by virtue. It is their virtues which allow them to make their request boldly.

Now, if this is the subject of the Psalm and someone says that Psalm 118 fits all saints everywhere and that one should always pray to God for the general resurrection, as the exiles in Babylon prayed for their return to Jerusalem, this is no violation of propriety. Being so rich and lavish, the Psalm adapted itself readily to the exiles in Babylon for their request and prayer, but it adapts itself even more precisely to those who fervently long for the general resurrection. Now the understanding of such a theōria must be left to those endowed with a fuller gift of grace. For the purpose of our exposition, let us concentrate on the historical prayer of the saints, the prayer about Jerusalem. But if anyone should doubt that there were saints in that captivity, he is totally mistaken. Yes, there were many saints; some of them were famous, others turned to the Lord humble and unknown, suffering no harm by being unknown to the world. Paul says about them: "Many went about in skins of sheep and goats, destitute, afflicted, ill-treated," and adds: "of whom the world was not worthy."[27] He added this clause so that no one may wonder why they were not known. There was no harm in being unknown, but the

27. Heb 11:37–38.

world proved unworthy of knowing such saints. There were, however, famous people also—I mean in Babylon—outstanding in piety and virtue, men such as Daniel and the three youths, Ezekiel, Zerubbabel, Jeshua son of Jozadak, Ezra, and others like them. But this Psalm is on the lips of all saints in captivity or on the way home. They all teach us that it is the practice of virtue and piety above all which has the strength and power to render our prayers effective before God. Thus, David the prophet begins the psalm with these words: "Blessed are those who are blameless in their way,"[28] and so on.

28. Ps 119:1.

10

Gregory of Nyssa

Born in Cappadocia (in modern Turkey) ca. 340 CE, Gregory of Nyssa is one of the three "Cappadocian Fathers," alongside his brother Basil of Caesarea and their friend Gregory of Nazianzus, who together definitively shaped Trinitarian theology in the late fourth century. Gregory of Nyssa was the youngest of the group. He owed his training in classical culture and Christian literature to his brother Basil and to his sister Macrina, whom he credits with convincing him to abandon his secular career and devote his life to the Church. No Christian in this period shows as much firsthand knowledge of Greek philosophy as Gregory of Nyssa. Having served the church as a lector ("reader") in his youth, Gregory was appointed bishop of the minor city of Nyssa in 372. He was briefly deposed in 376 following accusations made against him by the city's Arian faction, but he returned to his bishopric in 378 when Theodosius I became emperor. Gregory wrote little during these early years; one of his first works was an ascetical treatise *On Virginity*. After Basil's death in 379, Gregory's literary output increased considerably. Although he typically avoided public controversies, Gregory played an instrumental role in the Council of Constantinople in 381. Gregory continued to compose works devoted to theology, exegesis, and Christian life until his death ca. 395.

Among Gregory's most important theological writings are several works in defense of Jesus's divinity against the Arian Eunomius, two treatises explaining Jesus's full humanity in refutation of Apollinaris, a systematic theology called the *Great Catechetical Discourse*, and discussions of the Trinity such as *That There Are Not Three Gods* and *On the Holy Spirit*. In honor of his sister Macrina, Gregory wrote a *Life of Macrina* and a dialogue *On the Soul and the Resurrection* that was modeled after Plato's *Phaedo* with Macrina as the central figure. Other ascetical works and numerous letters and homilies from Gregory also touch on the ideals of Christian life. In terms of biblical interpretation, Gregory continued Basil's *Homilies on the Hexaemeron* (on the six days of Creation) by writing his own *Explanation of the Hexaemeron* and *On the Creation of Humanity*. Gregory composed several series of exegetical sermons including five homilies *On the Lord's Prayer* and eight homilies *On the Beatitudes*. In his most important writings on Scripture, which include *On the Titles of the Psalms*, *Homilies on Ecclesiastes*, *Homilies on the Song of Songs*, and the *Life of Moses*, Gregory emphasized eternal progress toward virtue and mystical encounter with God.

The *Life of Moses* is divided into two major sections: (1) the *historia* of Moses, which summarizes the biblical story of Moses essentially according to the "historical" account; and (2) a *theōria* on the life of Moses, a theological, pastoral, and devotional contemplation of Moses interpreted within the framework of Gregory's comprehensive Christian philosophy. Philo and Origen served as models for Gregory, but throughout the *Life of Moses* the bishop of Nyssa demonstrates his own creative synthesis of biblical themes, inherited Christian doctrine, Platonism, and Stoicism. Gregory often uses the vocabulary of "virtues" and "reason" to describe what should guide the Christian, and words such as "passions" and "impulse" for what leads the Christian astray. A range of traditional Christian terms appear in the *Life of Moses* for the spiritual sense, including *theōria,* "contemplation" (2.48), *dianoia,* "understanding" (1.14–15), *hyponoia,* "deeper sense" (2.219), *anagōgē,* "elevated sense" (2.223), and *tropikos,* "figurative" (2.43). The high point of the *Life of Moses* takes place in the second section (*theōria*) when Moses encounters the ineffable knowledge of God on Mount Sinai (*Life of Moses* 2.152–69) as he draws near to the thick darkness where God is (Exod 20:21).

In the first paragraphs of the Prologue, Gregory explains that the Divine One is the perfect Good and constitutes goodness without limit. Although Christians are called to be perfect as God is perfect (Matt 5:48), the one who pursues virtue can never fully attain perfection. Therefore, the Christian life is an eternal "straining forward to what lies ahead" (Phil 3:13). The first selection below is the conclusion to the prologue (*Life of Moses* 1.9–15). Then follows a section dealing with Moses's initial flight to Midian and his encounter with God at the Burning Bush (*Life of Moses* 2.12–26). Next comes a short segment where Gregory reflects on the goal of his discourse (*Life of Moses* 2.48–50). Finally, a substantial excerpt shows Gregory's spiritual interpretation of the Passover and the crossing of the Red Sea.

Life of Moses 1.9–15 (from the Prologue)

9. Although on the whole my argument has shown that what is sought for is unattainable, one should not disregard the commandment of the Lord which says, "Therefore be perfect, just as your heavenly Father is perfect."[1] For in the case of those things which are good by nature, even if people of understanding were not able to attain to everything, by attaining even a part they could yet gain a great deal.

10. We should show great diligence not to fall away from the perfection which is attainable, but to acquire as much as possible: To that extent let us make progress within the realm of what we seek. For the perfection of human nature consists perhaps in its very growth in goodness.

11. It seems good to me to make use of Scripture as a counselor in this matter. For the divine voice says somewhere in the prophecy of Isaiah, "Consider Abraham your father, and Sarah who gave you birth."[2] Scripture gives this admonition to those who wander outside virtue. Just as at sea those who are carried away from the direction of the harbor bring themselves back on course by a clear sign, upon seeing either a beacon light raised up high or some mountain peak coming into view, in the same way Scripture by the example of Abraham and Sarah may guide again to the harbor of the divine will those adrift on the sea of life with a pilotless mind.

12. Human nature is divided into male and female, and the free choice of virtue or of evil is set before both equally. For this reason the corresponding example of virtue for each sex has been exemplified by the divine voice, so that each, by observing the one to which he is akin (the men to Abraham and

1. Matt 5:48.
2. Isa 51:2.

the women to Sarah), may be directed in the life of virtue by the appropriate examples.

13. Perhaps, then, the memory of anyone distinguished in life would be enough to fill our need for a beacon light and to show how we can bring our soul to the sheltered harbor of virtue where it no longer has to pass the winter amid the storms of life or be shipwrecked in the deep water of evil by the successive billows of passion.[3] It may be for this very reason that the daily life of those sublime individuals is recorded in detail, that by imitating those earlier examples of right action those who follow them may conduct their lives to the good.

14. What then? Someone will say, "How shall I imitate them, since I am not a Chaldean as I remember Abraham was, nor was I nourished by the daughter of the Egyptian as Scripture teaches about Moses, and in general I do not have in these matters anything in life corresponding to anyone of the ancients? How shall I place myself in the same rank with one of them, when I do not know how to imitate anyone so far removed from me by the circumstances of his life?" To him we reply that we do not consider being a Chaldean a virtue or a vice, nor is anyone exiled from the life of virtue by living in Egypt or spending his life in Babylon, nor again has God been known to the esteemed individuals in Judea only, nor is Zion, as people commonly think, the divine habitation.[4] We need some subtlety of understanding and keenness of vision to discern from the history how, by removing ourselves from

---

3. This was a popular metaphor. For example, see Philo, *On the Sacrifices of Cain and Abel* 90, where Philo describes life as a journey through the eddy and swirl of the sea where reason is tossed to and fro, with the journey's goal being to reach the anchorage of virtue. In Porphyry, *On the Cave of the Nymphs* 34, Porphyry cites Plato to suggest that "sea" and "wave crash" refer to the material universe, and that Odysseus in the *Odyssey* was a symbol of the human person passing through the stages of life in order to reach the place "beyond all wave crash" (cf. *Odyssey* 11.122–23).
4. Cf. Ps 76:1–2.

such Chaldeans and Egyptians and by escaping from such a Babylonian captivity, we shall embark on the blessed life.

15. Let us put forth Moses as an example for life in our treatise. First we shall go through in outline his life as we have learned it from the divine Scriptures. Then we shall seek out the spiritual understanding which corresponds to the history in order to obtain suggestions for virtue. Through such understanding we may come to know the perfect life for humanity.

Life of Moses 2.12–26
(Moses flees to Midian and encounters the Burning Bush)

12. Now after living with the princess of the Egyptians for such a long time that he seemed to share in their honors, he must return to his natural mother. Indeed, he was not separated from her while he was being brought up by the princess, but was nursed by his mother's milk, as the history states.[5] This teaches, it seems to me, that if we should be involved with profane teachings during our education, we should not separate ourselves from the nourishment of the Church's milk, which would be her laws and customs.[6] By these the soul is nourished and matured, thus being given the means of ascending the height.

13. It is true that he who looks both to the profane doctrines and to the doctrines of the fathers will find himself between two antagonists. For the foreigner in worship is opposed to the Hebrew teaching and contentiously strives to appear stronger than the Israelite. And so he seems to be to many of the more superficial who abandon the faith of their fathers and fight on

5. Exod 2:5–10.
6. On milk as spiritual teaching, see 1 Cor 3:2; Heb 5:12–13; 1 Pet 2:2.

the side of the enemy, becoming transgressors of the fathers' teaching. On the other hand, he who is great and noble in soul like Moses slays with his own hand the one who rises in opposition to true religion.[7]

14. One may, moreover, find this same conflict in us, for each person is set before competitors as the prize of their contest. He makes the one with whom he sides the victor over the other. The fight of the Egyptian against the Hebrew is like the fight of idolatry against true religion, of licentiousness against self-control, of injustice against righteousness, of arrogance against humility, and of everything against what is deemed to be its opposite.[8]

15. Moses teaches us by his own example to take our stand with virtue as with a kinsman and to kill virtue's adversary. The victory of true religion is the death and destruction of idolatry. So also injustice is killed by righteousness and arrogance is slain by humility.[9]

16. The dispute of the two Israelites with each other occurs also in us.[10] There would be no occasion for wicked, heretical opinions to arise unless erroneous reasonings withstood the truth. If, therefore, we by ourselves are too weak to give the victory to what is righteous, since the bad is stronger in its attacks and rejects the rule of truth, we must flee as quickly as possible (in accordance with the historical example)[11] from the conflict to the greater and higher teaching of the mysteries.

7. Exod 2:11-12. The Greek for "true religion" is *ho logos tēs eusebeias,* "the *logos* of piety." In Philo, *Allegorical Interpretation* 3.37–38, the one (= Moses) who takes refuge in "the God who is" strikes down perishable human passion (= the Egyptian). Elsewhere Philo likens the Egyptian who was killed by Moses to pleasure (*On Flight and Finding* 148).
8. On Gregory's notion that realities such as Good and Life have no limit in themselves but are limited by the presence of their opposite, see *Life of Moses* 1.5. On the notion that every concept that admits of a contrary has only one opposite, see Plato, *Protagoras* 332a–e.
9. For a similar idea, see Philo, *Questions and Answers on Exodus* 2.17.
10. Exod 2:13-14.
11. Exod 2:15.

17. And if we must again live with a foreigner, that is to say, if need requires us to associate with profane wisdom, let us with determination scatter the wicked shepherds from their unjust use of the wells[12]—which means let us reprove the teachers of evil for their wicked use of instruction.

18. In the same way we shall live a solitary life, no longer entangled with adversaries or mediating between them, but we shall live among those of like disposition and mind who are fed by us, while all the movements of our soul are shepherded, like sheep, by the will of guiding reason.[13]

19. It is upon us who continue in this quiet and peaceful course of life that the truth will shine, illuminating the eyes of our soul with its rays. This truth, which was then manifested by the ineffable and mysterious illumination which came to Moses, is God.[14]

20. And if the flame by which the soul of the prophet was illuminated was kindled from a thorny bush, even this fact will not be useless for our inquiry. For if truth is God and truth is light—the Gospel testifies by these sublime and divine names to the God who made himself visible to us in the flesh—such guidance of virtue leads us to know that light which has reached down even to human nature.[15] Lest one think that the radiance did not come from a material substance, this light did not shine from some luminary among the stars but came

---

12. Exod 2:16–19.
13. Exod 2:21–22; 3:1. Cf. Philo, *On the Sacrifices of Cain and Abel* 45, who says that the mind that cleaves to virtue becomes like a shepherd of sheep who guides the chariot and controls the helm of the unreasoning faculties of the soul. Origen, *Homilies on Jeremiah* 5.6, identifies Jesus as the Good Shepherd who shepherds the irrational movements of the souls that lead to sin; see also Philo, *On Agriculture* 26–66; and *On the Sacrifices of Cain and Abel* 104–5, on the mind as shepherd of the irrational parts of the soul. It was a commonplace among Greek thinkers that reason governs the passionate and irrational parts of the soul (e.g., Plato, *Timaeus* 42a–d; Plutarch, *On Moral Virtue* 442a).
14. Exod 3:2–3.
15. John 1:4–5, 9–10, 14; 8:12; 14:6.

from an earthly bush and surpassed the heavenly luminaries in brilliance.

21. From this we learn also the mystery of the Virgin: The light of divinity which through birth shone from her into human life did not consume the burning bush, even as the flower of her virginity was not withered by giving birth.[16]

22. That light teaches us what we must do to stand within the rays of the true light: Sandaled feet cannot ascend that height where the light of truth is seen, but the dead and earthly covering of skins, which was placed around our nature at the beginning when we were found naked because of disobedience to the divine will,[17] must be removed from the feet of the soul. When we do this, the knowledge of the truth will result and manifest itself. The full knowledge of being comes about by purifying our opinion concerning nonbeing.

23. In my view the definition of truth is this: not to have a mistaken apprehension of Being.[18] Falsehood is a kind of impression which arises in the understanding about nonbeing:[19] as though what does not exist does, in fact, exist.

---

16. Matt 1:18–25; Luke 1:34–35.

17. Cf. Gen 3:21. See also Gregory's *Homilies on the Beatitudes* 8.1, where the "garments of skin" from Gen 3:21 represent dead skin that humanity put on following the disobedience of Adam and Eve, which is removed by spiritual circumcision.

18. In Exod 3:14, where the Hebrew has: "God said to Moses: '*hyh 'shr 'hyh* ('I will be who I will be'). . . . '*hyh* ('I will be') has sent me to you," the Septuagint translates: "God said to Moses: *egō eimi ho ōn* ('I am Being'). . . . *ho ōn* ('Being') has sent me to you." The precise significance of the Hebrew is unclear, but the Greek form of this passage readily lent itself to philosophical reflections such as Gregory gives here. For discussions of "Being," see for example Plato, *Timaeus* 27d–28a ("Being" is without cause and has no "becoming"); Plutarch, *The E at Delphi* 392a–b ("Being" is beyond full apprehension); and Plotinus, *Enneads* 3.6.6 ("Being" has no need of anything, but is cause to other things).

19. An "impression" or "mental picture" (*phantasia*) arises in the understanding through sense perception (*aisthēsis*); for the Stoic view, see Diogenes Laertius 7.45; Sextus Empiricus, *Against the Mathematicians* 7.227–41; see also Plotinus, *Enneads* 3.6.1–5. Plato, *Theaetetus* 184c–186e explains that knowledge, as in knowledge of existence and non-existence, does not reside in our sense perceptions but in our reflection on these perceptions (cf. *Phaedo* 65d–e). That sense perceptions (like the passions) can lead to error and need to be governed properly is a common theme in Philo (e.g., *On the Special*

But truth is the sure apprehension of real Being. So, whoever applies himself in quietness to higher philosophical matters over a long period of time will barely apprehend what true Being is, that is, what possesses existence in its own nature, and what nonbeing is, that is, what exists only in appearance, with no self-subsisting nature.

24. It seems to me that at the time when the great Moses was instructed in the theophany, he came to know that none of those things which are apprehended by sense perception and contemplated by the understanding really subsists, but that the transcendent essence and cause of the universe, on which everything depends, alone subsists.

25. For even if the understanding looks upon any other existing things, reason observes in absolutely none of them the self-sufficiency by which they could exist without participating in true Being. On the other hand, that which is always the same, neither increasing nor diminishing, immutable to change whether to better or to worse (for it is far removed from the inferior and it has no superior), standing in need of nothing else, alone desirable, participated in by all but not lessened by their participation—this is truly real Being. And the apprehension of it is the knowledge of truth.[20]

26. In the same way that Moses on that occasion attained to this knowledge, so now does everyone who, like him, divests himself of the earthly covering and looks to the light shining from the bramble bush, that is, to the Radiance which shines

---

Laws 2.89; *Allegorical Interpretation* 2.6, 50; 3.50; *Who Is the Heir?* 75–80, 111), who reflects the Platonic tradition (e.g., *Phaedo* 79c).

20. On the Platonic concepts in this paragraph, see for example Plato, *Phaedo* 80a–b; *Republic* 380d–381c; Alcinous, *The Handbook of Platonism*, ch. 10 (on "God"); Plotinus, *Enneads* 1.6.7; 3.6.6; 5.1.3–9. See also James 1:17; Acts 17:25. For further discussion of Gregory's appropriation of Greek philosophy, see H. F. Cherniss, *The Platonism of Gregory of Nyssa* (New York: Franklin, 1930); and David Balás, *Μεθουσία Θεοῦ: Man's Participation in God's Perfections According to Saint Gregory of Nyssa* (SA 55; Rome: IBC Libreria Herder, 1966).

upon us through this thorny flesh and which is (as the Gospel says) the true light and the truth itself.[21] A person like this becomes able to help others to salvation, to destroy the tyranny which holds power wickedly, and to deliver to freedom everyone held in evil servitude.[22]

Life of Moses 2.48–50
(reflection on the goal of this discourse)

48. If, while trying to parallel completely the historical account to the sequence of such intellectual contemplation, someone should somehow discover something in the account that does not coincide with our understanding, he should not reject the whole enterprise. He should always keep in mind our discussion's goal, to which we are looking while we relate these details. We have already said in our prologue that the lives of honored men would be set forth as a pattern of virtue for those who come after them.

49. Those who emulate their lives, however, cannot experience the identical literal events. For how could one again find the people multiplying during their sojourn in Egypt?[23] And how again find the tyrant who enslaves the people and bears hostility to male offspring and allows the feminine and weaker to grow in numbers?[24] And how again find all the other things which Scripture includes? Because therefore it has been shown to be impossible to imitate the marvels of these blessed men in these exact events, one might substitute a moral

21. John 1:4–5, 9; 8:12; 14:6.
22. Cf. Gen 4:7; John 8:34; Rom 6:16–18; 7:14; 2 Pet 2:19. Plato, *Republic* 577d–e, speaks of the "tyranny" which enslaves the soul that is driven by desire.
23. Exod 1:7, 12, 20.
24. Exod 1:13–16. On the male offspring as virtue and the female offspring as vice, see Gregory of Nyssa's *Life of Moses* 2.2–7. This interpretation follows Philo, *Allegorical Interpretation* 3.1, 243; *Questions on Exodus* 1.7–8; and Origen, *Homilies on Exodus* 2.1–3.

teaching for the literal sequence in those things which admit of such an approach. In this way those who have been striving toward virtue may find aid in living the virtuous life.

50. If the events require dropping from the literal account anything written which is foreign to the sequence of elevated understanding, we pass over this on the grounds that it is useless and unprofitable to our purpose, so as not to interrupt the guidance to virtue at such points.

Life of Moses 2.102–29
(The Passover and Crossing the Red Sea)

102. What follows agrees with our spiritual understanding of the text. For Scripture requires that the body of the lamb, whose blood was displayed on the doors and separated the people from the destroyer, become our food.[25]

103. The demeanor of those eating this food was to be intense and earnest, not like that of those who enjoy themselves at banquets, whose hands are relaxed and whose clothes are loose and whose feet are unprepared for travel. But everything was the opposite. Their feet were covered with sandals, a belt bound the clothing at the waist, and the staff to repel dogs was held in hand.[26]

104. And to them in this condition was presented meat without any artfully prepared sauces but cooked upon any fire that happened to be available. The guests eagerly devoured it in great haste until the entire body of the animal was

25. Exod 12:3–8, 12–13. Cf. Matt 26:19, 26; 1 Cor 5:7. Important early Christian interpretations of the Passover include Melito of Sardis, *On the Passover* (ca. 165 CE) and Origen, *Treatise on the Passover* (ca. 245 CE).

26. Exod 12:11. The explanation that the staff is meant to repel dogs may be connected to Exod 11:7: "not a dog shall growl at any of the Israelites." Philo, *Questions and Answers on Exodus* 1.19, says that the staff is useful for driving away poisonous reptiles and other beasts.

consumed. They ate whatever was edible around the bones, but they did not touch the entrails. To break the bones of this animal was one of the things forbidden. Whatever might be left of the meat was consumed by the fire.[27]

105. From all this it is evident that the letter looks to some higher understanding, since the law does not instruct us how to eat. Nature, which implants a desire for food in us, is a sufficient lawgiver with regard to these things.[28] The account rather signifies something different. For what does it matter to virtue or vice to eat your food this way or that, to have the belt loose or tight, to have your feet bare or covered with shoes, to have your staff in your hand or laid aside?

106. It is clear what the traveler's equipment figuratively stands for: It commands us explicitly to recognize that our present life is transient. Already at birth we are driven by the very nature of things toward our departure, for which we must carefully prepare our hands, feet, and the rest.

107. So that the thorns of this life (the thorns would be sins)[29] may not hurt our naked and unprotected feet, let us cover them with shoes. The shoes are the self-controlled and austere life which breaks and crushes the points of the thorns and prevents sin from slipping inside unnoticed.[30]

108. The tunic flowing down over the feet and reaching to the soles would be a hindrance to anyone who would diligently finish the divine course.[31] The tunic accordingly would be seen

27. Exod 12:8–11, 46. Cf. Exod 34:25; Num 9:11–12; Deut 16:4. On the removal of the entrails, see Lev 3:3–4; m. Pesahim 5.10; t. Pesahim 4.10.
28. According to the Stoics, Nature ordained that each animal has as its first impulse self-preservation, which includes the impulse to eat; see Diogenes Laertius 7.85–86; Cicero, *On Ends* 3.20–21.
29. Cf. Gen 3:18.
30. See also *Life of Moses* 2.2 on the need for "austerity and intensity of virtue." Regarding the "self-controlled" (*enkratēs*) life, self-control (*enkrateia*) was a Platonic virtue (*Republic* 430d–432a; Plutarch, *On Moral Virtue* 445b–c) and a Stoic virtue (Diogenes Laertius 7.92–93; Stobaeus 2.7; 60.9–24); see also Philo, *Life of Moses* 2.185; *On the Creation of the World* 164; and Acts 24:25; Gal 5:23; 2 Pet 1:6.

as the full enjoyment of the pursuits of this life, which the prudent reason, like a traveler's belt, draws in as tightly as possible. The place around which the belt passes shows that it is to be understood as prudence.[32] The staff for repelling animals is the message of hope, by which we support the weariness of the soul and ward off what threatens us.

109. The food placed before us from the fire I call the warm and fervent faith which we receive without having given thought to it. We devour as much of it as is easily eaten, but we leave aside the doctrine concealed in the thoughts which are hard and tough without investigating it thoroughly or seeking to know more about it. Instead we consign this food to the fire.

110. In order that these figures may be made clear, let us explain that whichever of the divine commands are readily perceived should not be followed sluggishly or by constraint, but we should be like those who are hungry and eagerly fill up on the things set before them, so that the food may become provision for our well-being. But such thoughts as are beyond our understanding—like the questions, What is the essence of God? What was there before the creation? What is there outside the visible world? Why do things which happen happen? and other such things as are sought out by inquiring

---

31. Cf. 1 Cor 9:24; Heb 12:1; 2 Tim 4:7.

32. Prudence was one of the four cardinal virtues, together with temperance, fortitude, and justice; see Plato, *Protagoras* 330b; 349b; 359a (five virtues: the four plus "piety"); *Republic* 4.427e; 433a–c; *Laws* 1.631c–d; 12.965d (four virtues); *Wisdom of Solomon* 8:7; Cicero, *On Ends* 5.23.67; *On Duties* 1.2.5. On the belt in Exod 12:11, cf. Philo, *Questions and Answers on Exodus* 1.19, who says that one must wrap the middle of the body with a belt in order to draw together the sensual pleasures and other passions which otherwise overtake the soul and hinder the traveler on the path that leads to virtue.

minds[33]—these things we concede to know only by the Holy Spirit, who "reaches the depths of God," as the Apostle says.[34]

111. Anyone instructed in the Scriptures surely knows that instead of "Spirit" Scripture often thinks of it and designates it as "fire."[35] We are also led to this understanding by the announcement of Wisdom: "Do not try to understand things that are too difficult for you," that is to say, Do not break the bones of Scripture, "for you have no need to see with your eyes those things that are hidden."[36]

112. Thus Moses led the people out of Egypt, and everyone who follows in the steps of Moses in this way sets free from the Egyptian tyrant all those guided by his word. Those who follow the leader to virtue must, I think, not lack the wealth of Egypt or be deprived of the treasures of the foreigners, but having acquired all the property of their enemies, must have it for their own use. This is exactly what Moses then commanded the people to do.[37]

113. No one who has listened to this casually[38] would accept the advice of the lawgiver if he enjoined those in want to rob,

33. The Greek word *periergos* (translated here as "inquiring mind") referred to a person who was meddlesome or overly inquisitive. This appears to be a reference to Eunomius and his followers. One of Gregory's charges against Eunomius was that the Arian bishop failed to recognize the limitations of human understanding, which led Eunomius to make rash and impious statements about divine mysteries (e.g., see Gregory of Nyssa, *Against Eunomius* 2.9; *Answer to Eunomius's Second Book* [*Nicene and Post-Nicene Fathers*, second series, 5:261]).

34. 1 Cor 2:10.

35. Matt 3:11; Luke 3:16; Acts 2:3–4; 1 Cor 3:12–17; cf. Exod 3:2; 13:21–22; 19:18; 24:17; Lev 6:12–13; Deut 4:24; 9:3; Ps 39:3; Isa 33:14; Jer 5:14; 20:9; 23:29; Mal 3:2–3; Luke 24:32; Heb 12:29. According to Origen (*Treatise on the Passover* 26–28; *Commentary on John* 10.103–5), we should not eat the flesh of the Passover sacrifice raw, that is, interpret Scripture literally, but we should roast it with the fire of the Spirit, that is, interpret Scripture spiritually.

36. Sir 3:22–23.

37. Exod 12:35–36; cf. Exod 3:21–22; 11:2–3.

38. Greek: *ek procheirou*, "off-hand," "rashly," or "ordinarily." Malherbe and Ferguson translate this as "carelessly." I am instead using "casually," that is: No one who gives this text a casual (obvious) reading would agree with Moses here, since it seems to contradict the laws that follow; but closer inspection will reveal a deeper meaning that is lofty and suitable.

and so became a leader in their wrongdoing. If someone looks to the laws which follow, which from beginning to end forbid wrongdoing to one's neighbor, he could not truthfully say that the lawgiver commanded these things, even though to some it seems reasonable that the Israelites should have exacted the wages for their work from the Egyptians by this device.[39]

114. Yet there is no less ground for complaint; this justification does not purify such a command of falsehood and fraud, for the person who borrows something and does not repay the lender is deceitful. If he borrows something not belonging to him, he does wrong because he commits fraud. But even if he should take what is rightly his own, he is still correctly called a deceiver since he misleads the lender into hoping that he will be repaid.

115. The loftier meaning is therefore more fitting than the obvious one. It commands those participating through virtue in the free life also to equip themselves with the wealth of pagan learning by which foreigners to the faith beautify themselves.[40] Our guide in virtue commands someone who "borrows" from wealthy Egyptians to receive such things as moral and natural philosophy, geometry, astronomy, dialectic, and whatever else is sought by those outside the Church, since these things will be useful when in time the divine sanctuary of mystery must be beautified with the riches of reason.

---

39. On the despoiling of Egypt as Israel receiving fair wages for their service, see Philo, *Life of Moses* 1.141; Clement of Alexandria, *Stromateis* 1.23.157; Tertullian, *Against Marcion* 2.20.1–3; 4.24.4; Irenaeus, *Against Heresies* 4.30.1–4; and Theodoret, *Questions on Exodus* 23. Earlier Gregory of Nyssa explained that Israel acquired Egyptian wealth under the pretext of taking a loan (*Life of Moses* 1.29). Augustine regarded the despoiling of Egypt as warranted because the Egyptians deserved to be deceived (*Eighty-three Different Questions* 53.2), or else as justified on the grounds that God's decrees should be obeyed, not evaluated (*Questions on the Heptateuch* 6).

40. On the despoiling of Egypt as the appropriation of pagan learning, see Origen, *Letter to Gregory,* and Augustine, *On Christian Teaching* 2.40.61. Gregory of Nazianzus interpreted the despoiling of Egypt as teaching Christians to make friends for themselves out of the mammon of unrighteousness (*Orations* 45.20; see Luke 16:9).

116. Those who treasured up for themselves such wealth handed it over to Moses as he was working on the tent of mystery, each one making his personal contribution to the construction of the holy places.[41] It is possible to see this happening even now. For many bring to the Church of God their profane learning as a kind of gift: Such a man was the great Basil, who acquired the Egyptian wealth in every respect during his youth and dedicated this wealth to God for the adornment of the Church, the true tabernacle.[42]

117. Let us return to the point where we digressed. When those who already look to virtue and follow the lawgiver in life have left the borders of the Egyptians' dominion behind, the assaults of temptations in some way pursue them and bring on distress and fears and threats of death. When frightened by these things, those newly established in the faith lose all hope for what is good. But if Moses or some leader of the people like him happens along, he will counsel them against fear and will strengthen their downcast minds with the hope of divine help.

118. This help will not come unless the heart of the leader speaks with God. Many of those who occupy a position of leadership are concerned only with outward appearances; of those hidden things that are observed only by God they have hardly a thought.[43] But in the case of Moses it was not so. While he exhorted the Israelites to be of good courage, he did cry out, although outwardly making no sound to God, as God himself bears witness.[44] The Scripture teaches us, I think, that the voice

---

41. Exod 25:1–9; 35:4–9, 20–29. On the tabernacle of mystery, see Gregory of Nyssa, *Life of Moses* 2.174, 188. Cosmological interpretations of the Tabernacle were offered by Philo, *On the Special Laws* 1.66–75; *Life of Moses* 88–93; and Clement of Alexandria, *Stromateis* 5.6.32.1–40.4. Gregory of Nyssa's exposition notably lacks cosmological elements and instead is oriented toward mystical interpretation.

42. Gregory compares Basil's virtue to that of Moses in his work, *In Praise of My Brother Basil.*

43. Cf. Matt 6:4, 6, 18.

44. In Exod 14:15 God says to Moses, "Why do you cry out to me?," even though it is not stated that Moses said anything. Origen, *Homilies on Exodus* 5.4, explains that Moses

which is melodious and ascends to God's hearing is not the cry made with the organs of speech but the meditation sent up from a pure conscience.[45]

119. To the one who finds himself in these circumstances, the brother appears limited in the help that he renders for the great struggles—I mean that brother who met Moses as he was going down to Egypt at the divine bidding, whom Scripture has understood as being in the rank of angels.[46] Then occurred the manifestation of the divine nature which manifests itself in the way that one is capable of receiving.[47] What we hear from the history to have happened, then, we understand from contemplation of the Word always to happen.

120. Whenever someone flees Egypt and, after getting outside its borders, is terrified by the assaults of temptation, the guide produces unexpected salvation from on high. Whenever the enemy with his army surrounds the one being pursued, the guide is forced to make the sea passable for him.

121. In this crossing the cloud served as a guide.[48] Those before us interpreted the cloud as the grace of the Holy Spirit, who guides toward the Good those who are worthy.[49] Whoever follows him passes through the water, since the guide makes a way through it for him. In this way he is safely led to freedom,

cried out to God without sound by means of the Spirit of the Son crying in Moses's heart, "Abba, Father," and interceding for Moses with indescribable groans (see Gal 4:6; Rom 8:23, 26–27).

45. See 1 Tim 1:5; Rom 8:26–27; 1 Cor 14:2.

46. Exod 4:14–17, 27–28. For Moses's brother Aaron representing an angel, see *Life of Moses* 2.42–47.

47. This is a reference to manna (see Exod 16:31; cf. Num 11:7). According to Basil (*Letter* 190.3), Philo explained that the manna adapted its taste to the wants of the eater. See also *Wisdom of Solomon* 16:21; t. Sotah 4.3; Mekilta of Rabbi Ishmael, Vayissa 5 and Amalek 3; Sifre Numbers 89; and b. Yoma 75a (cf. Ephrem, *Commentary on Exodus* 16.3). Origen, *Homilies on Exodus* 7.8, likens the manna to the Word of God that adjusts itself to suit the capacity of the one who receives it.

48. Exod 13:21–22.

49. On the pillar of cloud as the Holy Spirit, see Origen, *Homilies on Exodus* 5.1; Basil, *On the Holy Spirit* 14.31; Ambrose, *On the Mysteries* 3.12–13; Theodoret of Cyrus, *Questions on Exodus* 27.

and the one who pursues him to bring him into bondage is destroyed in the water. No one who hears this should be ignorant of the mystery of the water.[50] He who has gone down into it with the army of the enemy emerges alone, leaving the enemy's army drowning in the water.

122. For who does not know that the Egyptian army—those horses, chariots and their drivers, archers, slingers, heavily armed soldiers, and the rest of the crowd of the enemies' line of battle—are the various passions of the soul by which humanity is enslaved? For the undisciplined intellectual drives and the sensual impulses to pleasure, sorrow, and covetousness are indistinguishable from the aforementioned army. Reviling is a stone straight from the sling, and the spirited impulse is the quivering spear point. The passion for pleasure is to be seen in the horses who themselves with irresistible drive pull the chariot.

123. In the chariot there are three drivers whom the history calls "viziers."[51] Since you were previously instructed in the

---

50. Gregory interprets the water of the Red Sea as the water of baptism. The key to Gregory's exposition is 1 Cor 10:1–11, according to which Israel was "baptized into Moses in the cloud and in the sea" when they passed through the Red Sea. Moreover, they ate "spiritual food" (manna, Exod 16:14–35) and drank "spiritual drink" (Exod 17:6), since "they drank from the spiritual rock that followed them; and the rock was Christ" (v. 4). Still, God was displeased with most of them, and so they died in the wilderness (v. 5; see Num 14:20–35). According to the apostle Paul, "These things happened to them as an example [typikōs], and they were written down as a warning to us" (v. 11). For Gregory and other early Christians, this seemed like the proper interpretive trajectory to follow. The task of the interpreter was merely to extend the allegory throughout the passage: if passing through the sea was baptism, then what held them captive (= Egyptians) was sin ("the passions") or demons, the period leading up to the water involved catechesis, what guides the newly baptized (= the pillar) is the Holy Spirit, and so forth. Gregory's Life of Moses is part of an extensive Christian tradition that interprets the text along these lines, for example: Clement of Alexandria, Stromateis 5.8.52–53; Irenaeus, Demonstration 46; Tertullian, On Baptism 9.1–4; Origen, Homilies on Exodus 3–7; Homilies on Numbers 27.2–5; Commentary on John 6.227–37; Eusebius of Caesarea, Demonstration of the Gospel 3.2; Hilary of Poitiers, Commentary on the Psalms 134.15–19; Didymus of Alexandria, On the Trinity 2.14; Cyril of Jerusalem, Catechetical Lectures 19.2–3; Ambrose, On the Mysteries 3.12–14; On the Sacraments 1.4.12; 1.6.20–22; Basil, On the Holy Spirit 14.31–33; Augustine, Against Faustus 12.29–30; and Theodoret of Cyrus, Questions on Exodus 26–28.

mystery of the side posts and upper doorposts, you will perceive these three, who are completely carried along by the chariot, as the tripartite division of the soul, meaning the rational, the appetitive, and the spirited.[52]

124. So all such things rush into the water with the Israelite who leads the way in the baleful passage. Then as the staff of faith leads on and the cloud provides light, the water gives life to those who find refuge in it but destroys their pursuers.

125. Moreover the history teaches us by this what kind of people they should be who come through the water, bringing nothing of the opposing army along as they emerge from the water. For if the enemy came up out of the water with them, they would continue in slavery even after the water, since they would have brought up with themselves the tyrant, still alive, whom they did not drown in the deep. If anyone wishes to clarify the figure, this lays it bare: Those who pass through the mystical water in baptism must put to death in the water the whole phalanx of evil—such as covetousness, unbridled desire, rapacious thinking, the passion of conceit and arrogance, wild impulse, wrath, anger, malice, envy, and all such things. Since the passions naturally pursue our nature, we must put to death

---

51. In the Septuagint, the "officers" (Exod 14:7; 15:4) who lead Pharaoh's chariots are translated by the word *tristatēs,* "vizier," literally "the third one."

52. See *Life of Moses* 2.96 on the upper doorpost and the two side posts (Exod 12:23) as signifying the tripartite nature of the soul as rational, appetitive, and spirited. For this concept of the soul, see Plato, *Republic* 436a–441e; and Alcinous, *Handbook of Platonism,* ch. 24. Also relevant is Plato's metaphor in *Phaedrus* 246a–254e of the soul as a chariot, with a chariot driver (= reason, the soul's pilot) and two horses, one horse being noble and the other its opposite. Plutarch, *On Moral Virtue* 445b–d, applies Plato's chariot metaphor to the exercise of reason over the passions. Philo, *On Agriculture* 72–73, 93, and *On the Migration of Abraham* 62, 67, construes both horses as negative (desire and fierce-spirit), with the chariot driver as Mind or the Divine Word (see also *Allegorical Interpretation* 3.193, 223–24). For Clement of Alexandria, *Stromateis* 5.8.52–53, who cites Plato explicitly, the "horse and its rider" (Exod 15:1) signifies the impulsive passion of desire (= the horse) and the chariot driver who gives the reins to pleasure (= its rider). In Origen, *Homilies on Exodus* 6.3, the officers or "viziers" ("the third ones") of the chariot are described as threefold in order to signify the three ways that people sin: in deed, in speech, and in thought.

in the water both the base movements of the mind and the acts which issue from them.

126. Just as unleavened bread was eaten in the mystery of the Pasch (which is the name of the sacrificial victim whose blood prevents the death of the one using it), even so the Law now commands us to eat unleavened bread at the Pasch (unleavened would be unmixed with stale yeast).[53] The Law gives us to understand by this that no remnant of evil should mix with the subsequent life. Rather we should make a totally new beginning in life after these things, breaking the continuity with evil by a radical change for the better. Thus also he means here that after we have drowned the whole Egyptian person (that is, every form of evil) in the saving baptism, we emerge alone, dragging along nothing foreign in our subsequent life. This is what we hear through the history, which says that in the same water the enemy and the friend are distinguished by death and life, the enemy being destroyed and the friend given life.

127. Many of those who receive the mystical baptism, in ignorance of the commandments of the Law, mix the bad leaven of the old life with the new life. Even after crossing the water they bring along the Egyptian army, which still lives with them in their doings.

128. Take for instance the one who became rich by robbery or injustice, or who acquired property through perjury, or lived with a woman in adultery, or undertook any of the other things against life that have been forbidden before the gift of baptism. Does he think that even after his washing he may continue to enjoy those evil things that have become attached

---

53. Exod 12:8, 14–20, 39; 13:6–10. For Gregory's spiritual interpretation, see 1 Cor 5:6–8. For Christ as the Passover lamb, see also Justin Martyr, *Dialogue with Trypho* 111.3.

to him and yet be freed from the bondage of sin, as though he cannot see that he is under the yoke of harsh masters?

129. For uncontrolled passion is a fierce and raging master to the servile reasoning, tormenting it with pleasures as though they were scourges. Covetousness is another such master who provides no relief to the bondsman, but even if the one in bondage should slave in subservience to the commands of the master and acquire for him what he desires, the servant is always driven on to more. And all the other things which are performed by evil are so many tyrants and masters. If someone should still serve them, even if he should have happened to pass through the water, according to my thinking he has not at all touched the mystical water whose function is to destroy evil tyrants.

11

Jerome

Jerome was born ca. 347 CE and spent his early life in Stridon, a small town in the Roman province of Dalmatia. He received his primary education in his hometown under the supervision of his Christian parents, who were wealthy enough to employ teachers for Jerome and his brother. At the age of eleven or twelve Jerome's parents sent him to Rome in order to study literature and rhetoric. Among Jerome's teachers was the prominent scholar Aelius Donatus, who had composed widely read commentaries on classical authors and a popular Latin grammatical textbook.[1] Later Jerome also studied rhetoric and had some exposure to philosophical writers as part of his

---

1. From Donatus Jerome learned classical literary analysis (*grammaticē*), which Jerome then applied to the Bible; see Michael Graves, *Jerome's Hebrew Philology* (Leiden: Brill, 2007), 13–75; and *Jerome: Commentary on Jeremiah*, trans. M. Graves (ACT; Downers Grove, IL: InterVarsity, 2011), xxxvi–xl. Major elements of *grammaticē* included *lectio* ("reading aloud"), *enarratio* ("explanation"), *emendatio* ("textual criticism"), and *iudicium* ("literary evaluation"). Aspects of Jerome's exegesis directly influenced by *grammaticē* include his focus on linguistic issues, his utilization of historical background information, and his extensive use of paraphrase.

formal education. Jerome's parents were obviously intent on preparing their son for life as a Christian and also life as a Roman aristocrat. As he later recollects, "From my cradle, I have been nourished on Catholic milk" (*Letter* 82.2), and also, "Almost from the cradle, my life has been spent in the company of grammarians, rhetoricians, and philosophers" (Preface to IH Job).[2]

In the late 360s Jerome traveled to the city of Trier in Gaul, the residence of the emperor Valentinian. But instead of entering civil service, Jerome decided to give up his plans for a secular career and pursue instead a life devoted to Christian ideals. In ca. 372 Jerome went east to Antioch, and from there in 375 he ventured into the desert of Chalcis in Syria in order to try out the monastic life of withdrawal from society; but Jerome never took to this lifestyle, and within a year or two he returned to Antioch. While in Antioch Jerome heard lectures by Apollinaris of Laodicea, whom he later claimed proudly as a teacher in scriptural interpretation, even though he rejected Apollinaris's teaching on the person of Christ (*Letter* 84.3). Jerome eventually journeyed to Constantinople in order to attend the church council of 381. In Constantinople Jerome deepened his understanding of Greek theology and cultivated his early admiration for Origen through interactions with Gregory of Nazianzus. During his time in the east Jerome significantly improved his command of Greek, picked up some Syriac, and began his study of Hebrew under the tutelage of a Jewish convert to Christianity.

In 382 Jerome returned to Rome. With his knowledge of Greek language and theology, eastern monastic experience, and basic Hebrew competence Jerome quickly found favor with Pope Damasus, whom he served as a secretary. While in Rome,

2. See Graves, trans., *Jerome: Commentary on Jeremiah*, xxiv.

Jerome continued his Hebrew studies by reading with Jews and by studying the Hebrew text alongside the Greek hexaplaric versions. Jerome also showed enthusiasm for rigorous ascetic ideals, promoting poverty, fasting, self-denial, and virginity. Unfortunately for Jerome, some important members of the Christian community in Rome rejected his rigorous ascetic teaching and even criticized his biblical scholarship, for example, complaining that his revision of the Latin Gospels based on the original Greek changed too much of the traditional Latin wording. After Damasus's death, Jerome was forced to leave Rome in 385.

Following his stay in Rome Jerome decided to return to the east. For a time he resided in Egypt where he listened to the teaching of Didymus of Alexandria and visited monks in the Egyptian desert. Finally, in 386 Jerome returned to Bethlehem together with his wealthy friend Paula, who had accompanied him from Rome on his eastern trek. Through Paula's resources they established a pair of monasteries, one for men supervised by Jerome and the other for women overseen by Paula. These monasteries served as centers of refuge for the poor and for pilgrims from the west, where aid was given to those in need and Jerome was afforded the time he needed to write.

Jerome lived in Bethlehem for the rest of his life, devoting substantial energy to his Hebrew studies, biblical translations, commentaries, and learned correspondence. Jerome's reputation as a scholar continued to grow, although his return to the "Hebrew truth" (*hebraica veritas*) received criticism from those who favored the Septuagint as the traditional Christian Old Testament.[3] In the 390s a controversy broke out over the

---

3. As Jerome stated in the preface to his translation of Isaiah: "Therefore, with full knowledge and recognition (of the difficulties and potential criticisms), I send forth my hand into the flame" (see Graves, trans., *Jerome: Commentary on Jeremiah*, xxvii).

orthodoxy of Origen's writings; Jerome sided with those who condemned Origen and so he ceased speaking favorably about the great Alexandrian scholar whom he formerly admired, even though he continued to consult Origen's works. In the 410s Jerome entered into the Pelagian controversy and composed a *Dialogue Against the Pelagians*. The final fifteen years of Jerome's life saw him at the height of his powers as a biblical scholar. Jerome completed a commentary on the Minor Prophets in 401, wrote an abbreviated commentary on Daniel in 407, and then followed up with commentaries on Isaiah (408–10), Ezekiel (410–14), and Jeremiah. Jerome began his commentary on Jeremiah in 414, and reached the end of chapter thirty-two by the time of his death in 419.

Over the course of his long career Jerome composed a variety of works, including literary lives of saints, for example *The Life of Malchus the Captive Monk*; doctrinal treatises, such as *Against Jovinianus,* which defended ascetic practices such as fasting and virginity; historical works, such as *Lives of Illustrious Men*; and numerous letters that treat diverse topics, especially asceticism and Scripture. He also produced many Latin translations of Greek Christian authors, above all Origen. But Jerome is best known for his commentaries on Scripture, biblical reference works such as his *Book of Hebrew Names,* and his translation of the Hebrew Bible ("Old Testament") into Latin. Jerome's Hebrew-based Latin Old Testament together with his translation of the Gospels became the basis for what later came to be called the Latin "Vulgate." In Jerome's day the *editio vulgata* ("popular edition") was the Old Latin version based on the Septuagint. Jerome identified his own Hebrew-based translation as his edition *iuxta Hebraicum* ("according to the Hebrew"), so I will refer to this translation as the IH edition.

Examples of Jerome's biblical exegesis are given below from his *Commentary on Jeremiah*. Often in Jerome's commentaries he gives the biblical text upon which he is commenting (= the "lemma") in two forms: first according to his own Hebrew-based translation (the IH edition), and second according to the Septuagint (the "LXX"). Although he sometimes does this in the *Commentary on Jeremiah,* more often in this work Jerome gives only the IH edition in full, providing occasional alternative translations from the Septuagint. Whenever Jerome gives two options in the biblical lemma, it may be understood that the first option is his own IH edition and the second is the Septuagint. Usually Jerome associates the Hebrew-based version with the literal or historical sense, and the Septuagint with the spiritual sense. The exception to this rule is Hebrew proper name etymologies, which had been employed for allegorical interpretation since the time of Philo.[4]

Jerome makes extensive use of the Greek versions that were found in Origen's *Hexapla*: Aquila, Symmachus, and Theodotion. In a few instances Jerome makes reference to a "second edition" of Aquila and a "second edition" of Symmachus, which were probably alternative translations written here and there in the margins of Jerome's copies of Aquila and Symmachus.[5] Jerome's transcriptions of Hebrew words into Latin are presented in the English translation below just as Jerome wrote them in Latin. The Hebrew text utilized by Jerome is nearly identical with the Hebrew text known today, the medieval "Masoretic Text." Jerome's text of the Septuagint was a copy of Greek Jeremiah as it was available in Palestine in the early fifth century CE, containing various editorial accretions, and so it does not always match the modern critical

4. See Graves, *The Inspiration and Interpretation of Scripture,* 65–70.
5. Graves, *Jerome's Hebrew Philology,* 94.

edition of the Septuagint. A notable feature of Jerome's commentaries is his practice of explaining the sense of multiple versions of the text side by side without clearly indicating a preference.

Jerome saw himself as combining the best of literal and spiritual exegesis. He proudly acknowledged that he learned how to interpret Scripture both from the Antiochene Apollinaris and also from the Alexandrian Didymus. At times he described his exegetical task as "to mix together our [Christian] *tropologia* with the *historia* of the Hebrews."[6] Julian of Eclanum perceived Jerome to be an exegetical hybrid, criticizing the monk of Bethlehem as "content to go between two traditions . . . all of his eloquence drifts off either through the allegories of Origen or through the fictitious traditions of the Jews" (*Commentary on Hosea, Joel and Amos,* "Prologue"). In terms of hermeneutical method, Jerome's exegesis does not exhibit a strong sense of coherence. Jerome is significant as a compiler of interpretive traditions, and also because of his linguistic skills and creative solutions to textual difficulties.

---

6. *Commentary on Zechariah,* "Prologue." See also *Commentary on Zechariah* 6:9-15 and *Commentary on Jeremiah,* Book 3, "Prologue," for Jerome's sense that he is blending together Jewish *historia* with Christian spiritual interpretation. When early Christian interpreters encountered Jewish traditions related to Old Testament narratives, they often incorporated them into their exegesis as *historia;* see Adam Kamesar, "The Evaluation of the Narrative Aggada in Greek and Latin Patristic Literature," *Journal of Theological Studies* 45 (1994): 37–71.

Commentary on Jeremiah

2:33-34:

"Why do you endeavor to present your way as good, in order to seek love? And what is more, you have taught others your evils and your ways. (34) Also on your wings"—or "hands"[7]—"is found the life blood of the guiltless poor; I did not find them breaking in, but in all these things"—or—"under every oak tree."[8]

"In vain," he says, "you desire to defend yourself by skill of words and to present your deeds as good, so as to appear worthy of love. And what is more, you have even taught others your ways, and have become an example to all of evil deeds. And indeed on your wings"—or "hands"—"is found the blood of the innocent, whom you have sacrificed to idols, or whose lives you have destroyed just as if you had sacrificed them." We have added from the Hebrew the word "poor," which is not found in the LXX.[9] "And moreover," he says, "I have not found that these poor, innocent people were killed while breaking in"—it was common for a thief to be killed during his crime[10]—"but rather they were killed in all these circumstances that I have mentioned above"—or "under every oak tree." In Hebrew the word in question is *ella*,[11] which can signify "these things," so that the sense is "in all of these things that I mentioned," or else it can signify "oak tree," so that the sense is: "under the oak and terebinth trees under whose shade and foliage you enjoyed the evils of idolatry."

---

7. Jerome's translation ("wings") matches Aquila and Symmachus.
8. Jerome reads these words with v. 34, whereas the NRSV connects them to v. 35.
9. The Hebrew word is *ebyōn*, "poor." It was also supplied in the *Hexapla*.
10. Exod 22:2–3.
11. The two words are spelled with the same consonants in Hebrew, but are vocalized slightly differently: *'elleh* means "these (things)" (= the Masoretic Text), and *'ēlāh* means "oak tree" (= the Septuagint).

9:22:

Speak, "Thus says the Lord: 'The carrion of man'—or 'dead bodies of men'—'shall fall like dung upon the land'—or, 'field'—, 'like sheaves after the reaper, and none shall gather them.'"

Regarding the Hebrew word which is written with three letters, *daleth, beth,* and *res*—for it does not have the vowels within it—in view of the surrounding context and the decision of the reader if it is read as *dabar*, then it means "word"; if it is read *deber*, it means "death"; and if it is read *dabber*, it means "Speak!"[12] Out of all this, the Septuagint and Theodotion joined this word to the previous passage, so that they said: "cutting off the children from the streets and the young men from the squares by death."[13] But Aquila and Symmachus translated the word as *laleson*, "Speak!" so that God commands the prophet to say the things that follow, "Thus says the Lord, etc." This is the sense: When death has come up through our windows and has entered the palaces of Jerusalem, and when children and young men have perished from the streets and squares, then their "carrion"—or the "dead bodies" of the deceased—will be like the stubble that is left after the reapers, which remains ungathered because it is useless. Through these things he wishes to show that the carnage to come will be so great that there will be no one to bury those who have fallen.

---

12. The Hebrew consonants can be read as the noun *dābār*, "word," the noun *deber*, "bubonic plague," or as the Piel imperative *dabbēr*, "speak!"
13. Jer 9:21. What Jerome reports here for the Septuagint is attested for Theodotion and was apparently found in the hexaplaric edition of the Septuagint under asterisk. Most Septuagint manuscripts lack "by death" and also the following phrase, "Thus says the Lord."

15:12:

Will iron be joined in friendship with iron from the north, and bronze?
Symmachus: Will iron do harm to iron from the north, and bronze?
LXX and Theodotion: Will iron know? And a bronze wrap?[14]

The cause of the diversity is clear. The word *iare,* which is written in the present passage, can mean both "friendship" and "harm" in view of the ambiguity of its pronunciation. This same word, if the letter *daleth* is read instead of the letter *res* (which is similar to *daleth*), signifies "knowledge" or "recognition."[15] What is said should be understood in this way: "You should not be indignant that the people are hostile to you; it is not possible for the people, who are hard, to love you, since you are proclaiming to them hard things." Or: "The Babylonians, who come from the north and are like the hardest iron, cannot be joined in friendship with this people, who are hard and ungovernable like bronze." Or: "This hardest iron, that is, the people of Israel, are unworthy of the knowledge of God; they have attained such a level of evil that they have been surrounded by a hard metal, bronze."

14. Most preserved manuscripts of the Septuagint read: "Will iron be known? And your strength is a bronze wrap."
15. The Hebrew verb as it appears in the Masoretic Text is made up of three letters: *yōd, rēsh, 'ayin.* Jerome, following Aquila, interprets it as a Niphal verbal form of *rēaʿ* ("friend"), meaning "to be joined to" (the Hebrew root *ryʿ*). Symmachus takes the verb to be the Hiphil of *rʿʿ*, meaning "to do harm." The Septuagint and Theodotion read a *dālet* instead of the *rēsh* (which differ by only a small point, as Jerome points out in his *Commentary on Isaiah* 28:9), and so they interpret the word as a form of *ydʿ*, "to know." On Jerome's handling of the confusion between similar letters in Hebrew, see Graves, *Jerome's Hebrew Philology,* 57–59.

17:9-10:

The heart of all is perverse and inscrutable;[16] *who can understand it?* (10) *"I the Lord search the mind and try the heart, to give to every man according to his ways, according to the fruit of his doings." LXX: "Deep is the heart beyond all things, and it is man; who can understand him?" And the rest similarly . . .*

The Hebrew word *enos* is written with four letters, *aleph, nun, vav,* and *sin.* If it is read *enos,* it means "man"; but if it is read *anus,* it means "inscrutable" or "incurable," with the sense that no one is able to comprehend the human heart—although Symmachus interpreted the passage thus: "inscrutable is the heart of all; what man is there who could comprehend it?"[17] We [Christians] are accustomed—with good intention, to be sure, but not according to knowledge—to use this passage against the Jews, to the effect that the Lord and Savior is a man according to his assumed flesh, and that none can understand the mystery of his nativity (as it is written: "Who will describe his generation?"[18]) except God alone, who searches out hidden things and renders to each one according to his works.[19]

16. The first ambiguity of the text is the Hebrew *'qb* ("uneven terrain, deceitful"), which Jerome renders as "perverse," matching Aquila (Septuagint: "deep"). The next point of ambiguity is the Hebrew *mikkōl* ("from all"), which is either possessive ("the heart of all"—so Jerome) or comparative ("more deceitful than all"—so the Septuagint). On the third point of ambiguity, see Jerome's comments.

17. Jerome gives the "full" spelling of this Hebrew word (*'nwsh*), as is found in over forty medieval Hebrew manuscripts, as opposed to the defective spelling found in the Leningrad Codex (*'nsh*). Jerome is reading the word as *'ānūsh* ("incurable"), which he takes to mean "inscrutable," or else "incurable" (cf. Symmachus on Jer 15:18). Jerome seems uncertain as to the meaning of this word, since in his *Commentary on Isaiah* 17:11 he claims to have learned from "the Hebrews" that *'ānūsh* means "strongly" (cf. *Leviticus Rabbah* 18.3). But since "strongly" does not work here, Jerome must search for a more contextually appropriate meaning among the hexaplaric versions. The Septuagint reads the word as *'enōsh,* "man."

18. Isa 53:8.

19. Ps 62:12; Matt 16:27; Rom 2:6; Rev 2:23. For other examples where Jerome criticizes a Christian theological interpretation on linguistic or contextual grounds, see *Commentary on Jeremiah* 13:18–19; 23:18; see also *Commentary on Amos* 4:12–13;

20:3:

On the morrow when it was light, Pashhur released Jeremiah from prison, and Jeremiah said to him, "The Lord does not call your name Pashhur, but Terror on every side."

For this passage, all translated just as they did before regarding both the name of the high priest and the kind of torment.[20] But the high priest's name is now changed, so that his impending punishment may be indicated by his name. He says, "You will by no means have 'blackness of mouth' and the authority of unjust power, but you will be led captive to Babylon"—for "Terror on every side" or "Terror all around" signifies this—"so that you will look all around here and there, trembling and uncertain of your own safety, and you will dread the enemies who are coming against you." In place of "Terror," which in Hebrew is *magur*, the LXX and Theodotion translated *metoikon*, that is, "migrating," the second edition of Aquila put "foreigner," the first edition of Aquila put "looking around," and Symmachus translated "carried off" or "gathered together" and "collected."[21]

21:13-14:

"Behold, I am against you, O inhabitant of a firm and flat valley, says the Lord; you who say, 'Who shall strike'—or, 'terrify'[22]—'us, or who

---

Commentary on Isaiah 63:1 ("many, led astray by pious error, think . . ."). In other cases, Jerome uses the Hebrew to discover a Christian theological meaning that was absent from the Septuagint (e.g., *Commentary on Jeremiah* 23:36b–40; *Commentary on Isaiah* 2:22).

20. Jerome is referring to how all the Greek versions translated these words in Jer 20:1–2.

21. The concepts of "migrating" and "foreigner" come from associating this word with the verb *gwr*, "to dwell as a foreigner." Jerome is independent of all the Greek versions, the Aramaic Targum and the Syriac Peshitta in translating *mgwr* as "Terror," although he agrees in this with the medieval Jewish commentaries of Rashi and David Kimchi.

22. Both Jerome and the Septuagint are reading this word (*yēḥat*) as a Hiphil form of *ḥtt*, which could mean either "to shatter" or "to terrify." The Targum and the Peshitta both

175

shall enter our habitations?' (14) *I will punish you"*—and that which follows: *"according to the fruit of your doings, says the Lord,"* is not found in the LXX.[23] *"And I will kindle a fire,"* he says, *"in her forest, and it shall devour all that is round about her."*

In place of "O inhabitant of a firm and flat valley," the LXX translated: "Behold, I am against you, who inhabit the valley of Sor, the plain." In place of "Sor," Symmachus translated "rock," Theodotion put "enclosed," the first edition of Aquila translated "firm," and his second edition put "Tyre." For *sor* or *sur* in the Hebrew language can mean "Tyre," "stone," or "constrained."[24] And so he speaks against Jerusalem, which has been "enclosed" by a blockade, or is surrounded by the Babylonian army just as "Tyre" is surrounded by the Great Sea, or else thinks itself strong and impregnable like the hardest "rock" in view of its large, "firm" defenses.

Jerusalem says, "Who will be able to terrify us, or who shall enter our habitations?" God, on the contrary, says, "I will punish you. You will not be able to escape my notice. Indeed, I will punish you with destruction. I will render to you the fruit of your evil deeds. I will kindle a fire in your forest. My anger—not the Babylonians, as you think, or the king of the Chaldeans—shall accomplish all these things." He calls Jerusalem and all the surrounding region a "forest" that lacks

interpret the word as a form of *nḥt*, "to descend" (cf. the NRSV: "Who can come down against us?").

23. The Septuagint as preserved lacks not only the text indicated by Jerome but also the first phrase of the verse: "I will punish you." All of this was supplied in the *Hexapla* under asterisk from Aquila and Theodotion.

24. The Hebrew letters in question are *ṣwr*. The Septuagint and Aquila's second edition interpreted the word as *ṣōr*, "Tyre." Symmachus understood *ṣūr*, "rock." This same vocalization (*ṣūr*), with the same basic sense, was in many contexts interpreted by Aquila as "solid/firm" (Jer 21:13; Deut 8:15, 32:31; 2 Sam 2:16; Ps 27:5 [26:5], 28:1 [27:1], 61:2 [60:3], 62:7 [61:8]; Isa 8:14, 30:29; Hab 1:12). Jerome follows Aquila's first edition ("firm") in the commentary lemma and in the IH version. Theodotion's "enclosed" probably derives from reading a past participle of the verb *ṣwr*, "to surround."

trees bearing the fruit of good deeds, so that it is prepared for burning.[25] And beautifully he calls the valley "flat," so that it is accessible to the enemies, as it says in Isaiah: "a vision of the valley of Zion";[26] it is not a "high mountain,"[27] which would be difficult to ascend.

Whatever was prophesied to the royal house and the chief city we refer to the ecclesiastical order and the leaders of the churches—those, at least, who have given themselves over to pride, wealth, and lewdness.[28] It will not be spared from ruin simply because it is the royal house. Consider: of all those who were from the line of David, very few were found who pleased the Lord, such as David himself, Hezekiah and Josiah; the vast majority of the leaders from the royal line provoked the Lord's anger against the whole people.

22:13-17:

"Woe to him who builds his house by unrighteousness, and his upper rooms by injustice; who oppresses his friend without cause, and does not give him his wages; (14) who says, 'I will build myself a great house with spacious upper rooms,' and opens for himself windows, making roofs with cedar, and painting it with red ochre. (15) Do you think you are a king because you compare yourself with cedar? Did not your father eat and drink and do justice and righteousness? Then it was well with him. (16) He judged the cause of the poor and needy for his own good. Is not this to know me? says the Lord. (17) But your eyes and heart are set on greed, shedding innocent blood, trickery, and

---

25. Matt 7:19; Luke 3:9.
26. Isa 22:1.
27. Isa 40:9.
28. See also Jerome's *Commentary on Jeremiah* 30:18–22: "whatever took place carnally among the former people is fulfilled spiritually in the church"; and *Commentary on Ezekiel* 13:1–3a: "Whatever was said at that time to the Israelite people now is referred to the church, so that 'holy prophets' become 'apostles and apostolic men,' and 'lying and frantic prophets' become 'all the heretics'."

the path of evil work." LXX: "O you who build your house not with righteousness, and your upper rooms by injustice; his neighbor works for him for nothing, and he does not give him his wages. (14) You built for yourself a measured house with airy upper rooms adorned with windows, furnished with cedar, and anointed with red ochre. (15) Are you a king because you contend against Ahaz, your father? They will not eat and drink; it was better for you to do justice and noble righteousness. (16) They did not know; they did not perform justice for the lowly or justice for the poor. Is this not a case of them not knowing me? says the Lord. (17) Behold, your eyes are not right and your heart is not good, but they are set on your greed and iniquity, so that you may shed innocent blood."

I have put each edition as a whole, so that both the Hebrew truth and the difficulty of the popular edition may be easily recognized.[29] The message is against Jehoiakim, the son of Josiah king of Judah, about whom we spoke above.[30] Pharaoh Neco king of Egypt set Jehoiakim up as king in place of his brother Jehoahaz, whom the Pharaoh led bound in chains to Egypt. We read of it in both Kings and Chronicles,[31] and the *historia* narrates that Jehoiakim son of Josiah reigned cruelly for eleven years in Jerusalem, lived an impious life and afterwards died. Yet, his burial is not narrated, even though holy Scripture has this custom whereby it states that all the kings died and were buried. But Scripture narrates the death of this king, but not his burial; we will speak about this later on.[32]

And so he offers this lament over the aforementioned king,

---

29. The "popular edition" (*editio vulgata*) is the Old Latin version based on the Septuagint. The "Hebrew truth" (*hebraica veritas*) is reflected in Jerome's own translation based on the Hebrew text.

30. Jer 22:10–12.

31. The (Book) "of Kings" (*Regum*), and the (Book) "of Things Omitted" (*Paralipomenon* —based on the Greek: *paraleipomenōn*), which is the Greek title of Chronicles. On the titles of biblical books, see Jerome's preface to his IH translation of Samuel-Kings.

32. Jer 22:18–19.

that he trusts in injustice, thinks that his royal honor is everlasting, makes for himself upper rooms, oppresses friends, does not render the proper wage to those who work and regards the edifice of his palace as eternal. "Will you be able to rule forever," says the divine message, "because you think you are comparable to a lofty cedar, namely, your father Josiah,[33] who was a righteous king?" "Your father," he says, "ate and drank and enjoyed royal wealth. Yet, it did not offend God that he had riches; rather, he pleased God because he did righteousness and justice, and for this reason it was well with him in the present age and will be well with him in the future." He says, "He judged the cause of the poor and needy," both for the benefit of those whom he helped and "for his own good." And all these favorable things came to him because "he knew me, says the Lord." "But your eyes, O Jehoiakim, are bent on greed, trickery and the path of evil work, so as to shed innocent blood!"

As for the LXX, I cannot understand what sense this might make. For, although the rest of the passage fits together at least in some way, the statement: "Are you a king because you contend against Ahaz, your father?" makes no sense at all. In place of "Ahaz," in the Hebrew it is written *araz*, which means "cedar."[34] And that which follows, "They will not eat and drink, etc." is so tangled up and confused that without the truth of the Hebrew it would be unintelligible to read.

At the same time, we can take this passage according to anagogy[35] as against heretics, who build for themselves a house that is measured, not great and wide with the richness of the

---

33. The Targum also takes the "cedar" to be a reference to king Josiah.
34. Heb: *'rz*, "cedar." The LXX read *'ḥz*, "Ahaz." Both Symmachus and Aquila read "cedar" as Jerome does, but in this case Jerome agrees with Symmachus (not Aquila) in his reading of the syntax of the sentence.
35. The Greek term *anagōgē*, "elevation," refers to the higher or spiritual sense.

church. Moreover, they do not build with righteousness and justice, since they desire to plunder other people's things. Thus it says, "You built for yourself a measured house with airy upper rooms," which are carried about with every wind of doctrine.[36] And they are "adorned with windows," since they do not have a lasting structure or firm stability. They are "furnished," he says, "with cedar." Indeed, they appear to have a most beautiful array of beams, but when the rains and storms of persecution come they quickly rot and collapse. Lastly, they are "anointed with red ochre." For they claim to adhere to the suffering and blood of the Lord,[37] but their rule is not lasting because they contend against and provoke to anger *araz*, that is "Cedar," their father. For every heretic is born in the church, but when they are cast out from the church they fight against their parent. And when it says, "They will not eat and drink," one should understand "the body and blood of the Savior." And so on with the rest of the passage.

He says that all their error comes from the fact that they do not know God and do not have right eyes; instead, they have a heart that is prone to greed, so that they plunder other people's things and shed the blood of those who have been deceived. For this is what it means to commit murder. Obscure matters should be discussed more extensively.[38]

23:18:

For who has stood in the counsel of the Lord to perceive and to hear his word, or who has given heed to his word and listened?

---

36. Eph 4:14.
37. Origen, *Fragments on Jeremiah* 13 applied this passage to false teachers, similarly explaining the red color as a deceptive allusion to the blood of Christ.
38. Jerome adds this final comment to justify the extensive length of his discussion on this passage.

Where we have translated, "in the *counsel* of the Lord," and in the Hebrew is written *bassod*, Aquila translated "secret," Symmachus "speech," and the LXX and Theodotion translated "substance" or "essence."[39] This is the sense: "O you ignorant mob, do not believe the prophets who are announcing lies to you, who say, 'The Lord says: there shall be peace for you; no evil shall come upon you.'[40] For how could they know the 'secrets' of God? Or, by what conversation could they have learned of the Lord's 'counsel'? How did the 'speech' of the divine arrangement come to them?" Certain of our interpreters think that they have found in this passage a place where the "substance" of God is addressed.[41]

31:2:

Thus says the Lord: "The people left remaining from the sword found grace in the wilderness; Israel shall go to his rest." LXX: The Lord said thus: "I found heat in the wilderness with those who perished by the sword; Go, and do not slay Israel!"

In this passage the Latin codices gave the absurd translation "lupines" in place of the word "heat," due to the ambiguity of the Greek word. For the Greek word *thermon* can signify either.[42] Yet, even this is not what is found in the Hebrew. For

39. The Hebrew word is *besōd*, made up of the preposition *b* ("in") and the noun *sōd* ("confidential discussion," or "secret, scheme"). Jerome gives all of the hexaplaric evidence. The Targum and the Peshitta both agree with Aquila ("secret"). Jerome's rendering ("counsel") matches the meaning of the word in Rabbinic Hebrew.

40. Jer 23:17.

41. Jerome is referring to Christians who saw in this passage, as it appears in the Septuagint and in the Old Latin, a reference to God's "substance" in the Trinitarian sense. Through his discussion of the translation options Jerome makes clear that this Trinitarian interpretation is based on the Septuagint's mistranslation. See n. 19 on Jer 17:9–10.

42. The ambiguity of the Greek word is a question of accent. For the Greek *thermos*, if the accent is on the first syllable it means "lupine," but if the accent is on the second syllable it means "heat." But the Septuagint itself represents a misunderstanding of the Hebrew *ḥn*, "grace" (Greek: *charis*), which the Septuagint interpreted as *ḥm*, "heat."

in the Hebrew it is written *hen,* which Aquila, Symmachus and Theodotion translated *charin,* that is, "grace." Only the LXX put "heat," since they thought that the final letter was an "m." For if we read *hen* with the letter "n," it means "grace"; but if we read with an "m," it means "heat."

This is the sense according to the Hebrew: The Jewish people left remaining from the Roman sword, who were indeed able to evade the anger of the Lord's fury, "found grace in the wilderness" of the Gentiles, so that amidst the throng of nations they might be saved in the Church. Thus Israel shall go and find his rest, in which he had always hoped and which the oracles of the prophets had promised to him. And now, this is the understanding according to the LXX: The Lord found the apostles and their associates, who were filled with heat and life, in the wilderness of the Gentiles, among those who had been slain because they lacked faith and the heat of life. This is why he commands the angels and those in God's service not to slay everyone or to wipe out Israel completely. He says to them: "Go, and do not slay Israel." There are some who are alive, who are hot with the ardor of faith, and who have shunned the coldness of infidelity and death. These are the ones whom the Lord will find in the wilderness!

12

Theodore of Mopsuestia

Born ca. 350 CE, Theodore studied rhetoric together with John Chrysostom under the sophist Libanius, the most prominent teacher of rhetoric in Antioch. Later, John Chrysostom, Theodore, and a certain Maximus of Seleucia abandoned their secular careers and entered into a Christian ascetic community led by Diodore of Tarsus (Socrates Scholasticus, *Ecclesiastical History* 6.3). Theodore was ordained a priest ca. 383, and in 392 he became bishop of Mopsuestia, where he served until his death in 428.

Throughout his life Theodore was deeply involved in theological discussions. He composed a refutation of the emperor Julian's anti-Christian treatise *Against the Galileans,* and he also addressed internal Christian disputes, such as in his works *Against Apollinaris* and *Against Eunomius.* We know of a substantial theological composition by Theodore called *On the Incarnation.* In the practical sphere, Theodore produced a number of ascetical works and also series of catechetical lectures (extant in Syriac translation) on the Lord's Prayer and the Nicene Creed. Shortly after his death Theodore was described as "a doctor of the whole Church and effective combatant against every heretical army" (Theodoret, *Ecclesiastical History* 5.39).

Doctrinally, Theodore did not accept the Augustinian position on original sin, and he was one of the leading advocates for the so-called "Antiochene Christology," which placed particular emphasis on the full humanity of Jesus as assumed by the Divine Logos.[1] Theodore was the teacher of Nestorius, and in connection with Nestorianism Theodore was condemned at church councils held under the auspices of the emperor Justinian in 551 and 553. Consequently, most of Theodore's writings are lost. Fragments of certain works are preserved in Greek, and even more of his writings survive in Syriac translation, because Theodore was held in high esteem in the Syriac churches that inhabited the Sasanian Empire. This is still reflected today in the Church of the East (known in the West as the "Nestorian" church).

Regarding Theodore's exegetical writings, later sources mention numerous commentaries, including works on Genesis, Job, Psalms, Song of Songs, the prophets, Matthew, Luke, John, Acts, and Paul's letters. Substantial portions are extant for the commentaries on Psalms, the Minor Prophets, John, and some of Paul's letters. Theodore's exegesis is marked by clarity and brevity. Most of his interpretive energy is devoted to explaining the basic flow of thought, often through simple paraphrase as set against the backdrop of the text's historical

---

1. For helpful discussions of Theodore's Christology in biblical and historical contexts, see Frederick McLeod, "Theodore of Mopsuestia Revisited," *Theological Studies* 61 (2000): 447–80; and Rowan Greer, *Theodore of Mopsuestia: Exegete and Theologian* (Westminster, UK: Faith Press, 1961).

setting as he understands it.[2] Peculiar expressions are explained as necessary. Theological elaboration is minimal. One cannot assume a direct correlation between the style of Theodore's commentaries and how he preached to his congregation. For Theodore, the task of the commentator is different from the task of the preacher, as he explained: "Indeed we think that the duty of the interpreter is to explain those words which are difficult to many, while the duty of the preacher is to speak about those topics which are already clear enough. Even superfluous topics can sometimes be useful to a preacher, but the interpreter must explain and say things concisely."[3]

Selections from three different works are offered here as examples of Theodore's approach to biblical interpretation. The first selection (1) is a pair of excerpts taken from Theodore's treatise *Against the Allegorists*, which is preserved only in Syriac translation. In the first excerpt, Theodore takes up the claim that certain biblical texts cannot be interpreted literally; in answer, Theodore explains that these texts simply reflect the biblical writer's use of metaphor. In the second excerpt, Theodore charges Origen with misinterpreting the Bible because he followed Philo in reading Scripture like pagans read their myths. The second selection (2) is from Theodore's *Commentary on Joel*, which was likely written early in his ecclesiastical career. In this passage, Theodore explains

---

2. For each of the Minor Prophets and for each Psalm, Theodore composed a preface in which he set forth the main subject matter (*hypothesis*) of the prophetic book or Psalm as situated within its specific historical context. Theodore's use of the term *hypothesis* is strikingly similar to introductions written by his teacher Libanius for the speeches of Demosthenes. In each introduction (*hypothesis*), Libanius identified the speech's historical setting, described the main point of the speech, and surveyed the content. See Michael Graves, "The 'Pagan' Background of Patristic Exegetical Methods," in *Ancient Faith for the Church's Future,* ed. M. Husbands and J. P. Greenman (Downers Grove, IL: InterVarsity, 2008), 105–7.

3. *Theodore of Mopsuestia: Commentary on the Gospel of John,* trans. Marco Conti (ACT; Downers Grove, IL: InterVarsity, 2010), 2.

how the historical sense of the prophet's message, that is, what he was saying to his original audience, relates to the text's meaning in connection with its quotation in the New Testament. The third selection (3) is a short passage from Theodore's *Commentary on the Psalms*, which is perhaps his first exegetical work, where he explains the historical sense of Psalm 68:18 and also the nature of its quotation in Ephesians 4.

Against the Allegorists (selections)

Come, then, let us also discuss those passages that some interpreters present to us from the divine Scriptures as texts that absolutely cannot be understood according to the subject matter itself,[4] because these passages are thought to contain lofty things that are above the subject matter. We acknowledge that there are passages relevant to this discussion. Here is one of them: "(Rescue) my only one from the paw of the dog";[5] and this: "the rivers will clap their hands altogether";[6] and this: "You rode your horses on the sea";[7] and again this: "Then the wolf shall feed with the lamb, and the leopard shall lie down with the goat";[8] and all other passages like these. We will not collect all of these passages, so that we do not extend our discussion needlessly. In fact, it is not necessary to mention all of them, because all of these passages reflect a single idiomatic usage[9] employed in the divine Scriptures. This comes from the use of a particular mode of expression found in passages such as these.

The divine Scriptures chose to express many things through

---

4. *pwšq' dmnhwn dptgm'*, "the interpretation which (is) from the matters themselves."
5. Ps 22:20.
6. Ps 98:8.
7. Hab 3:15.
8. Isa 11:6.
9. *'yd'*, "idiomatic usage."

comparisons,[10] because the Hebrew language possesses a certain idiomatic usage of this kind. Sometimes Scripture expresses a comparison in the form of a simile,[11] and sometimes it sets forth a comparison as equivalent to the reality[12] so as to function like a simile.[13] For example, when[14] it says: "he is like . . ." as in "I became like a wineskin in the frost";[15] or "I went astray like a lost sheep";[16] or "I became like a man without help";[17] or "The arrows of the mighty are sharp like the embers of the oak";[18] or "we became like those who rejoice";[19] or "I have become like an owl in ruin";[20] or "My bones became white as if burned";[21] and other passages that are expressed using this kind of comparison, it obviously sets forth each one as a proper simile using a form that is suitable for the things being expressed.

On the other hand, when it says: "He made my arms a bow of bronze,"[22] or: "to shoot in secret at the innocent,"[23] and other statements of this kind, it does not strictly use simile to express

---

10. *dmwt'*, "comparison."
11. *'whdt'*, "simile."
12. *sw'rn'*, "reality," "fact," "the actual thing."
13. I.e., a metaphor.
14. I am reading *'mty*, "when" instead of *'mr*, "said," following Lucas Van Rompay, ed., *Théodore de Mopsueste: Fragments syriaques du Commentaire des Psaumes* (CSCO 435; Louvain: Peeters, 1982), 3.
15. Ps 119:83.
16. Ps 119:176.
17. Ps 88:4.
18. Ps 120:4.
19. Ps 126:1. The Septuagint (Ps 125:1), which was Theodore's text, reads: "as those who were comforted." The text here, "like those who rejoice" matches the Syriac Peshitta. Apparently, the Syriac translator or copyist supplied the biblical quotation from the Syriac version, rather than translating from Theodore's own Septuagint text.
20. Ps 102:6. This ("in ruin") is the Peshitta. The Septuagint (Ps 101:7) has "in a building-house."
21. Ps 102:3. This is the Peshitta. The Septuagint (Ps 101:4) reads: "My bones were burnt up like firewood."
22. Ps 18:34. The biblical quotation supplied by the translator or copyist adds the word *'yk*, "like" ("like a bow of bronze"), in keeping with the Peshitta; but based on the context it is obvious that Theodore's text lacked the word "like," in accordance with the Septuagint (Ps 17:35).
23. Ps 64:4.

these comparisons, but it gives the appearance of presenting them as equivalent to the reality itself. For it should have said: "He made my arms *like* a bow of bronze," because he did not in fact make his arms into a bow of bronze, but rather he depicted[24] them as being *like* a bow, such that one is similar to the other. As another example, it says: "to shoot in darkness at the upright in heart,"[25] whereas it might have said, "to shoot *as if* in darkness." For this is what it intends to say: "They are doing everything *as if* in thick darkness; that is: they are bold only because they are concealing what they are doing." But to express this it simply says: "to shoot in darkness." In fact, it employs this idiomatic usage frequently.

Scripture often adopts this idiomatic usage, which functions like a simile, in order to express a comparison in a striking way. I will give an example: (Please note that Blessed David calls a young lion a "lion cub.") At Psalm fifty-seven he speaks thus: "God sent his mercy and his truth and he delivered my soul from the midst of lion cubs."[26] (The Greek says "lion cubs" where it means "strong lions.") Now, he should have said: "God sent his mercy and his truth and he delivered my soul *as if* from the midst of lions." But here he expresses the comparison without "as if," which was necessary for him to do in this case, because the force is thereby greater than if he had used the form of a simile. Furthermore, because it is customary for lions to tear with their teeth and to lick blood with their tongue, he develops[27] this and compares his enemies to lions. So he

---

24. I am interpreting *dlm'* as a form of *dm'*, "to liken," "to represent" (see L. Van Rompay, trans., *Théodore de Mopsueste*, 4).

25. Ps 11:2.

26. Ps 57:3–4. The Syriac biblical quotation supplied in the manuscript follows the Peshitta in having "dogs" instead of "lion cubs," but it is clear from the context that Theodore's biblical text was that of the Septuagint (Ps 56:4–5): "he delivered my soul from the midst of lion cubs."

27. The meaning of this Syriac word (*g'š*) is uncertain.

goes on to say: "men, whose teeth are weaponry and arrows, and whose tongue is a sharp sword,"[28] offering "teeth" and "tongue" as equivalents for their implements of war. He did not say, "their weaponry and their arrows are *like* teeth" or "their swords are *like* tongues," but he said that these things *are* their teeth, and they *are* their tongues. He did not say these things as similes using "like," but rather as comparisons presented as equivalent to the realities—that is, according to the form of the words. Yet, according to the sense he clearly expressed all these things in the manner of similes.

Therefore, a person will not be mistaken who recognizes this idiomatic usage when explaining all those passages in the divine Scriptures that some interpreters present to us as texts that cannot be understood according to the subject matter itself. . . .

[Theodore goes on to discuss the difference between "allegorical" interpretation as practiced by the apostle Paul (e.g., Gal 4:24) and pagan allegory. According to Theodore, Paul did not intend to undercut the historical narrative but rather based his figurative interpretation on the historical and literal sense. Pagans, on the other hand, invented allegories in order to explain away the absurdities found in their myths, especially regarding their gods. Of course, Christian Scripture recounts some indecent events, but these were meant to serve as negative examples. This was made sufficiently clear by biblical figures such as Moses, Samuel, David, and Stephen].[29]

But it did not seem good to the "noble" Origen to pay attention to the explanations offered by these people.[30] Rather, Origen reckoned Philo, a Jew, as far superior to them. Because Philo

---

28. Ps 57:4. The Syriac biblical quotation supplied in the manuscript follows the Peshitta in having "spears" instead of "weaponry" and in adding the word ʾyk, "like" ("like a sharp sword"), but it is clear that Theodore's text had "weaponry" and lacked the word "like," as in the Septuagint (Ps 56:5).

29. A substantial part of the section summarized here is available in English translation in Frederick McLeod, *Theodore of Mopsuestia* (ECF; London & New York: Routledge, 2009), 75–79.

30. I.e., people such as Moses, Samuel, David, and Stephen.

was instructed in "outside" learning,[31] he regarded the intention[32] of the divine Scriptures, i.e., what seems evident from the narratives themselves, as something insignificant and contemptible. He was the first who introduced pagan allegorical accounts taken from the teaching of the Gentiles, for he supposed that the divine Scriptures were similarly furnished with the trappings of allegory. Yet, he did not perceive that he was greatly dishonoring the divine Scriptures by dismissing the accounts of the narratives themselves, making them seem untrue like pagan stories.

It is no surprise that Philo treated the divine Scriptures in this conniving fashion, seeing that he also dared to introduce numerology based on human speculation into the teaching of Moses, that is, into the teaching of the divine Scriptures. Indeed, he ventured to show that in the ordering of its creation the world was founded according to this numerology, and that Moses himself taught this to us by his words.[33] Still, although in many places Philo repudiated[34] the narrative accounts and composed his discourses according to this numerological content, he was compelled to acknowledge some of the accounts, partly because he revered the ancient glory, partly because of the reputation he had acquired, and partly because of the truth that was preserved among his people. But it was out of love for vainglory that Philo inserted pagan teaching

31. I.e., "pagan" learning.

32. *r'yn'*, "mind," "conscience," "sentence." Theodore seems to mean the "thought" or "intention" of the (human) biblical writer.

33. See Philo, *On the Creation of the World* 89–128; *Allegorical Interpretation* 1.8–15. On Pythagorean philosophy and Philo's "arithmological" exegesis, see Gregory E. Sterling, "'The Jewish Philosophy': Reading Moses via Hellenistic Philosophy according to Philo," in *Reading Philo: A Handbook to Philo of Alexandria*, ed. T. Seland (Grand Rapids: Eerdmans, 2014), 143–45.

34. The preserved Syriac text has *šlm*, "to ratify," which does not fit the context. L. Van Rompay, *Théodore de Mopsueste*, 12, proposes *šr'*, "to loosen, dissolve, repudiate," which at the very least makes good sense in context and is a valid conjecture until better evidence comes to light.

into the divine Scriptures, not realizing that embellishment based on this teaching is shameful when applied to the Scriptures.

So then, our "noble master" Origen, because he did not find anyone who was able to teach him about these things in accordance with the truth of the divine Scriptures, took Philo as his teacher in allegorical interpretation, by which Philo presumed to distort everything that is written in the Scriptures.[35]

Commentary on Joel 2:28-32

It will happen after this that I shall pour out my spirit on all flesh, your sons and daughters will prophesy, your elders will dream dreams, your young people will see visions. Even on my slaves and on my female slaves I shall pour out my spirit in those days, and they will prophesy. I shall provide portents in heaven and on earth, blood and fire and clouds of smoke. The sun will revert to darkness and the moon to blood before the great and striking day of the Lord comes. It will happen that everyone who calls on the name of the Lord will be saved, because on Mount Zion and in Jerusalem they will be saved, as the Lord said; good news will come to those whom the Lord has called (vv. 28-32):

I shall provide my wealth and care to all—the meaning of "I shall pour out my spirit." The people in the time of the Old Testament did not understand the Holy Spirit to be a unit as a

---

35. Theodore's criticism of Origen is reminiscent of a charge leveled against Origen by the third-century philosopher Porphyry of Tyre, who claimed that Origen illegitimately introduced Greek philosophy into Jewish fables [i.e., the Old Testament], employing (among others) Plato, Numenius, leading Pythagoreans, Chaeremon the Stoic, and "Cornutus, from whom he learnt the figurative interpretation, as employed in the Greek mysteries, and applied it to the Jewish writings" (quoted in Eusebius, *Ecclesiastical History* 6.19.4-8; see *Eusebius: Ecclesiastical History, Books VI-X*, trans. J. E. L. Oulton [LCL 265; Cambridge, MA: Harvard University Press, 1932], 57-59).

person distinct from the others, being both God and from God; by "spirit of God," "holy spirit," and every other such name at the time they referred to His grace, care, and affection, as in applying to God also "soul": "My soul hates your new moons and your Sabbaths,"[36] meaning the affection by which He hated the festivals. A similar example is "Your good spirit will guide me on level ground,"[37] meaning, "out of care for me you will provide this on account of great goodness." A similar example is "Take not your holy spirit from me,"[38] as if to say, "Do not remove your care for me"—and so on, not to provide scriptural texts beyond need. Here, too, he is saying something of the kind: In this way I shall provide you with my care so that you may be accorded all visions and be in a position to disclose something of the future. I shall work marvels in heaven and on earth for everyone, great slaughter of my adversaries and punishment of them, as well as clouds of smoke betraying the divine wrath; the sun will be changed into darkness and the moon into blood in the perception of the onlookers, which they will experience owing to the magnitude of the problems befalling them.[39] This will happen before that day, which he will render "striking" by the punishment of the adversaries. In the midst of them, all those who call upon the divine name will attain salvation, and those who will go up to Mount Zion and

36. Cf. Isa 1:14.
37. Ps 143:10.
38. Ps 51:11.
39. Aristarchus of Samothrace (ca. 216–145 BCE) was an important classical scholar of the Hellenistic period, whose literary-critical mindset has sometimes been compared to that of Theodore. Theodore's description of the original meaning of Joel 2:30–31 ("in the perception of the onlookers . . .") is similar to Aristarchus's explanation of *Odyssey* 20.356–58, where the Seer Theoclymenus foretells the destruction of the suitors (". . . the sun has perished from heaven and an evil mist settles over all"). As Aristarchus explains: "It is not that an eclipse of the sun would actually take place, but Theoclymenus, prophesying by a certain inspiration, sees that the sun would perish *for them*" (G. Dindorf, *Scholia Graeca in Homeri Odysseam* [Oxford, 1855], 2:694). On Theodore and Aristarchus, see Graves, "The 'Pagan' Background of Patristic Exegetical Methods," 107–8.

Jerusalem will be saved, since God promised this and allowed all those whom He summoned to this return to hear the good news.

While this is in fact the obvious sense of the passage, blessed Peter at any rate used it in speaking to Jews on the occasion of the descent of the Holy Spirit. And rightly so, since the Law contained a shadow of all things to come,[40] whereas the people were vouchsafed care owing to the expectation of what would appear at the coming of Christ the Lord. What happened in their time was all insignificant and like a shadow so that the account was given with use of hyperbole rather than containing facts, whereas the reality of the account was found to be realized in the time of Christ the Lord, when everything was important and awesome, novel and really baffling, surpassing what had happened under the Law to the greatest extent imaginable. So whereas what happened in the time of the Old Testament had the function of a puzzle, the magnitude of what happened in the time of Christ the Lord was in the order of reality. Blessed David likewise says about the people, "Its soul was not abandoned to Hades, nor did its flesh see corruption," which cannot be understood at the level of fact; rather, by the use of hyperbole or metaphor he says it was rescued from danger or corruption.[41] The factual reality of the text, on the other hand, is demonstrated by Christ the Lord, when it happened that neither was his soul abandoned to Hades, being restored to the body in resurrection, nor did his body suffer any corruption, so that not only did it remain

---

40. Col 2:17; Heb 10:1.
41. Ps 16:10. Ps 16:8–11 is quoted in Acts 2:25–28, where Peter says that David spoke this Psalm as a prophet foretelling the resurrection of Christ (see also Acts 13:35–37). As Theodore interprets it, in its original context this Psalm was a hyperbolic statement about God preserving the life ("soul") of the people from destruction, but the precise wording of the Psalm in its reality (i.e., not just hyperbolically) properly fit the resurrection of Christ, which was to come about later.

with its own appearance in which it actually died but it was also transformed into an immortal and incorruptible nature. So, while the former situation was a puzzle, the latter was reality. Hence blessed Peter used the passage as something expressed metaphorically at a particular time for a particular reason, but now having an outcome in reality at the time of the facts themselves. The moral is that we should have faith in the events of this time to a much greater extent than they felt wonderment at that event in the past.

Now, since there are many instances of this kind in the divine Scripture, the present one is obviously also of much the same character. You see, while the Lord God in speaking to Jews in the manner then customary promised to provide them generously with His care, and so on in the way we have interpreted, everything turned out in reality in the time of Christ the Lord—the sun was actually darkened and the moon with it, great portents occurred in heaven and many on earth, the saving blood of Christ the Lord appeared, as well as fire, in keeping with the particular action of the Spirit's visit, preceded by clouds of smoke,[42] to suggest by way of proof the punishment wreaked on those guilty of the crucifixion. At that time also everyone received a share of the grace of the Holy Spirit in being vouchsafed many and varied gifts of grace, with which some foretold the future, others worked a great number of marvels as confirmation of the greatness of what had happened and as proof of the glory concerning Christ the Lord. The result is that what had formerly been said through the prophet as metaphor or hyperbole had its demonstration in reality with the promise being superseded by the fulfillment; such could reasonably be thought to be the reason why the blessed Apostles applied either this passage or the others as

42. See Matt 27:45–54; 28:2–3; Acts 2:1–4.

well as everything else said by the Prophets on different subjects to the Incarnation of Christ the Lord. As a result, the story of events at that time does not have the appearance of being concocted, and the magnitude of events today is more clearly established by comparison with them, and through them all there is more precise proof that there is a certain relationship between former and latter, and that the previous events are surpassed by the present to the extent that shadow is surpassed by reality, even if it seems to be related to it.

Commentary on Psalms 68:18

You ascended to the heights, taking captivity captive; you received gifts from among human beings:[43]

The people were enslaved as though held captive in Egypt, and God snatched them from slavery and freed them by the norms of war, punishing the adversaries, and thus took the people for himself. So the complete capture by norms of war is referred to as "captivity," namely, ourselves serving as though in captivity, whom you captured like a strong general conquering by norms of war, reclaiming and rescuing. "You

---

43. Theodore believed that David wrote many Psalms in the persona of other people, addressing various historical occasions in Israel's history either in the past or else (since David was a prophet) in the future. Theodore identifies the historical setting for Psalm 68 as the occasion when Moses set forth with the ark in order to lead the people in the wilderness (Num 10:35; cf. Ps 68:1). Therefore, in the preface to Psalm 68 Theodore offers an overview of the ark's history. At the end of the preface, Theodore says: "Now, even among profane writers to this day the practice occurs of people speaking in the person of people living long ago and mentioning what would have been appropriate for them to say—something they usually call 'speech-in-character' [*ēthopoiia*]" (*Theodore of Mopsuestia: Commentary on Psalms 1-81*, trans. Robert C. Hill [Atlanta: SBL 2006], 859). Theodore's theory about David composing psalms in the character of persons living at other times reflects his appropriation of one of the preparatory exercises (*progymnasmata*) used in ancient rhetorical schools, an exercise called *ēthopoiia*, where a student would introduce a character into his work and allow that character to speak in his or her own person; see R. Dean Anderson, Jr., *Glossary of Greek Rhetorical Terms* (Leuven: Peeters, 2000), 60–61, 106–7.

ascended to the heights" means, You were shown to be great and elevated; hence "you received gifts from among human beings": God gave them orders to ask for "silver and gold vessels," and upon asking they were given them.[44] Then when the death of the firstborn occurred, they abandoned Egypt at God's command with the vessels in their possession. So he is saying, It was not only that you removed us and freed us from slavery: "you also received gifts from human beings," as if everyone dispatched them with gifts. Now, the apostle cited this text, not as a prophecy about Christ, but as one applicable to Christ in that while we were captives of the Devil, he was victorious in battle with him and carried us off for himself. Hence, since the phrase "you received gifts" did not apply, in our normal practice in using it in ecclesiastical usage he replaced "you received" with "he gave," this being more applicable to Christ, who did not receive but gave the gifts of the Spirit after the ascension into heaven.[45] "Even those resisting your dwelling." As he had spoken in similar terms above of "the embittered,"[46] so too here: You did this, he is saying, though we resisted, freeing us by your lovingkindness, and allotting us a habitation to have as our own place and reside in it.

---

44. Exod 3:21–22; 11:2–3; 12:35.
45. Eph 4:7–13. In Ps 68:18, the Psalmist says to God, "You received (Hebrew: *lāqaḥtā;* Septuagint: *elabes*) gifts among human beings." In Ephesians, this text is given as "he gave (Greek: *edōken*) gifts to human beings." Also, God's ascending is taken to suggest Christ's descent to the lower parts of the earth and ascent above all the heavens (Eph 4:9–10). In Theodore's view, the Psalm originally described Israel's despoiling of Egypt when God defeated the Egyptians in the time of the Exodus, and Paul reapplied the text to Christ, who defeated the Devil and gave gifts to the church. The change in wording was required by the new context.
46. In Ps 68:6 (Ps 67:7 in the Septuagint), the end of the verse in Greek reads: "the embittered, those living in tombs."

13

John Chrysostom

John "Chrysostom" of Antioch was the most renowned preacher of his era. Within a century after his death he came to be known by the epithet *Chrysostomos*, "golden-mouthed." Chrysostom was born ca. 349 CE in or around Antioch. His father died when he was young, but his family had the resources to provide him with an excellent education. Like Theodore of Mopsuestia, Chrysostom studied rhetoric under the sophist Libanius. Later, both Chrysostom and Theodore studied Christian Scripture with Diodore of Tarsus. Raised in the church, Chrysostom was baptized in the late 360s and was ordained as a lector ("reader") in 371. After his mother's death in the early 370s, Chrysostom spent four years living in the desert outside of Antioch under the direction of a Syrian monk. He then spent two years in monastic seclusion where he continued to read Scripture. Upon his return to the city, Chrysostom was ordained a deacon in 381, and then a priest in 386. For twelve years as a priest in the Church at Antioch Chrysostom preached regularly and wrote numerous pastoral treatises.

In 398 Chrysostom was elevated to the office of bishop of Constantinople. In a short time, however, the new bishop made powerful enemies in the capital and beyond. His zeal for moral reform, his disapproval of luxuriant court life, and his forthrightness in homilies all provoked opposition. Eventually, Chrysostom's attempts to address financial corruption in the Church and his sympathies with Egyptian monks put him at odds with Theophilus, bishop of Alexandria, and his sharp criticism of imperial opulence and the empress Eudoxia (e.g., comparing her to Jezebel and Herodias) invoked hostility from the Palace. In 403, at the "Synod of the Oak" held near Constantinople, a gathering of bishops led by Theophilus condemned Chrysostom *in absentia* and temporarily deposed him from office. After a brief reinstatement as bishop, Chrysostom was again deposed in 404 and driven into exile, at first to Armenia and then after three years to the eastern shore of the Black Sea. As a result of the severe conditions of his exile and forced marches, Chrysostom died in 407. Yet, support for Chrysostom remained strong among many Christians throughout the empire. One of his key allies was Innocent I, bishop of Rome. Palladius of Helenopolis wrote a *Dialogue on the Life of Chrysostom* ca. 408 that served as an apology for the monastic preacher from Antioch who became bishop of Constantinople. Chrysostom came to be greatly admired in subsequent years throughout Christendom.

The body of writings ascribed to John Chrysostom is enormous. Many works written by others were transmitted under Chrysostom's name. Since the Renaissance a major task in the study of Chrysostom's corpus has been to identify his authentic works. Most of Chrysostom's genuine compositions are homilies on various topics and treatises on the Christian life. Many of the homilies in particular are devoted to biblical interpretation.

Early works on the monastic vocation include *Against Critics of the Monastic Life* and *Conflict between the King and the Monk*. Chrysostom promoted monastic ideals in compositions such as *On Virginity* and *On Not Remarrying*. A slightly later treatise from his time as a presbyter at Antioch is *On the Priesthood*, which was widely read in his lifetime (see Jerome, *Lives of Illustrious Men* 129). Chrysostom preached numerous homilies on liturgical themes, such as *On the Day of the Birth of Our Lord Jesus Christ* (preached Dec. 25, 386), and series of sermons on Holy Thursday, Good Friday, Easter, Ascension, and Pentecost. He also delivered homilies in honor of martyrs, such as his *Homily on St. Babylas*. Some homilies focused on theological topics, such as *On Repentance, On Almsgiving,* and *On the Incomprehensibility of God*. Others addressed immediate pastoral concerns, such as his *Homilies Against the Jews,* in which he fulminated against Christians who were participating in Jewish practices, and his *Homilies on the Statues,* delivered to the inhabitants of Antioch as they awaited possible imperial repercussions for a riot during which they destroyed statues of the emperor and his family. Above all, Chrysostom preached numerous homilies on Scripture, typically working through key passages of a given book serially. At Antioch major sermon series were devoted to Genesis, Psalms, Matthew, John, and Paul's letters. Shorter series were devoted to Isaiah, 1 Samuel (on Hannah, David, and Saul), the story of Lazarus (Luke 16:19–31), and other biblical texts. At Constantinople Chrysostom preached on various books, including extensive treatments of Acts and Hebrews. Over 200 letters are preserved in Chrysostom's corpus, mostly from the latter part of his career. Two of his last compositions offer pastoral and philosophical reflection on his hardships: *Let No One Be Offended Except by Himself* (a Stoic theme) and *To Those Scandalized by Adversity.*

In his approach to Scripture Chrysostom may be compared with Theodore of Mopsuestia, his friend and fellow student of Diodore of Tarsus. Unlike Theodore's commentaries, which are typically concise and analytical, Chrysostom's homilies are lively, expressive, and geared toward moral instruction. Like Theodore, however, Chrysostom normally sought to base his pastoral exposition on the text's flow of thought, keeping in view the biblical writer's message to his original audience (as Chrysostom understood it). In Old Testament expositions, christological interpretations are not prominent and are often reserved for the conclusion. As a general rule, Chrysostom does not pursue theological themes at much depth, even when he is expounding the New Testament. Instead, his biblical interpretation aims to commend essential Christian faith and provide spiritual and moral guidance.

The first selection below is the beginning of Chrysostom's fifteenth homily on Genesis, which he delivered in Antioch. It illustrates the homiletical style of his biblical interpretation and sets forth some of his key principles, such as his concern for "precision" and his belief in God's "considerateness" (or "condescension") in communicating with humanity through Scripture. The second selection is taken from a homily on 1 Cor 10:1–11, titled *Homily on the Words of Paul: "I Do Not Want You to Be Ignorant"* (1 Cor 10:1). In the course of explaining Paul's christological understanding of Israel's experience in the wilderness, Chrysostom offers his own account of how the Old

Testament foreshadows the New Testament, employing New Testament terminology in an Antiochene way.

Homilies on Genesis 15.1–11

For Adam, however, there proved to be no helpmate of his kind. God caused a drowsiness to come upon Adam, and he fell asleep. God took one of Adam's ribs and closed up the flesh in its place. The Lord God fashioned the rib that He had taken from Adam into a woman (Gen 2:20–22):

1. I am very gratified by you for the fact that yesterday you received with great enthusiasm the exhortation we gave and, far from being upset at the length of the discourse, you followed it to the very end in such a way that your desire for listening reached great heights and continued at that level. Hence the sound hopes communicated to us that you would translate our advice into practice. I mean, the person who listens with such relish would clearly be prepared for practice of good works; and in a particular way your attendance today would provide a proof of your health of soul. You see, just as hunger is a sign of bodily well-being, so love for divine sayings proves to be the surest sign of the soul's health.

2. So, when the fruit of your zeal shows the outcome of your attention, well then, let us in turn pay to you, dear people, the reward we promised yesterday—I mean the reward of this spiritual teaching, which has the capacity both to increase my own resources while I am paying it, and to render you its recipients wealthy. All spiritual goods are like this, after all—something that cannot be said for material things. In the latter case, in other words, the one who pays reduces his own substance and makes the recipient better off, whereas in the former case, on the contrary, things are different: the one who

pays increases his own wealth by so doing, and also the resources of the recipients become greater.

3. So, since we are well disposed for kindness and you are ready to receive this spiritual wealth, keep the recesses of your mind in a state of readiness. Come now, let us fulfill our promise; let us take up again the thread of the reading from blessed Moses, and discharge our debt to you at this point. We need, therefore, to give an open explanation of the words read yesterday with a view to exploring with precision[1] the richness of thought concealed in the words and setting it forth to you, my dear people. In other words, listen now to the words of sacred Scripture: "For Adam, however, there proved to be no helpmate of his kind." What is the force of this brief phrase, "For Adam, however"? Why did he add the particle?[2] I mean, would it not have been enough to say, "For Adam"? Let us not be heedless in our anxiety to explore these matters, acting out of excessive ambition;[3] instead, let us act so as to interpret everything with precision and instruct you not to pass by even a brief phrase or a single syllable contained in the holy Scriptures. After all, they are not simply words, but words of the Holy Spirit, and hence the treasure to be found in even a single syllable is great. So attend carefully, I beseech you: let everyone give an alert attention, I ask you, let no one be sluggish, no one drowsy; let no one be distracted in thinking of outside concerns, or bring here the worries of daily life and stay wrapped in them. Instead, consider the dignity of this

1. The idea that Scripture communicates with "precision" (Greek: *akribeia*) and therefore should be interpreted with precision is a key principle of Chrysostom's exegesis; see Robert C. Hill, "*Akribeia*: A Principle of Chrysostom's Exegesis," *Colloquium* 14 (1981): 32–36.
2. The beginning of this sentence in the Septuagint contains the conjunctive particle *de*, which Chrysostom understands in a contrastive sense, "however."
3. Greek: *philotimias heneken perittēs*, "out of excessive ambition." Robert C. Hill, *St. John Chrysostom: Homilies on Genesis 1–17* (FC 74; Washington, DC: Catholic University of America Press, 1986), 195, translates this phrase as "out of great curiosity."

spiritual gathering and the fact that we are listening to God speaking to us through the tongue of the inspired authors. Give your attention in this way and keep your mind alert lest any of the seeds sown by us will fall on rock, or by the roadside, or among thistles; instead, let the whole batch of seeds be sown on good ground—I mean the field of your mind—and thus be in a position to yield you a generous crop and multiply the amount sown by us.[4]

4. Let us see, now at long last, what is the conjunctive force of this particle. "For Adam, however," the text says, "there proved to be no helpmate of his kind." Notice, I remind you, the precision of sacred Scripture. After saying, "For Adam, however, there proved to be no helpmate," it did not stop there but added, "of his kind," clarifying for us by the addition the reason why it formed the conjunction with the particle. I would think the sharper ones among you would probably by now be in a position to apply yourselves to predicting what is about to be said. Since, however, we must keep our instruction addressed to you all alike and make our words clear to everybody, come now, let us teach you why he spoke in that way. But wait just a moment: you remember in what was mentioned before that after sacred Scripture said, "Let us make him a helpmate like himself,"[5] it immediately taught us about the creation of wild beasts, reptiles and all the irrational animals, saying as it did, "Further, God formed from the earth all the wild beasts of the field and all the birds of heaven; he led them to Adam to see what he would call them."[6] Like their master he imposed names on them, and to each species he assigned its own name: wild beasts, birds, and all irrational

---

4. See the Parable of the Sower (Matt 13:3–23; Mark 4:3–20; Luke 8:5–15).
5. Gen 2:18.
6. Gen 2:19.

animals according to the intelligence granted him, so that we at this stage might be in a position to know that all those creatures, despite the ministering role they play and the assistance they give human beings in their labors, are nonetheless irrational and in great measure inferior to humans—just in case we might think it was about the animals that God said, "'Let us make a helpmate for him." You see, although they are helpful and make a very useful contribution to the service of human beings, they are nonetheless irrational.

5. The fact that they are helpful, after all, emerges from experience. I mean, some are suited to bearing loads for us, while others to working the soil: an ox draws the plough, cuts furrows, and provides for us much other assistance in farming; likewise an ass makes itself very useful in bearing loads; and many other of the irrational animals service our bodily needs. Sheep, after all, meet our needs from their wool for making clothes, and again in similar fashion goats provide a service for us from their coat, their milk and other things related to our living. So in case you think it was in reference to them it was said above, "Let us make him a helpmate," it now begins its statement with the words, "For Adam, however, there proved to be no helpmate of his kind," as if blessed Moses were teaching us in saying these words that, while all these animals were created and received from Adam the assignment of names, nevertheless none of them proved to be adequate for helping him. Accordingly he wants to teach us about the formation of the being about to be brought forth and the fact that this being due for creation is the one he was speaking about. "Let us make him a helpmate like himself," meaning of his kind, with the same properties as himself, of equal esteem, in no way inferior to him.[7] Hence his words, "For Adam,

---

7. Chrysostom's views on women are complex. Chrysostom's affirmation here that

however, there proved to be no helpmate of his kind," by which this blessed author shows us that whatever usefulness these irrational animals bring to our service, the help provided for Adam by woman is different and immeasurably superior.

6. So, now that all the animals were created and had received their names from the first man, the loving Lord made it His concern to create a helpmate for him of his kind; having arranged everything with this creature of His in mind and having brought forth all this visible creation for his sake, after all the other beings He creates also woman. Notice how He teaches us precisely the process of her creation, too. I mean, after teaching us that He wanted to produce for man a helpmate like him by saying previously, "Let us make him a helpmate like himself," and then adding, "There proved to be no helpmate of his own kind," accordingly he set about the formation of this creature of similar properties to him, and the text says, "God caused drowsiness to come upon Adam, and he slept. God took one of Adam's ribs and closed up the flesh in its place. The Lord God fashioned the rib He had taken from Adam into a woman and brought her to Adam." There is great force in these words, surpassing all human reasoning. I mean, it is not possible to comprehend their grandeur in any other way

---

women share the same properties as men, are equal in esteem, and are in no way inferior can be contrasted with statements of a different character elsewhere, for example: that women are assigned to less important, inferior domestic matters, whereas men are assigned to the more beneficial, necessary aspects of public affairs (*The Kind of Women Who Ought to Be Taken as Wives* 4); and that women do not bear the divine image, which pertains strictly to authority according to Chrysostom's interpretation of Gen 1:26 and 1 Cor 11:7, although women and men do share the same form (*Homilies on Genesis* 8.9–10). On Chrysostom's views on women, see Patricia Cox Miller, *Women in Early Christianity: Translations from Greek Texts* (Washington, DC: Catholic University of America Press, 2005), 123–50, 268–76; and Nonna Verna Harrison, "Women and the Image of God according to St. John Chrysostom," in *In Dominico Eloquio. In Lordly Eloquence: Essays on Patristic Exegesis in Honor of Robert Louis Wilken*, ed. P. M. Blowers, A. R. Christman, D. G. Hunter, and R. D. Young (Grand Rapids: Eerdmans, 2002), 259–79.

than by viewing everything with the eyes of faith. "God caused drowsiness to come upon Adam," the text says, "and he slept."

7. Notice the precision of the teaching. This blessed author has stipulated both things, or rather the Holy Spirit through his tongue, teaching us the sequence of what happened. "God caused drowsiness to come upon Adam," the text says, "and he slept." It wasn't simply drowsiness that came upon him nor normal sleep; instead, the wise and skillful Creator of our nature was about to remove one of Adam's ribs. Lest the experience cause him pain and afterwards he be badly disposed towards the creature formed from his rib, and lest through memory of the pain he bear a grudge against this being at its formation, God induced in him this kind of sleep: He caused a drowsiness to come upon him and bid him be weighed down as though by some heavy weight. Like some excellent craftsman, His purpose was to do away with mere appearances, supply for any deficiencies, and in His own loving kindness create what had thus been taken from man, not allowing man to suffer any sense of what was happening. The text says, remember, "God caused drowsiness to come upon Adam, and he slept. God took one of Adam's ribs and closed up the flesh in its place," so that after the release of sleep he could not feel the loss he was suffering. You see, even if he was unaware at the time of the removal, nevertheless afterwards he would be likely to realize what had happened. So lest He cause him pain in removing the rib, or the loss of it cause him any distress later, He thus provided for both eventualities by making the removal painless and supplying for the loss without letting him feel anything of what had happened. So, the text says, the Lord God took the rib and fashioned it into a woman. A remarkable expression, defying our reasoning with its extraordinary boldness. After all, everything done by the Lord has this

character: forming the human being from dust is no less remarkable than this.[8]

8. Notice the considerateness[9] of sacred Scripture in the words employed with our limitations in mind: "God took one of his ribs," the text says. Don't take the words in human fashion; rather, interpret the concreteness of the expressions from the viewpoint of human limitations. You see, if he had not used these words, how would we have been able to gain knowledge of these mysteries which defy description? Let us therefore not remain at the level of the words alone, but let us understand everything in a manner proper to God[10] because applied to God. That phrase, "He took," after all, and other such things are spoken with our limitations in mind.

9. Now consider how here again He follows the same practice as in the case of Adam. I mean, just as in that case He said once, a second time and in fact frequently, "The Lord God took the human being that he had formed,"[11] and again, "The Lord God instructed Adam,"[12] and further, "The Lord God said, 'Let us make him a helpmate like himself,'"[13] so here too it says, "The Lord God fashioned the rib He had taken from Adam into a woman," and previously, "The Lord God caused drowsiness to come upon Adam," so that you might know that there is no difference between Father and Son in these expressions; instead, on account of both of them having the one essence,

---

8. Gen 2:7.

9. The Greek word *sunkatabasis* can be translated into English as "condescension" (Latin: *condescendo*; Greek *sunkatabainō*, "go down together with"). Yet, Hill favors "considerateness" as the best English translation for *sunkatabasis*, in order to avoid giving the sense that God is being patronizing. As Hill argues, it is an act of divine love when God speaks in Scripture clothed in human limitations so as to accommodate the human capacity to understand; see Robert C. Hill, *Reading the Old Testament in Antioch* (Leiden: Brill, 2005), 36–39.

10. Greek: *theoprepōs*, "in a manner proper to God."

11. Gen 2:15.

12. Gen 2:16.

13. Gen 2:18.

sacred Scripture applies the names indiscriminately.[14] See at any rate how, in the case of the formation of woman as well, it followed the same practice, saying, "The Lord God fashioned the rib he had taken from Adam into a woman."

10. What would be said in this case by those heretics who are always intent on calling everything into question and who hold the opinion that the origin of the Creator of all has been comprehended? What words can express the full sense of this? What kind of mind can grasp it? He took one rib, the text says—and how from this single rib did He fashion the complete being? Yet why do I say, how from this single thing did He fashion the being? Tell me, how did the removal happen? How was it he felt nothing of the removal? You can tell me none of these things; only the One who did the creating knows. So if we cannot comprehend these things with which we are familiar and what has to do with the formation of a being of the same race as ourselves, how much madness and folly does it betray to meddle in what concerns the Creator and to allege that we can comprehend matters that not even incorporeal and divine powers understand but continuously praise in fear and trembling?

11. "The Lord God," the text says, "fashioned the rib he had taken from Adam into a woman." See the precision of Scripture. I mean, it no longer said, "He formed," but "He fashioned," since He took part of what was already formed and, so to say, made up for what was lacking. Hence it says, "He fashioned"; He did not perform further shaping, but took some small part of the shaping already done, fashioned this

14. In each of these passages the Hebrew text has *yhwh 'elōhīm,* "YHWH God," which the Septuagint translated as *kyrios ho theos,* "Lord God." Following typical New Testament usage, Chrysostom understands *kyrios,* "Lord," to be a reference to Jesus the Son, and *theos,* "God" to be a reference to God the Father. According to Chrysostom, by using the names together in this fashion Scripture affirms the Trinitarian doctrine that the Father and the Son are one in essence.

part and made a complete being. How great the power of God, the master Craftsman, making a likeness of those limbs from that tiny part, creating such wonderful senses, and preparing a creature complete, entire and perfect, capable both of speaking and of providing much comfort to man by a sharing of her being. For it was for the consolation of this man that this woman was created. Hence Paul also said, "Man was not created for woman, but woman for man."[15] Do you see how everything is made for him? I mean, after the act of creation, after the brute beasts were brought forth, some suited for eating and some capable of assisting with man's service, the human being that had been formed stood in need of someone to talk to and able to offer him much comfort by a sharing of her being. So, from man's rib God creates this rational being, and in His inventive wisdom He makes it complete and perfect, like man in every detail—rational, capable of rendering him what would be of assistance in times of need and in the pressing necessities of life. It was God, you see, who was arranging everything in His wisdom and creative power. After all, we for our part, even though unable with the limitations of our reasoning to comprehend the way things happen, nevertheless believe that everything yields to His will and that whatever He directs is in fact brought forth. "The Lord God," the text says, "fashioned the rib He had taken from Adam into a woman, and led her to Adam," showing that it was for him that He had made her. He led her to Adam, it says. That is, since among all the other creatures there proved to be no helpmate of his kind (so the text says), behold, the promise I made—having guaranteed as I did to provide you with a helpmate of your kind—I kept by giving you one.

15. 1 Cor 11:9.

Homily on the Words of Paul:
"I Do Not Want You to Be Ignorant"
(1 Cor. 10:1-11) [selection]

Since the former "passing through" was a type of the baptism to come,[16] it was necessary that it first be depicted in general terms. And just as all benefited from these things formerly,[17] so also now all partake of the same things equally. "And how is it possible," someone says, "that the former event was a type of the present reality?" You must first learn what a type is, and what the reality is. Then, I can offer you an account of this matter.

What, then, is a shadow? And what is the reality? Come, let us consider the example of a picture that a painter might draw.[18] You have often seen the picture of a king in which the color has been filled in with dark blue paint. First, the painter traces a white outline, making a king, a royal throne, bodyguards, horses standing nearby, and enemies in chains lying on the ground. At this point, you can see these things sketched out in shadow. You do not know everything, but neither are you totally unaware of what is there. You understand vaguely that a man and a horse are drawn. But you cannot tell with much precision which king is drawn or what specific enemies are depicted, until the reality of the color comes to elucidate the picture and make it clearer. With

---

16. See Exod 14:22; 1 Cor 10:1.

17. In the portion of the homily leading up to this point, Chrysostom has been discussing the word "all" in 1 Cor 10:1–4: "our ancestors were *all* under the cloud, and *all* passed through the sea, and *all* were baptized into Moses in the cloud and in the sea, and *all* ate the same spiritual food, and *all* drank the same spiritual drink."

18. On this metaphor, see also Cyril of Alexandria, *On Worship in Spirit and Truth,* Book 1 (PG 68, pp. 140c–141a). Cyril employs the metaphor of a painter filling in a preliminary sketch with color, and also a bronzesmith making a statue by pouring hot liquid metal into a mold, in order to illustrate how Christ fulfills the Mosaic writings as suggested by John 5:45–46.

a picture you do not expect to recognize everything before the truth of the color is added, but you consider the sketch to be sufficiently complete if it gives you even a general understanding of what is being drawn. Similarly, this is how I think you should understand the Old Testament and the New Testament: you should not expect from the type all the precision of the reality.

We can now explain to you how the Old Testament possesses a certain kinship with the New Testament, and how the former "passing through" possesses a certain kinship with our Baptism. Back then it involved water, and now it involves water. Formerly it was the sea, but now it is a pool. Back then all the people went into the water, and likewise now all enter into the water. This is the manner of the kinship. So, do you wish to understand the reality that is brought out by the color? Previously they escaped from Egypt through the sea, but now they escape from idolatry. Back then Pharaoh was drowned, but now it is the Devil. Formerly the Egyptians were suffocated, but now the old self of sin is buried.[19]

Notice the kinship between the type and the reality, and the superiority of the reality over the type. The type should not be entirely different from the reality, or else it would not be a type. But neither should the type be equal to the reality, or else it would itself be the reality. Between the type and the reality there must be a fitting symmetry, such that the type does not possess all of the reality, but neither does it entirely fall short of it. Indeed, if it had everything, it would itself be the reality, but if it entirely fell short, it could not serve as a type. The type must partake of the reality, but it must also hold something back in reserve for the reality. Therefore, you should not expect everything from the Old Testament. Rather,

19. See Rom 6:4–6; Eph 4:22; Col 2:12; 3:9.

learn to be content even with minor enigmas that you perceive only vaguely.

What, then, is the kinship between the type and the reality? All were involved then, and all are involved now. It was through water then, and it is through water now. Those people were rescued from slavery, and we are also rescued from slavery, although not from the same kind. They were rescued from slavery to the Egyptians, whereas we are rescued from slavery to demons. They were rescued from being slaves to Barbarians, whereas we are rescued from being slaves to sin. They were led forth to freedom, and so are we, but not to the same kind of freedom. The freedom to which we are led is more illustrious by far. And do not be surprised if our freedom is greater and surpasses their freedom. For surely it belongs to the nature of the reality that it is far superior to its type, but without contradicting the type or being in conflict with it.

What, then, does it mean: "all were baptized into Moses"?[20] Perhaps what is said here is a bit unclear. Therefore, I will endeavor to make it clearer. At that time, the water separated before their eyes and they were commanded to pass through a strange and marvelous land which no one had ever crossed before. They wandered around, hesitated, and were distressed. So Moses passed through first, and he enabled all the others to be able to follow him with ease. In this way, "all were baptized into Moses." Having put their trust in Moses, they were emboldened to advance through the waters, since they had taken him to be the leader of their journey. This also happened with Christ. For He led us out of error and set us free from idolatry, and He guides us into the Kingdom. Christ was the first to embark on this journey, since He was the first to ascend into the heavens. Therefore, just as the former people were

20. 1 Cor 10:2.

emboldened by Moses to undertake their journey, so also let us be emboldened by Christ to undertake our voyage. That this is the sense of "all were baptized into Moses" is clear from the *historia*. Now, they were not baptized into the "name" of Moses. Do not be surprised that we not only have Jesus as our leader but also are baptized into His name, whereas they were not baptized into the "name" of Moses. As I said, it is necessary that the reality should have some vast and inexpressible superiority over the type.

14

Augustine

Augustine was born in 354 CE in the city of Thagaste, located in the northeast corner of modern Algeria. In Augustine's day, important cities in North Africa such as Thagaste were dominated by Roman culture and language. Augustine's father Patricius was apparently of Roman background and possessed sufficient means to provide a solid Roman education for his son. Augustine credited his mother Monica with providing him with a foundation in Christian faith and persistent urgings to remain loyal to it. By his own account, a love for literature and wisdom took root in Augustine in 373 as a result of his reading Cicero's dialogue on philosophy *Hortensius.* Around this time Augustine joined a group called the Manichees, followers of the teaching of the Persian prophet Mani (d. 276), who addressed the existence of evil by positing a dualistic worldview involving conflict between good and evil powers. The Manichees practiced a kind of asceticism, claimed to base their doctrines on reason, and included a significant role for Christ within their system. Augustine adhered to Manichean teachings for at least nine years, during which time he taught rhetoric in the city of Carthage in North Africa. In 382 Augustine took the next logical step in his career by traveling to Rome, where he met the influential pagan senator Symmachus, who recommended Augustine for a professional rhetorical post in the city of Milan in 384.

Soon after arriving in Milan to teach rhetoric, Augustine came into contact with the learned, articulate, and prestigious bishop Ambrose. From Ambrose Augustine came to appreciate Catholic Christian philosophy and piety, and also learned about the spiritual interpretation of the Old Testament. These realizations helped Augustine to leave behind his Manichean identity and rediscover the Catholic Christian faith of his mother. In 386 Augustine spent time at a villa in Cassiciacum outside of Milan and composed there a number of dialogues expounding Christian Neoplatonist philosophy, such as *On the Happy Life* and *On the Immortality of the Soul*. Augustine was baptized in 387. Within the next two years Augustine relinquished his career in rhetoric and his mother died. So he returned to North Africa and began writing works aimed at refuting Manichaeism, such as *On Genesis Against the Manicheans*. His first stop in returning to Africa was his hometown of Thagaste. His continued interest in intellectual matters can be seen in his treatise *On Music*, which was part of a projected series of writings on the liberal arts. Augustine's talent as an orator, Christian devotion, leadership qualities, and social network caused his reputation to grow throughout Christian North Africa. By 391 Augustine had become a presbyter in the Church of Hippo Regius (in modern Algeria), and in 395 he was selected as bishop. Augustine served as bishop of Hippo until his death in 430.

Augustine's literary output was immense and diverse, including tightly argued philosophical treatises, pastoral and ascetic writings, works directed at specific theological and ecclesiastical controversies, expositions of Scripture, more than 500 sermons, and over 200 letters. The general course of Augustine's literary career is often traced by noting three major interlocutors who engaged his primary attention at different stages of his life: (1) the Manichees (starting ca. 388), against whom he wrote many refutations, including *Against Fortunatus* and *Against Faustus the Manichean*; (2) the Donatists (ca. 401–411), a major presence in Christian North Africa with rigorous standards for ecclesiastical purity who recognized their own bishops and were not in communion with the Church outside of North Africa, against whom Augustine debated and whom he eventually succeeded in suppressing by appealing to imperial laws (for example, *On Baptism Against the Donatists*); and (3) the followers of Pelagius (starting ca. 412), a monk who emphasized the human capacity to respond affirmatively to God's commands by means of the grace already present in creation, against whom Augustine emphasized original sin, continuing grace, and predestination (for example, *Guilt and Remission of Sins* and *Nature and Grace*). Perhaps Augustine's most widely influential writings are the *Confessions* (397–401), a theological account of his own Christian experience; *On the Trinity* (ca. 400–418); and *City of God* (412–426), a massive apologetic and theological work written after the sack of Rome in 410, meant to distinguish between a spiritual city of God devoted to the love of God and an earthly city devoted to self-love.

After his ordination as presbyter, Augustine immersed

himself in the study of Scripture. His writings in the final thirty years of his life reflect increasing familiarity with Scripture and use of scriptural categories. Major exegetical works include *On Genesis Literally Interpreted, Enarrations on the Psalms, Tractates on the Gospel of John, On the Lord's Sermon on the Mount,* and *Questions on the Heptateuch.*

The passages presented here to illustrate Augustine's approach to Scripture are taken from *On Christian Teaching,* a treatise whose purpose is to communicate "certain precepts for interpreting the Scriptures" (*Christian Teaching,* "Prologue" 1). The broad structure of this work is set forth at the beginning of Book 1 when Augustine identifies two things necessary for scriptural interpretation: discovering what we need to understand and presenting what we have understood. Books 1–3 address the process of discovering what Scripture says and Book 4 addresses how this truth should be presented.[1] In Book 1 Augustine establishes key theological foundations: first, that God alone is to be enjoyed, human beings can be enjoyed in God, and everything else should be used in relation to God (*Christian Teaching* 1.3.3; 1.5.5; 1.23.22; 1.33.37); and second, that the words of Scripture are "signs" (*signa*) that point to the ultimate subject matter (*res,* "things") of Scripture,[2] namely, love of God and love of neighbor, so that

1. Among ancient Romans the system of oratory consisted of five parts: invention (*inventio*), disposition (*dispositio*), elocution (*elocutio*), memory (*memoria*), and performance (*actio*). See Quintilian, *Institutes of Oratory* 3.3.1; and Cicero, *On the Orator* 1.142–43. In *On Christian Teaching,* Augustine devotes Books 1–3 to "invention," the "process of discovering" (*modus inveniendi*) through scriptural exegesis what to say, and Book 4 to "elocution," the "process of presenting" (*modus proferendi*) what has been learned from Scripture, with special attention to the relationship between style and content (*Christian Teaching* 1.1.1; 4.1.1).

2. Aristotle used the term "sign" in the context of rhetorical argumentation to refer to an indication of something else (*Prior Analytics* 2.27.70a; *Rhetoric* 1.1357a; *Sophistical Refutations* 167b; see also Cicero, *On Invention* 1.30.47–48; Quintilian, *Institutes of Oratory* 5.9.9). The early Stoic theory of language envisioned three categories: a verbal utterance as "that which signifies" (*sēmainon*), the concept that is "signified" (*sēmainomenon*), and the real "existing" (*tynchanon*) object that corresponds to these

any proper understanding of Scripture must build up this double love (*Christian Teaching* 1.2.2; 1.36.40; cf. 2.1.1–2.5.6). Early in Book 2 Augustine identifies two reasons why things written are not understood: they are obscured either by "unknown signs" (*signa ignota*) or by "ambiguous signs" (*signa ambigua*). Moreover, both of these types of signs can be used in a "literal" (*propria*) or "metaphorical" (*translata*) sense (*Christian Teaching* 2.10.15). Book 2 treats unknown signs: in order to explain unknown signs in their literal sense (*signa ignota propria*) we must have a knowledge of languages (*Christian Teaching* 2.11.16); in order to comprehend the meaning of unknown signs in their metaphorical sense (*signa ignota translata*) we must understand the realities behind the signs (*Christian Teaching* 2.16.23). This leads to a survey of the liberal arts, such as the study of animals, stones, plants, numbers, music, history, cultural convention, astronomy, and philosophy. Book 3 treats ambiguous signs: ambiguous signs in their literal sense (*signa ambigua propria*) are clarified through literary analysis as employed by ancient grammarians, guided where necessary by the Rule of Faith (*Christian Teaching* 3.2.2); ambiguous signs in their metaphorical sense (*signa ambigua translata*) serve as the gateway into the figurative, theological meaning of Scripture (*Christian Teaching* 3.5.9). Book 4 offers

(Sextus Empiricus, *Against the Mathematicians* 8.11–12, 270–71; Diogenes Laertius 7.55–59, 62–63; see also Seneca, *Letters* 117.13). For the use of "signification" to describe the distinction between words and content, Quintilian was likely an important resource: "every speech consists either of things signified or of things that signify, that is, of content (*res*) or of words (*verba*)" (*Institutes of Oratory* 3.5.1; see also 3.3.1; 8. Preface 6). For Augustine, "a sign is a thing which of itself makes some other thing come to mind, besides the impression that it presents to the senses" (*Christian Teaching* 2.1.1; cf. 1.2.2). Augustine also discusses words as signs and the relationship between words and things in *On Dialectic* (e.g., 5.9–10) and *On the Teacher* (e.g., 2.3.1; 4.8.35–36). For further discussion, see Giovanni Manetti, *Theories of the Sign in Classical Antiquity* (trans. C. Richardson; Bloomington and Indianapolis: Indiana University Press, 1993); and Tarmo Toom, "Augustine's Hermeneutics: The Science of Divinely Given Signs," in *Patristic Theories of Biblical Interpretation: The Latin Fathers,* ed. T. Toom (Cambridge: Cambridge University Press, 2016), 77–108.

a distinctively Christian vision for presenting scriptural truth through didactic oratory.

Books 1–2 and much of Book 3 (through 3.25.35) were composed shortly after Augustine became bishop, between the years 395 and 397. For much of Augustine's career *On Christian Teaching* remained unfinished. He finally completed the remainder of Book 3 and Book 4 in the year 427. Augustine realized that no one person possesses all the knowledge presupposed in *On Christian Teaching*. This work was meant as a guidebook for scriptural interpretation for the Church as a whole. As a resource for biblical interpretation, as a model for Christian appropriation of the liberal arts, and as a paradigm for Christian rhetoric, *On Christian Teaching* had an enormous impact on the Latin Middle Ages.

On Christian Teaching (selections)

On Christian Teaching 1.36.40–41

1.36.40. So anyone who thinks that he has understood the divine scriptures or any part of them, but cannot by his understanding build up this double love of God and neighbor,[3] has not yet succeeded in understanding them. Anyone who derives from them an idea which is useful for supporting this love but fails to say what the writer demonstrably meant in the passage has not made a fatal error, and is certainly not a liar. In a liar there is a desire to say what is false, and that is why we find many who want to lie but nobody who wants to be misled. Since a person lies knowingly but is misled unknowingly, it is clear enough that in any given situation the person misled is better than the one who lies, since it is better to suffer injustice

---

3. Lev 19:18; Deut 6:5; Matt 22:34–40; Mark 12:28–31; Luke 10:25–28.

than to commit it. Everyone who lies commits injustice; so anyone who believes that a lie is sometimes useful believes that injustice is sometimes useful. No one who lies keeps faith while lying—he certainly desires that the person he lies to should put faith in him, but when lying he does not keep faith—and everyone who breaks faith is unjust. So either injustice is sometimes useful—which is impossible—or lying is always useless.[4]

1.36.41. Anyone with an interpretation of the Scriptures that differs from that of the writer is misled, but not because the Scriptures are lying. If, as I began by saying, he is misled by an idea of the kind that builds up love, which is the end of the commandment, he is misled in the same way as a walker who leaves his path by mistake but reaches the destination to which the path leads by going through a field. But he must be put right and shown how it is more useful not to leave the path, in case the habit of deviating should force him to go astray or even adrift.[5]

On Christian Teaching 2.9.14–2.11.16

2.9.14. These are all the books in which those who fear God and are made docile by their holiness seek God's will.[6] The

---

4. Augustine works out a definition of lying and explains different views on the possible utility of lying in his treatise *On Lying* (written ca. 395), concluding that lying cannot be justified under any circumstance. He addresses this topic with greater directness in *To Consentius, Against Lying* (written in 420).

5. Here Augustine warns against deviating in one's interpretation from what the author wrote. For a different angle on the role of authorial intention in interpreting Scripture, see below *Christian Teaching* 3.27.38–3.28.39.

6. Augustine has just given a list of the "complete canon of Scripture" (*Christian Teaching* 2.8.13). This list includes for the Old Testament: the five books of Moses, Joshua, Judges, Ruth, the four books of Kings (= 1–2 Samuel and 1–2 Kings), Chronicles, Job, Tobit, Esther, Judith, 1–2 Maccabees, Ezra, Nehemiah, Psalms, Proverbs, Song of Songs, Ecclesiastes, Wisdom of Solomon, Ecclesiasticus, the Twelve Prophets, Isaiah, Jeremiah, Daniel and Ezekiel; and for the New Testament: the four Gospels, the fourteen letters of Paul (including Hebrews), 1–2 Peter, 1–3 John, Jude, James, Acts, and Revelation. On Augustine's understanding of the biblical canon, see Anne-Marie Bonnardière, "The

first rule in this laborious task is, as I have said, to know these books; not necessarily to understand them but to read them so as to commit them to memory or at least make them not totally unfamiliar. Then the matters which are clearly stated in them, whether ethical precepts or articles of belief, should be examined carefully and intelligently. The greater a person's intellectual capacity, the more of these he finds. In clearly expressed passages of Scripture one can find all the things that concern faith and the moral life (namely hope and love, treated in my previous book).[7] Then, after gaining a familiarity with the language of the divine Scriptures, one should proceed to explore and analyze the obscure passages, by taking examples from the more obvious parts to illuminate obscure expressions and by using the evidence of indisputable passages to remove the uncertainty of ambiguous ones.[8] Here memory is extremely valuable; and it cannot be supplied by these instructions if it is lacking.

2.10.15. There are two reasons why written texts fail to be understood: their meaning may be veiled either by unknown signs or by ambiguous signs. Signs are either literal or metaphorical.[9] They are called literal when used to signify the things for which they were invented: as, for example, when we say *bovem* [ox], meaning the animal which we and all speakers

---

Canon of Scripture," in *Augustine and the Bible*, ed. and trans. Pamela Bright (Notre Dame, IN: University of Notre Dame Press, 1986), 26–41.

7. See *Christian Teaching* 1.37.41–1.40.44. For example: "So when someone has learnt that the aim of the commandment is 'love from a pure heart, and good conscience and genuine faith' [1 Tim 1:5], he will be ready to relate every interpretation of the holy Scriptures to these three things [i.e., faith, hope, and love] and may approach the task of handling these books with confidence" (*Christian Teaching* 1.40.44).

8. On the idea that clear passages should be used to interpret ambiguous ones, see Tertullian, *On Modesty* 17.18; *Against Marcion* 1.9; *On the Resurrection* 19, 21; *Against Praxeas* 20; Irenaeus, *Against Heresies* 2.27.1; Origen, *Philocalia* 2.3. See also Quintilian, *Institutes of Oratory* 5.10.8.

9. Augustine distinguishes between "unknown signs" (*signa ignota*) and "ambiguous signs" (*signa ambigua*), either of which may be "literal" (*propria*) or "metaphorical" (*translata*).

of Latin call by that name. They are metaphorical when the actual things which we signify by the particular words are used to signify something else: when, for example, we say *bovem* and not only interpret these two syllables to mean the animal normally referred to by that name but also understand, by that animal, "worker in the gospel," which is what Scripture, as interpreted by the apostle Paul, means when it says, "You shall not muzzle the ox that treads out the grain."[10]

2.11.16. An important antidote to the ignorance of literal signs is the knowledge of languages. Users of the Latin language—and it is these that I have now undertaken to instruct—need two others, Hebrew and Greek, for an understanding of the divine Scriptures, so that recourse may be had to the original versions if any uncertainty arises from the infinite variety of Latin translators. Though we often find Hebrew words untranslated in the texts, like *amen, alleluia, raca, hosanna.*[11] In some cases, although they could be translated, the original form is preserved for the sake of its solemn authority (so *amen, alleluia*); in others, like the other two that I mentioned, they are said to be incapable of being translated into another language. There are certain words in particular languages which just cannot be translated into the idioms of another language. This is especially true of interjections, which signify emotion rather than an element of clearly conceived meaning: two such words, it is said, are *raca,* a word expressing anger, and *hosanna,* a word expressing joy. But it is not because of these few words, which it is easy enough to note down and ask other people about, but because of the aforementioned diversity of translators that a knowledge of languages is

---

10. Deut 25:4; 1 Cor 9:9; 1 Tim 5:18.
11. In the Latin Bible, examples include *amen*: Num 5:22; Deut 27:15; Psalm 41:13; Rom 1:25; Gal 1:5; Rev 1:6; *alleluia*: Ps 146:1; Rev 19:1; *raca*: Matt 5:22; and *hosanna*: Matt 21:9; John 12:13.

necessary. Translators of Scripture from Hebrew into Greek can be easily counted, but not so translators into Latin, for in the early days of the faith any person who got hold of a Greek manuscript and fancied that he had some ability in the two languages went ahead and translated it.[12]

On Christian Teaching 2.16.23–24

2.16.23. As for metaphorical signs, any unfamiliar ones which puzzle the reader must be investigated partly through a knowledge of languages, and partly through a knowledge of things. There is a figurative significance and certainly some hidden meaning conveyed by the episode of the pool of Siloam,[13] where the man who had his eyes anointed by the Lord with mud made from spittle was ordered to wash his face. If the evangelist had not explained this name from an unfamiliar language, this important meaning would have remained hidden. So too, many of the Hebrew names not explained by the authors of these books undoubtedly have considerable significance and much help to give in solving the mysteries of the Scriptures, if they can be explained at all. Various experts

---

12. Augustine's comment reflects the chaotic state of the text of the Old Latin Bible in his day. Translations of Old and New Testament books from Greek into Latin were made in the second and third centuries CE through a gradual and anonymous process, and revisions of the Latin Bible on the basis of diverse and evolving Greek texts continued up to Augustine's time. Augustine recognized the "Seventy" translators who supposedly produced the Septuagint as authoritative (*Christian Teaching* 2.15.22), and he was also aware of the "hexaplaric" translators from Hebrew into Greek: Aquila, Symmachus, and Theodotion. As for translators from Hebrew into Latin, at this point in time (ca. 396) Augustine was critical of Jerome's Hebrew-based Latin translation project (see Augustine's *Letter* 28 written in 394 or 395; *Letter* 71 written in 403; and *Letter* 82 written in 405). Yet, in *City of God* 18.42–44 (written sometime after 420) Augustine acknowledges the value of Jerome's Hebrew-Latin translations alongside the Septuagint and he refers to Jerome as "a most learned man, skilled in all three languages" (i.e., Hebrew, Greek, and Latin). Moreover, in *Christian Teaching* 4.7.15 (composed ca. 427), Augustine chooses to quote Amos in Jerome's Hebrew-based version rather than the Septuagint.
13. John 9:7.

in the language have rendered no small service to posterity by explaining all these individual words from the Scriptures and giving the meaning of the names Adam, Eve, Abraham, and Moses, and of place names such as Jerusalem, Zion, Jericho, Sinai, Lebanon, Jordan, and any other names in that language that are unfamiliar to us.[14] Once these are clarified and explained many figurative expressions in Scripture become quite clear.

2.16.24. Ignorance of things makes figurative expressions unclear when we are ignorant of the qualities of animals or stones or plants or other things mentioned in Scripture for the sake of some analogy. The well-known fact about the snake, that it offers its whole body to assailants in place of its head, marvelously illustrates the meaning of the Lord's injunction to be as wise as serpents,[15] which means that in place of our head, which is Christ,[16] we should offer our body to persecutors, so that the Christian faith is not as it were killed within us when we spare our body and deny God. And the fact that a snake confined in its narrow lair puts off its old garment and is said to take on new strength chimes in excellently with the idea of imitating the serpent's astuteness and putting off the old man (to use the words of the apostle)[17] in order to put on the new, and also with that of doing so in a confined place, for the Lord said "enter by the narrow gate."[18] Just as a knowledge of the habits of the snake clarifies the many analogies involving this

14. In terms of what was available in Latin, Jerome had produced two works explaining the meanings of proper nouns in Scripture: *Book of Hebrew Names* and *Book of Hebrew Place Names*. In the Greek tradition, both Eusebius of Caesarea (*Ecclesiastical History* 2.18.7) and Origen (cited in the preface to Jerome's *Book of Hebrew Names*) credited Philo with composing the prototype Hebrew-Greek proper name list, although it is doubtful whether Philo knew enough Hebrew to have done this. In any case, Philo certainly made use of such a list in his commentaries.
15. Matt 10:16.
16. Eph 4:15.
17. Eph 4:22–24; Col 3:9–10.
18. Matt 7:13.

animal regularly given in Scripture, so too an ignorance of the numerous animals mentioned no less frequently in analogies is a great hindrance to understanding. The same is true of stones, herbs, and anything that has roots. Even a knowledge of the carbuncle, a stone which shines in the dark, explains many obscure passages in Scripture where it is used in an analogy; and ignorance of the beryl and adamant often closes the door to understanding. It is easy to understand that unbroken peace is signified by the olive branch brought by the dove when it returned to the ark,[19] simply because we know that the smooth surface of oil is not easily broken by another liquid and also that the tree itself is in leaf all year round. And because of their ignorance about hyssop many people, unaware of its power to cleanse the lungs or even (so it is said) to split rocks with its roots, in spite of its low and humble habit, are quite unable to discover why it is said, "You will purge me with hyssop, and I shall be clean."[20]

On Christian Teaching 3.1.1–3.2.2

3.1.1. The student who fears God earnestly seeks his will in the holy Scriptures. Holiness makes him gentle, so that he does not revel in controversy; a knowledge of languages protects him from uncertainty over unfamiliar words or phrases, and a knowledge of certain essential things protects him from ignorance of the significance and detail of what is used by way of imagery. Thus equipped, and with the assistance of reliable texts derived from the manuscripts with careful attention to the need for emendation,[21] he should now approach the task

---

19. Gen 8:11.
20. Ps 51:7. On the cleansing power of hyssop, see also *Christian Teaching* 2.41.62.
21. The emendation (*emendatio*) of copying errors found in manuscripts was a foundational step in ancient literary analysis.

of analyzing and resolving the ambiguities of the Scriptures. To prevent himself from being misled by ambiguous signs, in so far as I can instruct him (it may indeed be the case that either because of great intellectual gifts or a clarity of mind that is the result of greater illumination than I have he scorns as elementary the methods which I wish to demonstrate)—but, as I began to say, in so far as I can instruct him, the student who is in the proper state of mind to accept my instruction should know that ambiguity in Scripture resides either in literal or in metaphorical usages (as the terms were described in Book 2).[22]

3.2.2. When it is literal usages that make Scripture ambiguous, we must first of all make sure that we have not punctuated or articulated the passage incorrectly. Once close consideration has revealed that it is uncertain how a passage should be punctuated and articulated,[23] we must consult the Rule of Faith, as it is perceived through the plainer passages of the Scriptures and the authority of the Church.[24] (I dealt adequately with this matter when speaking of things in Book 1.[25]) But if both interpretations, or indeed all of them, if there are several sides to the ambiguity, sound compatible with the Faith, then it remains to consult the context—the preceding and following passages, which surround the ambiguity—in

22. See *Christian Teaching* 2.10.15.
23. Expressing punctuation (*distinctio*) and articulating the text in such a way as to distinguish between homographs or identify a sentence as a statement, question, or exclamation belonged to the sphere of *lectio* ("reading aloud") in ancient literary analysis.
24. The "Rule of Faith" in the second and third centuries served as a summary of the defining beliefs of Christianity. Augustine offers a statement on the teaching of the Catholic Faith to be used in guiding the interpretation of Scripture in *Two Books on Genesis Against the Manichees* 2.2.3. Examples of Augustine's appeal to the Rule of Faith can be found in *On the Trinity* 15.28.51; *On Original Sin* 2.34.29; and *On Baptism Against the Donatists* 2.1.2.
25. See *Christian Teaching* 1.18.17: "He accordingly gave keys to His Church so that whatever it loosed on earth should also be loosed in heaven, and whatever it bound on earth should also be bound in heaven" (see Matt 16:19). On the use of plainer passages to interpret more obscure passages, see *Christian Teaching* 2.9.14.

order to determine which of the several meanings that suggest themselves is supported by it, and which one lends itself to acceptable combinations with it.

On Christian Teaching 3.5.9

3.5.9. But the ambiguities of metaphorical words, about which I must now speak, require no ordinary care and attention. To begin with, one must take care not to interpret a figurative expression literally. What the apostle says is relevant here: "the letter kills but the spirit gives life."[26] For when something meant figuratively is interpreted as if it were meant literally, it is understood in a carnal way. No "death of the soul" is more aptly given that name than the situation in which the intelligence, which is what raises the soul above the level of animals, is subjected to the flesh by following the letter. A person who follows the letter understands metaphorical words as literal, and does not relate what the literal word signifies to any other meaning. On hearing the word "Sabbath," for example, he interprets it simply as one of the seven days which repeat themselves in a continuous cycle; and on hearing the word "sacrifice" his thoughts do not pass beyond the rituals performed with sacrificial beasts or fruits of the earth. It is, then, a miserable kind of spiritual slavery to interpret signs as things, and to be incapable of raising the mind's eye above the physical creation so as to absorb the eternal light.

On Christian Teaching 3.10.14–3.22.32

3.10.14. As well as this rule, which warns us not to pursue a figurative (that is, metaphorical) expression as if it were literal,

26. 2 Cor 3:6.

we must add a further one: not to accept a literal one as if it were figurative. We must first explain the way to discover whether an expression is literal or figurative. Generally speaking, it is this: anything in the divine discourse that cannot be related either to good morals or to the true faith should be taken as figurative.[27] Good morals have to do with our love of God and our neighbor, the true faith with our understanding of God and our neighbor. The hope that each person has within his own conscience is directly related to the progress that he feels himself to be making towards the love and understanding of God and his neighbor. All this has been dealt with in Book 1.

3.10.15. But since the human race is prone to judge sins not by the strength of the actual lust, but rather by the standard of its own practices, people generally regard as culpable only such actions as men of their own time and place tend to blame and condemn, and regard as commendable and praiseworthy only such actions as are acceptable within the conventions of their own society. And so it happens that if Scripture enjoins something at variance with the practices of its readers, or censures something that is not at variance with them, they consider the relevant expression to be figurative (always assuming that their minds are governed by the authority of the Word). But Scripture enjoins nothing but love, and censures nothing but lust, and molds people's minds accordingly. Similarly, if their minds are taken over by a particular prejudice, people consider as figurative anything that Scripture asserts to the contrary. But it asserts nothing except

27. In this formulation, one can discern a figurative sense not only when the literal sense is problematic, but also when the literal sense fails to relate to good morals or the true faith. Even details such as genealogies or proper names, although they pose no special problems, can be taken figuratively in order to derive from them moral and theological teaching. The logic is as follows: since all inspired Scripture is profitable for instruction (cf. 2 Tim 3:16), it would be a "problem" for any scriptural text if it failed to yield meaningful Christian teaching.

the Catholic Faith, in time past, present, and future. It narrates the past, foretells the future, and demonstrates the present, but all these things serve to nourish and strengthen this love, and to overcome and annihilate lust.

3.10.16. By love I mean the impulse of one's mind to enjoy God on his own account and to enjoy oneself and one's neighbor on account of God; and by lust I mean the impulse of one's mind to enjoy oneself and one's neighbor and any corporeal thing not on account of God.[28] What unbridled lust does to corrupt a person's own mind and body is called wickedness; what it does to harm another person is called wrongdoing. All sins can be divided into these two kinds, but wickedness comes first. Once it has depleted the mind and as it were bankrupted it, it rushes on to commit wrongdoing in order to remove the obstacles to wickedness or to find assistance for it. Similarly, what love does to benefit itself is self-interest, and what it does to benefit a neighbor is known as kindness. And here self-interest comes first, because nobody can do good to another out of resources which he does not possess.[29] The more the realm of lust is destroyed, the more the realm of love is increased.

3.11.17. Any harsh and even cruel word or deed attributed to God or his saints that is found in the holy Scriptures applies to the destruction of the realm of lust.[30] If the message is clear, it should not be treated as figurative and related to something else. For example, Paul's saying: "You are storing up wrath for yourself on the day of wrath, the day of the revelation of the just judgment of God, who will repay all people according to

---

28. See *Christian Teaching* 1.3.3–1.5.5; 1.22.20–1.23.22; 1.33.37, where Augustine explains that only God should be enjoyed as the goal of joy, and people should be enjoyed in God.

29. On love of self and then of neighbor, see *Christian Teaching* 1.24.24–1.26.27.

30. Augustine gives here a version of the principle that a proper understanding of Scripture must offer theological teaching that is "worthy of God."

their works; eternal life to those who by persistence in well-doing seek glory and honor and immortality, but anger and fury to those who fractiously refuse to obey the truth and put their trust in iniquity. There will be tribulation and distress to every human soul that does evil, first to the Jew and then to the Greek."[31] But this was written to those whose destruction must accompany that of the lust itself, those who refused to overcome it. In cases where the realm of lust is overcome by a person once dominated by it, this perfectly clear saying applies: "Those who belong to Jesus Christ have crucified their flesh along with its passions and desires."[32] Even here, admittedly, some words are used metaphorically, such as "wrath of God" and "crucified," but they are not so many, or so unclear in expression, as to hide the sense and create allegory or obscurity, which is what I mean by figurative expression in the strict sense. On the other hand, Jeremiah's phrase, "Behold today I have established you over nations and kingdoms, to uproot and destroy, to lay waste and scatter,"[33] is, without doubt, entirely figurative, and so must be related to the aim that I mentioned above.

3.12.18. Matters which seem like wickedness to the unenlightened, whether merely spoken or actually performed, whether attributed to God or to people whose holiness is commended to us, are entirely figurative. Such mysteries are to be elucidated in terms of the need to nourish love. A person who makes more limited use of transient things than the moral conventions of his own society allow is either self-controlled or superstitious; a person whose use of them exceeds the limits set by the practice of good people in his society is either guilty

---

31. Rom 2:5–9.
32. Gal 5:24.
33. Jer 1:10.

of wickedness or an indication of some special significance. In all such matters what is reprehensible is not the use made of things but the user's desire. No person in his right mind should ever think that the Lord's feet were anointed by a woman with precious ointment in the same way as the feet of self-indulgent and evil men are anointed at the sort of banquets which we abhor.[34] A good perfume signifies a good reputation: anyone who enjoys this through the deeds of an upright life anoints Christ's feet in a figurative sense with a most precious perfume by following in his footsteps. Again, what is generally speaking wicked in other people is the sign of something great in one who is divine or a prophet. Consorting with a prostitute is one thing in a depraved society, but something quite different in the prophecy of Hosea.[35] And the fact that some people strip in their drunken, uninhibited parties does not make it immoral to be naked in the bath.

3.12.19. We must therefore pay careful attention to the conduct appropriate to different places, times, and persons, in case we make rash imputations of wickedness. It is possible for a wise man to take some kind of costly food without any taint of greed or gluttony, and for an unwise one to yearn for junk food with a most disgusting outburst of greed. Or someone might have a healthy preference for eating fish, like our Lord,[36] rather than lentils, like Abraham's grandson Esau,[37] or barley, like cattle. The fact that most animals are more restrained than we are is not the result of their cheaper diet. In all matters of this kind actions are made acceptable or unacceptable not by the particular things we make use of, but by our motives for using them and our methods of seeking them.

34. Matt 26:6–13; John 12:1–8.
35. Hos 1:2–3.
36. Luke 24:42; John 21:7–14.
37. Gen 25:34.

3.12.20. Righteous men of long ago visualized the kingdom of heaven as an earthly kingdom, and predicted it accordingly. In the interests of perpetuating the race[38] there was a perfectly blameless practice for one man to have several wives. For the same reason it was not honorable for one woman to have several husbands; that does not make a woman more fertile, and it is indeed a form of immoral prostitution to seek either profit or progeny through promiscuity. Given such social conventions,[39] things that the saints of those ages could do without any lust—although they were doing something which cannot be done without lust nowadays—are not censured by Scripture. Anything of this kind related there is to be understood not only historically and literally but also figuratively and prophetically, and interpreted according to the aim of love, whether it be love of God or love of one's neighbor, or both. In ancient Rome it was considered wicked to wear ankle-length tunics or ones with sleeves,[40] whereas now it is thought immoral for the upper classes not to have them when wearing tunics; so we must observe that in the use of all other such things there must be an absence of lust, which not only wickedly exploits the actual practice of its society but also, by going beyond those limits in an outburst of total wickedness, often makes a disgraceful exhibition of its own ugliness, which had previously been concealed behind the barriers of traditional morality.

3.13.21. Whatever accords with the social practices of those with whom we have to live this present life—whether this manner of life is imposed by necessity or undertaken in the

---

38. "In the interests of perpetuating the race," *Sufficiendae prolis causa*; cf. Virgil, *Georgics* 3.65: *atque aliam ex alia generando suffice prolem* ("and perpetuate the race one after another [i.e., cattle] by breeding").

39. "Given such social conventions," *in huiuscemodi moribus* (literally: "in [view of] 'mores' of such kind").

40. See Cicero, *Against Catiline* 2.22.

course of duty—should be related by good and serious men to the aims of self-interest and kindness, either literally, as we ourselves should do, or also figuratively, as is allowed to the prophets.

3.14.22. When those who are unfamiliar with different social practices come up against such actions in their reading, they think them wicked unless restrained by some explicit authority. They are incapable of realizing that their own sort of behavior patterns, whether in matters of marriage, or diet, or dress, or any other aspect of human life and culture, would seem wicked to other races or other ages. Some people have been struck by the enormous diversity of social practices[41] and in a state of drowsiness, as I would put it—for they were neither sunk in the deep sleep[42] of stupidity nor capable of staying awake to greet the light of wisdom—have concluded that justice has no absolute existence but that each race views its own practices as just. So since the practices of all races are diverse, whereas justice ought to remain unchangeable, there clearly is no such thing as justice anywhere.[43] To say no more, they have not realized that the injunction "do not do to another what you would not wish to be done to yourself" can in no way be modified by racial differences.[44] When this injunction is related to the love of God, all wickedness dies; and when it is related to the love of one's neighbor, all wrongdoing dies. For nobody wants his own dwelling to be wrecked, and so he should not wish to wreck God's dwelling (which is himself).

---

41. "By the enormous diversity of social practices," *Qua varietate innumerabilium consuetudinum* (*consuetudo* = "social practice").

42. "They were neither sunk in the deep (*alto*) sleep," *neque alto somno . . . sopiebantur;* cf. Virgil, *Aeneid* 1.680–81: *hunc ego sopitum somno super alta Cythera . . . recondam* ("him sunk in sleep I will bury on the height [*alta*] of Cythera . . .").

43. In Cicero's dialogue *On the Republic* 3.9.14–3.11.19, the character Philus employs an argument such as Augustine presents here in the course of making a hypothetical defense of injustice.

44. Tobit 4:15.

Nobody wants to be harmed by anybody; so he should not do harm to anybody.

3.15.23. So when the tyranny of lust has been overthrown love rules with laws that are utterly just: to love God on His account, and to love oneself and one's neighbor on God's account. Therefore in dealing with figurative expressions we will observe a rule of this kind: the passage being read should be studied with careful consideration until its interpretation can be connected with the realm of love. If this point is made literally, then no kind of figurative expression need be considered.

3.16.24. If the expression is a prescriptive one, and either forbids wickedness or wrongdoing, or enjoins self-interest or kindness, it is not figurative. But if it appears to enjoin wickedness or wrongdoing or to forbid self-interest or kindness, it is figurative. Scripture says, "Unless you eat the flesh of the Son of Man and drink his blood, you will not have life in you."[45] This appears to enjoin wickedness or wrongdoing, and so it is figurative, a command to participate in the Lord's passion and to store in our memory the pleasurable and useful knowledge that his flesh was crucified and wounded for our sake. Scripture says, "If your enemy is hungry, feed him; if he is thirsty, give him a drink."[46] Here no one can doubt that it enjoins kindness. But one would think that the following words, "for by doing this you will pile coals of fire on his head,"[47] advocate malicious wrongdoing; so one

45. John 6:54. Augustine sometimes speaks of the Eucharist as the Church's true sacrifice, which was symbolized in Old Testament sacrifices, by which the Church offers itself to God, and also as a sacrament or visible sign of an invisible sacrifice (e.g., *Tractates on the Gospel of John* 26.1.4; *Responses to Januarius* [= *Letters* 54–55] 1.2, 4; *Letter* 98.9; *City of God* 10.5, 6, 20; 17.20). For further discussion, see Pamela Jackson, "Eucharist," in *Augustine Through the Ages: An Encyclopedia*, ed. Allan D. Fitzgerald (Grand Rapids: Eerdmans, 1999), 330–34.
46. Rom 12:20a.
47. Rom 12:20b.

can be sure that it was meant figuratively. Given that it can be interpreted in two ways, in the sense of causing harm and in the sense of offering something, the principle of love should lead you to the interpretation involving kindness, so that you understand by "coals of fire" the agonized groans of penitence which cure the pride of a person who regrets having been the enemy of someone who helped him in distress. Similarly, when the Lord says, "He who loves his own soul shall lose it,"[48] this should not be taken as forbidding self-interest (everyone must seek to preserve his own soul) but as meaning "lose one's soul" in a figurative sense—that is, to destroy and lose one's current perverse and disordered way of using it, by which one is inclined to what is temporal and prevented from seeking what is eternal. It is written: "give to the merciful and do not support a sinner."[49] The second part of this statement seems to forbid kindness ("do not support a sinner"); so understand "sinner" figuratively as "sin," the meaning being "do not support his sin."

3.17.25. It often happens that someone who is, or thinks he is, at a higher stage of the spiritual life regards as figurative instructions which are given to those at a lower stage. So, for example, a man who has embraced a life of celibacy and castrated himself for the sake of the kingdom of heaven[50] might maintain that any instructions given in the sacred books about loving or governing one's wife should be taken not literally but figuratively; or someone who has resolved to keep his own daughter unmarried might try to interpret as figurative the saying "Marry off your daughter, and you will have done a great deed."[51] This too, then, will be one of our

48. John 12:25.
49. Sir 12:4.
50. Matt 19:12.
51. Sir 7:25; cf. 1 Cor 7:36–38.

rules for interpreting Scripture: we must understand that some instructions are given to all people alike, but others to particular classes of people, so that the medicine may confront not only the general pathology of the disease but also the particular weakness of each part of the body. What cannot be raised to a higher level must be healed at its own level.

3.18.26. Likewise we must take care not to regard something in the Old Testament that is by the standards of its own time not wickedness or wrongdoing, even when understood literally and not figuratively, as capable of being transferred to the present time and applied to our own lives. A person will not do this unless lust is in total control and actively seeking the complicity of the very Scriptures by which it must be overthrown. Such a wretch does not realize that these things are written down for a useful purpose, to enable men of good conscience to see, for their own spiritual health, that a practice which they embrace can be damnable, if the love shown by its followers (in the first case) or their greed (in the second) is taken into account.

3.18.27. For if one man according to the custom of his time could be chaste with many wives, another today can be lustful with a single wife. I approve the man who exploits the fertility of many women for a purpose other than sexual gratification more highly than one who enjoys one woman's flesh for its own sake. In one case there is the motive of self-interest, in accordance with the conditions prevailing at the time; in the other, the satisfaction of a lust caught up in the pleasures of the world. In God's eyes the men to whom the apostle allowed sexual intercourse with their individual wives, because of their lack of self-control,[52] are at a lower stage than those who each had several wives but looked only to the procreation of

52. See 1 Cor 7:1–2.

children in the sexual act (just as in eating and drinking a wise man looks only to physical health). And so if the Lord's advent had found them still in this life, when it was time not "to throw away stones but collect them,"[53] they would have immediately castrated themselves for the sake of the kingdom of heaven. For there is no difficulty in forgoing sex, except where there is lust in practicing it. Those men of old knew that the enjoyment of sex with their wives was a form of unrestrained abuse. This is shown by Tobit's prayer when he married his wife: "You are blessed, Lord of our fathers, and your name is blessed for ages to come. Let the heavens and all creation bless you. You made Adam and gave him the assistance of Eve. And now, Lord, you know that it is not for enjoyment that I am taking my sister, but in all honesty, so that you may have mercy on us, O Lord."[54]

3.19.28. But promiscuous people who with unbridled lust go through one affair after another, or people who, just with a single wife, not only exceed the limit appropriate to the procreation of children but also in their inhuman incontinence pile filth upon filth with an utterly shameless exercise of their slavish kind of freedom, do not consider it possible that the men of old treated their many wives with self-control and in so doing simply fulfilled the duty, required by their times, of continuing the race. What they themselves, entangled as they are in the toils of lust, do not even achieve with one wife, they think totally impossible with several.

3.19.29. But they may as well say that good and holy men should not even be honored or praised, just because they themselves, when honored and praised, swell with pride, and because the more frequent, and the more widespread, the publicity of flattering tongues becomes, the more greedy they

---

53. Eccles 3:5.
54. Tob 8:5–7.

are for empty praise. This makes them vain, and so the wind of rumor, whether it is seen as favorable or unfavorable, draws them into various whirlpools of wickedness or drives them against the rocks of wrongdoing. So they should realize what a difficult and demanding thing it is not to be enticed by the bait of praise or pierced by the barbs of insult, and not measure others by themselves.

3.20.29. They would do better to reckon that our apostles were neither puffed up when admired by men nor cast down when despised. They escaped neither of these temptations, being fêted by the accolades of believers and slandered by the abuse of persecutors. So just as the apostles experienced all this in accordance with the custom of their times without being corrupted, so those men of old, relating their treatment of women to the conventions of their times, did not tolerate the domination of lust, the lust which enslaves men who find all this incredible.

3.20.30. And so if they discovered that their wives or concubines had been accosted or violated by their sons, these men would be quite unable to restrain themselves from implacably hating them, supposing that something of this kind had happened to them.

3.21.30. But King David, when he suffered this at the hands of his wicked and brutal son, not only put up with his cruelty but even lamented his death.[55] He was not trapped in the net of carnal jealousy, since it was not his own injuries but the sins of his son that worried him. He had in fact deliberately given orders that if his son were overcome he should not be killed, so as to leave him some scope for repentance when overthrown.[56] After failing to save him he grieved over his son's death not

---

55. 2 Sam 16:22; 18:33.
56. 2 Sam 18:5.

because of his bereavement, but because he knew the penalties to which a soul guilty of such wicked adultery and murder was heading. For on the death of his earlier son (who was innocent) whose illness had been distressing him, he was pleased.[57]

3.21.31. The following episode makes it very clear what moderation and self-control those men showed towards women. The same king, his head turned by youthful passion and worldly success, unlawfully violated a woman after ordering her husband to be killed, and was accused by a prophet.[58] When he came to David to convict him of his sin, Nathan put to him the analogy of a poor man with one sheep, and a neighbor of the poor man, who, although he himself had several, nevertheless served his poor neighbor's one and only sheep to greet the arrival of a guest. This appalled King David, who ordered the neighbor to be killed and the poor man to be compensated for his sheep four times over—and so condemned himself unawares for the sin he was aware of having committed.[59] When apprised of this and warned of divine punishment he atoned for his sin by repentance.[60] But in this analogy it is only the sexual sin that is signaled by the sheep of the poor neighbor. David was not asked in this analogy about the murder of the woman's husband—the killing of the poor man himself, that is, with his single sheep—and so it was on his adultery alone that he issued his self-condemnatory verdict. From this one can infer the self-control with which he treated his many women, since in the case of the one woman with whom he had overstepped the limit he was compelled to punish himself. But in David's case there was no permanence to this extravagant lust, it was a passing phase; that is why

57. 2 Sam 12:15–23.
58. 2 Sam 11:2–5, 14–17; 12:7–12.
59. 2 Sam 12:1–6.
60. 2 Sam 12:13. Cf. Psalm 51.

his illicit appetite was called a "guest" by the prophet who convicted him.[61] He did not say that the man had offered his poor neighbor's sheep in a feast for his king, but for his "guest." But in David's son Solomon this lust was no guest paying a passing visit, but took over the whole kingdom. Scripture did not remain silent about this, but condemned him as a womanizer.[62] In his early life he had a passionate desire for wisdom;[63] but then, after gaining it through spiritual love, he lost it through carnal love.

3.22.32. So all, or nearly all, of the deeds contained in the books of the Old Testament are to be interpreted not only literally but also figuratively; but (in the case of those which the reader interprets literally) if agents are praised but their actions do not agree with the practices of the good men who since the Lord's coming in the flesh have been the guardians of the divine precepts, one should take up the figurative meaning into the understanding but not take over the deed itself into one's own behavior. Many things were done in those times out of duty which cannot be done now except out of lust.

On Christian Teaching 3.27.38–3.28.39

3.27.38. Sometimes not just one meaning but two or more meanings are perceived in the same words of Scripture. Even if the writer's meaning is obscure, there is no danger here, provided that it can be shown from other passages of the holy Scriptures that each of these interpretations is consistent with the truth. The person examining the divine utterances must of course do his best to arrive at the intention of the writer through whom the Holy Spirit produced that part of Scripture;

61. 2 Sam 12:4.
62. 1 Kgs 11:1–6.
63. 1 Kgs 3:7–9; 2 Chron 1:8–12.

he may reach that meaning or carve out from the words another meaning which does not run counter to the faith, using the evidence of any other passage of the divine utterances. Perhaps the author too saw that very meaning in the words which we are trying to understand. Certainly the spirit of God who worked through the author foresaw without any doubt that it would present itself to a reader or listener, or rather planned that it should present itself, because it too is based on the truth.[64] Could God have built into the divine eloquence a more generous or bountiful gift than the possibility of understanding the same words in several ways, all of them deriving confirmation from other no less divinely inspired passages?[65]

3.28.39. When one unearths an equivocal meaning which cannot be verified by unequivocal support from the holy Scriptures it remains for the meaning to be brought into the open by a process of reasoning, even if the writer whose words we are seeking to understand perhaps did not perceive it. But this practice is dangerous; it is much safer to operate within the divine Scriptures. When we wish to examine passages made obscure by metaphorical expressions, the result should be something which is beyond dispute or which, if not beyond dispute, can be settled by finding and deploying corroboratory evidence from within Scripture itself.

---

64. Cf. *Christian Teaching* 1.36.41 on the role of authorial intent in interpreting Scripture.
65. On the idea that the words of Scripture can convey multiple valid meanings, see also Augustine, *Confessions* 12.18.27–12.32.43.

15

John Cassian

John Cassian was born ca. 360 CE in Scythia, the region encompassed by the Danube River and the Black Sea. While still a young man perhaps in his early twenties (ca. 382), Cassian left behind his family's estate and traveled east together with a friend named Germanus in order to stay at a monastery in Bethlehem. Shortly afterward, Cassian and his friend journeyed to Egypt, desiring to learn about the monks in the Egyptian desert who lived the anchoritic life, that is, a solitary life withdrawn from the world. Cassian stayed in Egypt for at least ten years and probably more, absorbing everything he could from the monks in the desert. Sometime around 401 Cassian spent at least a year in Constantinople, where John Chrysostom ordained him a deacon. In 405 Cassian made his way to Rome carrying letters from the clergy of Constantinople, who were petitioning bishop Innocent of Rome to intervene on behalf of John Chrysostom during the latter's exile. Their efforts did not ultimately succeed, since Chrysostom died in exile in 407; but Cassian was ordained an elder while he was in Rome. Eventually Cassian settled at Marseille in Gaul ca. 415, where he established a monastery for men and another for women. He devoted the remainder of his life to overseeing these communities until his death ca. 435.

In his youth John Cassian received a solid classical education. He complained that his thoughts were sometimes led away to sin by the recollection of pagan literature, the best remedy for this ailment being meditation on sacred Scripture (*Conferences* 14.12–13). Among fifth-century Latin authors Cassian was one of the finest writers. Through his extensive travels he also attained fluency in Greek. Cassian's main purpose in his writings was to transmit the monastic traditions of Egypt to his Latin-speaking contemporaries. Between 420 and 428 Cassian wrote two works on monasticism: the *Institutes,* which in the first four books describes the customs of the Egyptian monks and in the final eight books treats the eight principal vices (gluttony, lust, greed, anger, melancholy, sloth, vainglory, and pride); and the *Conferences,* which is comprised of twenty-four discourses on various topics (for example: discretion, renunciation, prayer, and friendship) in which Cassian recounts the instruction he and Germanus received from specific Egyptian monks in the course of their numerous conversations. Cassian paints an idealistic picture of the devoted Christian saint who lives a solitary life away from the world (anchorite), but his appropriation of this tradition laid the groundwork for monastic communities that share all things (cf. Acts 2:14; 4:32), follow common disciplines, and live apart from the world in community (cenobites).

During his time in Egypt, Cassian learned theological piety in the tradition of Origen and was deeply influenced by Evagrius

Ponticus, from whom he borrowed many important concepts, such as the catalogue of eight vices (see Evagrius, *Praktikos* 6). In terms of his own theological writing, Cassian composed a treatise *On the Incarnation of the Lord, Against Nestorius,* in which he also sharply criticized Pelagius. Unlike Augustine, however, Cassian still allowed for some involvement of the human will in salvation. Moreover, in *Conferences* 13, "On God's Protection," Cassian offered an account of divine grace that was incompatible with Augustine's anti-Pelagian position. As a result, Cassian's views were censured by Prosper of Aquitaine, and Cassian's writings were rejected by the "Gelasian Decree," a somewhat prominent Latin text from the sixth century. Nevertheless, because of his positive reception among Latin authorities such as Isidore of Seville, Thomas Aquinas, and the Rule of St. Benedict, Cassian has been widely influential on western monasticism. Cassian has always been highly regarded in the eastern churches.

The following selection comes from chapter fourteen of the *Conferences,* which presents a conversation between Cassian, his friend Germanus, and a certain Egyptian monk Abba Nesteros ("Father" Nesteros), who speaks to the two young men on the topic of "spiritual knowledge," that is, the understanding and use of Scripture.

Conferences 14.1–3, 8

14.1.1. Both our promise and the sequence of our itinerary demand that the instruction of Abba Nesteros, a man of the highest knowledge and outstanding in every regard, should follow. When he heard that we had committed some parts of holy Scripture to memory and desired to understand them, he addressed us in words like these:

14.1.2. "There are indeed as many kinds of knowledge in this world as there are different sorts of arts and disciplines. But, although all are either completely useless or contribute something of value only to the present life, still there is not one that does not have its own order and method of instruction by which it can be grasped by those who are interested in it.

14.1.3. "If, then, those arts follow their own defined principles when they are taught, how much more does the teaching and profession of our religion, which is directed to contemplating the secrets of invisible mysteries rather than to present gain and which seeks instead the reward of eternal prizes, consist in a defined order and method. Its knowledge is in fact twofold. The first kind is *praktikē*, or practical, which reaches its fulfillment in correction of behavior and in cleansing from vice. The other is *theōrētikē*, which consists in the contemplation of divine things and in the understanding of most sacred meanings.[1]

14.2.1. "Whoever, therefore, wishes to attain to the *theōrētikē* must first pursue practical knowledge with all his strength and power. For the *praktikē* can be possessed without the theoretical, but the theoretical can never be seized without the practical. For certain steps have been arranged and distinguished in such a way that human lowliness can mount to the sublime. If these follow one another according to the method that we have mentioned, a person can attain to a

---

1. Cassian employs the Greek terms *praktikē* and *theōrētikē*. This basic distinction belongs to Aristotle, *Metaphysics* 2.1 (993b): "Moreover, philosophy is rightly called a knowledge of Truth. The object of theoretic [*theōrētikē*] knowledge is truth, while that of practical [*praktikē*] knowledge is action" (*Aristotle: Metaphysics, Books 1–9*, trans. Hugh Tredennick [LCL 271; Cambridge, MA: Harvard University Press, 1933], 87). The application of the term *praktikē* to Christian monasticism can be traced to Evagrius Ponticus, *Praktikos* 1: "Christianity is the dogma of Christ our Savior. It is composed of *praktikē*, of the contemplation of the physical world (*physikē*), and of the contemplation of God (*theologikē*)" (*Evagrius Ponticus: The Praktikos and the Chapters on Prayer*, trans. John E. Bamberger [Kalamazoo, MI: Cistercian, 1981], 15). For Cassian, *praktikē* refers to the practice of the spiritual life, and *theōrētikē* refers to contemplative spirituality.

height to which he cannot fly if the first step has not been taken. In vain, therefore, does someone who does not reject the contagion of vice strive for the vision of God.[2] 'For the Spirit of God hates deception, and it does not dwell in a body subject to sin.'[3]

14.3.1. "Now this practical perfection exists in a twofold form. Its first mode is that of knowing the nature of all the vices and the method of remedying them. The second is that of discerning the sequence of the virtues and forming our mind by their perfection in such a way that it is obedient to them not as if it were coerced and subjected to an arbitrary rule but as taking pleasure in and enjoying what is so to say a natural good, thus mounting with delight the hard and narrow way. For how will a person who does not understand the nature of his vices and has not striven to uproot them be able to attain either to the method of the virtues, which is the second step in practical discipline, or to the mysteries of spiritual and heavenly realities, which are found on the higher step of *theoria*?[4]

14.3.2. "It follows that a person who has not conquered the level places cannot progress to the heights, and much less will he grasp things that are outside himself if he has been unable to understand things that are within himself. Yet we should know that we must exert ourselves twice as hard to expel vice as to acquire virtue. We do not come to this by our own guesswork, but we are taught by the words of him who

---

2. On the need for a virtuous life in order to understand Scripture, see also Athanasius, *On the Incarnation* 57: "But in addition to the study and true knowledge of the Scriptures are needed a good life and pure soul and virtue in Christ, so that the mind, journeying in this path, may be able to obtain and apprehend what it desires, in so far as human nature is able to learn about God the Word. For without a pure mind and a life modeled on the saints, no one can apprehend the words of the saints" (*Athanasius: Contra Gentes and De Incarnatione*, trans. Robert W. Thomson [Oxford: Clarendon, 1971], 275).

3. Wisdom of Solomon 1:5, 4.

4. This is the Latin term *theoria*, "contemplation."

alone knows the ability and intelligence of what he has made: 'Behold,' he says, 'today I have set you over nations and over kingdoms, to root up and to pull down and to disperse and to scatter and to build and to plant.'[5]

14.3.3. "He has pointed out that four things are necessary for expelling what is harmful—namely, rooting up, pulling down, dispersing, and scattering. But for perfecting the virtues and for acquiring what pertains to righteousness there are only building and planting. Hence it is quite clear that it is more difficult to pluck out and eradicate the ingrown passions of body and soul than it is to gather and plant spiritual virtues.

14.8.1. "But let us return to discussing the knowledge that was spoken of at the beginning. As we said previously, the *praktikē* is dispersed among many professions and pursuits. The *theōrētikē*, on the other hand, is divided into two parts—that is, into historical interpretation and spiritual understanding. Hence, when Solomon had enumerated the different forms of grace in the Church, he added: 'All who are with her are doubly clothed.'[6] Now, there are three kinds of spiritual knowledge —tropology, allegory, and anagogy—about which it is said in Proverbs: 'But you describe those things for yourself in threefold fashion according to the largeness of your heart.'[7]

5. Jer 1:10.
6. Prov 31:21 in the Septuagint reads: "all who are with her are 'clothed' [from *endiduskō*]." A common word for "to clothe" in Greek is *enduō*, and the Old Latin translator of the Septuagint interpreted the *-di-* within this word (*en-di-duskō*) as the *di-* prefix that means "double." Therefore, in Cassian's Latin translation the text reads: "are doubly clothed" (*vestiti sunt dupliciter*).
7. Prov 22:20 according to the Septuagint. On this use of Proverbs 22:20, see Origen, *First Principles* 4.2.4. Unlike Origen, Cassian recognizes three spiritual senses beyond the historical sense, resulting in a total of four senses. A different paradigm involving four senses was suggested by Augustine, *The Usefulness of Believing* 5 (history, aetiology, analogy, allegory). The four senses of Scripture popular in the Latin Middle Ages are expressed in this epigram of Nicholas de Lyra (d. 1349): "The letter teaches events, allegory what you should believe, morality teaches what you should do, anagogy what mark you should be aiming for" (*Littera gesta docet, quid credas allegoria, moralis quid agas, quo tendas anagogia*); see Henri de Lubac, *Medieval Exegesis: The Four Senses of Scripture* (trans. Mark Sebanc; Grand Rapids: Eerdmans, 1998), 1:1.

14.8.2. "And so history embraces the knowledge of past and visible things, which is repeated by the Apostle thus: 'It is written that Abraham had two sons, one from a slave and the other from a free woman. The one from the slave was born according to the flesh, but the one from the free woman by promise.'[8] The things that follow belong to allegory, however, because what really occurred is said to have prefigured the form of another mystery. 'For these,' it says, 'are two covenants, one from Mount Sinai, begetting unto slavery, which is Hagar. For Sinai is a mountain in Arabia, which is compared to the Jerusalem that now is, and which is enslaved with her children.'[9]

14.8.3. "But anagogy, which mounts from spiritual mysteries to certain more sublime and sacred heavenly secrets, is added by the Apostle: 'But the Jerusalem from above, which is our mother, is free. For it is written: Rejoice, you barren one who do not bear, break out and shout, you who are not in labor, for the children of the desolate one are many more than of her who has a husband.'[10] Tropology is moral explanation pertaining to correction of life and to practical instruction, as if we understood these same two covenants as *praktikē* and as theoretical discipline, or at least as if we wished to take Jerusalem or Zion as the soul of the human being, according to the words: 'Praise the Lord, O Jerusalem; praise your God, O Zion.'[11]

14.8.4. "The four figures that have been mentioned

8. Gal 4:22–3.
9. Gal 4:24–25.
10. Gal 4:26–27.
11. Ps 147:12. Jerome, *Homily 57* (perhaps reflecting Origen), interprets Jerusalem as the ecclesiastical soul or the Church (*The Homilies of Saint Jerome*, trans. M. L. Ewald [FC 48; Washington, DC: Catholic University of America Press, 1964], 1:408–9). Chrysostom states that this verse addresses not the city but the inhabitants of the city (*St. John Chrysostom: Commentary on the Psalms*, trans. Robert C. Hill [Brookline, MA: Holy Cross Orthodox Press, 1998], 353).

converge in such a way that, if we want, one and the same Jerusalem can be understood in a fourfold manner. According to history it is the city of the Jews. According to allegory it is the Church of Christ. According to anagogy it is that heavenly city of God 'which is the mother of us all.'[12] According to tropology it is the soul of the human being, which under this name is frequently either reproached or praised by the Lord. Of these four kinds of interpretation the blessed Apostle says thus: 'Now, brothers, if I come to you speaking in tongues, what use will it be to you unless I speak to you by revelation or by knowledge or by prophecy or by instruction?'[13]

14.8.5. "Now, 'revelation' pertains to allegory, by which the things that the historical narrative conceals are laid bare by a spiritual understanding and explanation. Suppose, for example, that we tried to make clear how 'all our fathers were under the cloud, and all were baptized in Moses in the cloud and in the sea, and all ate the same spiritual food and drank the same spiritual drink from the rock that followed them. And the rock was Christ.'[14] This explanation, which refers to the prefiguration of the body and blood of Christ that we daily receive, comprises an allegorical approach.

14.8.6. "But 'knowledge,' which is also mentioned by the Apostle, is tropology, by which we discern by a prudent examination everything that pertains to practical discretion, in order to see whether it is useful and good, as when we are ordered to judge for ourselves 'whether it befits a woman to pray to God with unveiled head.'[15] This approach, as has been said, comprises a moral understanding.

---

12. Gal 4:26.
13. 1 Cor 14:6. The four key words in this verse, "revelation" (= allegory), "knowledge" (= tropology), "prophecy" (= anagogy), and "instruction" (= history), are correlated to Cassian's four senses of Scripture.
14. 1 Cor 10:1–4.
15. 1 Cor 11:13.

"Likewise, 'prophecy,' which the Apostle introduced in the third place, bespeaks anagogy, by which words are directed to the invisible and to what lies in the future, as in this case: 'We do not want you to be ignorant, brothers, about those who are asleep, so that you may not be saddened like others who have no hope. For if we believe that Christ has died and has arisen, so also God will bring those who have fallen asleep in Jesus with him. For we say this to you by the word of the Lord, that we who are alive at the coming of the Lord shall not anticipate those who have fallen asleep in Christ, for the Lord himself shall descend from heaven with a command, with the voice of an angel and with the trumpet of God, and the dead who are in Christ shall arise first.'[16] **14.8.7.** The figure of anagogy appears in this kind of exhortation.

"But 'instruction' lays open the simple sequence of a historical exposition in which there is no more hidden meaning than what is comprised in the sound of the words, as in this case: 'I delivered to you first what I also received, that Christ died for our sins according to the Scriptures, that he was buried on the third day, and that he was seen by Cephas.'[17] And: 'God sent his Son, made of woman, made under the law, to save those who were under the law.'[18] And this: 'Hear, O Israel: The Lord your God is one Lord.'"[19]

16. 1 Thess 4:13–16.
17. 1 Cor 15:3–5.
18. Gal 4:4–5.
19. Deut 6:4.

Bibliography

Primary Sources

Augustine. *Christian Teaching*. Published as *Saint Augustine: On Christian Teaching*. Translated by R. P. H. Green. Oxford World's Classics. Oxford: Oxford University Press, 1999.

Barnabas, Epistle of. Pages 177–98 in *The Apostolic Fathers in English*. Edited and translated by Michael W. Holmes. 3rd ed. Grand Rapids: Baker Academic, 2006.

Cyprian. *To Quirinus: Testimonies against the Jews*. Pages 507–57 in *The Ante-Nicene Fathers, Vol. 5: Hippolytus, Cyprian, Caius, Novatian, Appendix*. Edited by Alexander Roberts and James Donaldson. Revised by A. Cleveland Coxe. Buffalo: Christian Literature, 1886. Reprint, Grand Rapids: Eerdmans, 1971.

Diodore of Tarsus. *Prologue to Psalm 118*. Pages 87–94 in *Biblical Interpretation in the Early Church*. Edited and translated by Karlfried Froehlich. Sources of Early Christian Thought. Philadelphia: Fortress Press, 1984.

Ephrem the Syrian. *Hymns on Paradise*. Published as *St. Ephrem the Syrian: Hymns on Paradise*. Translated by Sebastian Brock. Crestwood, NY: St. Vladimir's Seminary Press, 1990.

Eusebius. *Commentary on Isaiah*. Published as *Eusebius of Caesarea:*

Commentary on Isaiah. Translated by Jonathan J. Armstrong. Ancient Christian Texts. Downers Grove, IL: InterVarsity, 2013.

Gregory of Nyssa. *The Life of Moses.* Published as *Gregory of Nyssa: The Life of Moses.* Translated by Abraham J. Malherbe and Everett Ferguson. HarperCollins Spiritual Classics. New York: HarperCollins, 2006.

Irenaeus. *Against Heresies,* Book 1. Published as *St. Irenaeus of Lyons: Against the Heresies, Book 1.* Translated by Dominic J. Unger. Revised by John J. Dillon. Ancient Christian Writers 55. New York: Newman, 1992.

_____. *Against Heresies,* Book 3. Published as *St. Irenaeus of Lyons: Against the Heresies, Book 3.* Translated by Dominic J. Unger. Revised by Matthew C. Steenberg. Ancient Christian Writers 64. New York: Newman, 2012.

_____. *Against Heresies,* Book 4. Pages 462–525 in *The Ante-Nicene Fathers, Vol. 1: The Apostolic Fathers, Justin Martyr, Irenaeus.* Edited by Alexander Roberts and James Donaldson. Revised by A. Cleveland Coxe. Buffalo: Christian Literature, 1885. Reprint, Grand Rapids: Eerdmans, 1971.

Jerome. *Commentary on Jeremiah.* Published as *Jerome: Commentary on Jeremiah.* Translated by Michael Graves. Ancient Christian Texts. Downers Grove, IL: InterVarsity, 2011.

John Cassian. *The Conferences.* Published as *John Cassian: The Conferences.* Translated by Boniface Ramsey. Ancient Christian Writers 57. New York: Newman, 1997.

John Chrysostom. *Homilies on Genesis.* Published as *St. John Chrysostom: Homilies on Genesis 1–17.* Translated by Robert C. Hill. Fathers of the Church 74. Washington, DC: Catholic University of America Press, 1986.

_____. *Homily on the Words of Paul: "I Do Not Want You to Be Ignorant."* Pages 241–52 in vol. 51 of *Patrologia Graeca.* Edited by J. P. Migne. Paris: Imprimerie Catholique, 1862.

Justin Martyr. *Dialogue with Trypho.* Published as *St. Justin Martyr: Dialogue with Trypho.* Edited by Michael Slusser. Translated by Thomas B. Falls. Revised by Thomas P. Halton. Washington, DC: Catholic University of America Press, 2003.

Origen. *First Principles.* Published as *Origen: On First Principles.* Translated by G. W. Butterworth. New York: Harper & Row, 1966.

Tertullian. *On Baptism.* Published as *Tertullian's Homily on Baptism.* Translated by Ernest Evans. London: SPCK, 1964.

_____. *Prescription against Heretics.* Pages 35–96 in *Tertullian: On the Testimony of the Soul and on the "Prescription" of Heretics.* Translated by T. Herbert Bindley. London: SPCK, 1914.

Theodore of Mopsuestia. *Commentary on the Psalms.* Published as *Theodore of Mopsuestia: Commentary on Psalms 1-81.* Translated by Robert C. Hill. Writings from the Greco-Roman World. Atlanta: Society of Biblical Literature, 2006.

_____. *Against the Allegorists.* Published as *Théodore de Mopsueste: Fragments syriaques du Commentaire des Psaumes.* Edited by Lucas Van Rompay. Corpus Scriptorum Christianorum Orientalium 435. Leuven: Peeters, 1982.

_____. *Commentary on the Twelve Prophets.* Published as *Theodore of Mopsuestia: Commentary on the Twelve Prophets.* Translated by Robert C. Hill. Fathers of the Church 108. Washington, DC: Catholic University of America Press, 2004.

Secondary Literature

Anderson, R. Dean, Jr. *Glossary of Greek Rhetorical Terms.* Leuven: Peeters, 2000.

Arnold, Duane W. H., and Pamela Bright, eds. *De doctrina christiana: A Classic of Western Culture.* Notre Dame, IN: University of Notre Dame Press, 1995.

Ashby, G. W. *Theodoret of Cyrrhus as Exegete of the Old Testament.* Grahamstown, South Africa: Rhodes University, 1972.

Baghos, Mario. "The Conflicting Portrayals of Origen in the Byzantine Tradition." *Phronema* 30 (2015): 69–104.

Balás, David L. Μετουσία Θεοῦ: *Man's Participation in God's Perfections According to Saint Gregory of Nyssa.* Studia Anselmiana 55. Rome: IBC Libreria Herder, 1966.

Bamberger, John E., trans. *Evagrius Ponticus: The Praktikos and the Chapters on Prayer.* Kalamazoo, MI: Cistercian, 1981.

Behr, John. *The Case against Diodore and Theodore: Texts and Their Contexts.* Oxford: Oxford University Press, 2011.

Bonnardière, Anne-Marie. "The Canon of Scripture." Pages 26–41 in *Augustine and the Bible.* Edited and translated by Pamela Bright. Notre Dame, IN: University of Notre Dame Press, 1986.

Briggs, Charles. *A Critical and Exegetical Commentary on the Book of Psalms.* International Critical Commentary. New York: Scribner's, 1907.

Bright, Pamela, ed. and trans. *Augustine and the Bible.* Notre Dame, IN: University of Notre Dame Press, 1986.

Brock, Sebastian. *The Harp of the Spirit: Eighteen Poems of Saint Ephrem.* 2nd ed. San Bernardino, CA: Borgo, 1984.

Cain, Andrew, and Josef Lössl, eds. *Jerome of Stridon: His Life, Writings and Legacy.* Farnham, UK: Ashgate, 2009.

Cameron, Michael. *Christ Meets Me Everywhere: Augustine's Early Figurative Exegesis.* Oxford: Oxford University Press, 2012.

Cherniss, Harold Frederik. *The Platonism of Gregory of Nyssa.* New York: Franklin, 1930.

Crouzel, H., and E. Prinzivalli. "Origen." Pages 977–83 in vol. 2 of *Encyclopedia of Ancient Christianity.* Edited by A. Di Berardino. Downers Grove, IL: InterVarsity, 2014.

Daniélou, Jean. *From Shadows to Reality: Studies in the Biblical Typology of the Fathers.* Translated by Wulstan Hibberd. London: Burns & Oates, 1960.

Dindorf, G. *Scholia Graeca in Homeri Odysseam.* Oxford, 1855.

Ernest, James D. *The Bible in Athanasius of Alexandria.* Leiden: Brill, 2004.

Ferguson, Everett. *The Rule of Faith: A Guide.* Eugene, OR: Cascade, 2015.

Friedländer, M., trans. *Moses Maimonides: The Guide for the Perplexed.* 2nd ed. London: Routledge, 1904.

Graves, Michael. *The Inspiration and Interpretation of Scripture.* Grand Rapids: Eerdmans, 2014.

_____. *Jerome's Hebrew Philology.* Leiden: Brill, 2007.

_____. "The Literary Quality of Scripture as Seen by the Early Church." *Tyndale Bulletin* 61 (2010): 161–82.

_____. "The 'Pagan' Background of Patristic Exegetical Methods." Pages 93–109 in *Ancient Faith for the Church's Future.* Edited by M. Husbands and J. P. Greenman. Downers Grove, IL: InterVarsity, 2008.

Greer, Rowan. *Theodore of Mopsuestia: Exegete and Theologian.* Westminster, UK: Faith Press, 1961.

Griffith, Sidney. *'Faith Adoring the Mystery': Reading the Bible with St. Ephrem the Syrian.* Milwaukee: Marquette University Press, 1997.

Harrison, Nonna Verna. "Women and the Image of God according to St. John Chrysostom." Pages 259–79 in *In Dominico Eloquio. In Lordly Eloquence: Essays on Patristic Exegesis in Honor of Robert Louis Wilken.* Edited by P. M. Blowers, A. R. Christman, D. G. Hunter, and R. D. Young. Grand Rapids: Eerdmans, 2002.

Hays, Robert Stephen. "Lucius Annaeus Cornutus' *Epidromē* (Introduction to the Traditions of Greek Theology): Introduction, Translation, and Notes." PhD dissertation, University of Texas at Austin, 1983.

Heine, Ronald. *Origen: Scholarship in Service of the Church.* Oxford: Oxford University Press, 2010.

Hill, Robert C. "*Akribeia:* A Principle of Chrysostom's Exegesis." *Colloquium* 14 (1981): 32–36.

_____. *Reading the Old Testament in Antioch.* Leiden: Brill, 2005.

Hollerich, M. J. *Eusebius of Caesarea's* Commentary on Isaiah: *Christian Exegesis in the Age of Constatine.* Oxford Early Christian Studies. Oxford: Clarendon, 1999.

Jackson, Pamela. "Eucharist." Pages 330–34 in *Augustine Through the Ages: An Encyclopedia.* Edited by Allan D. Fitzgerald. Grand Rapids: Eerdmans, 1999.

Kamesar, Adam. "The Evaluation of the Narrative Aggada in Greek and Latin Patristic Literature." *Journal of Theological Studies* 45 (1994): 37–71.

Kamptner, M. "Testimonies, Collections of." Pages 558–59 in *Dictionary of Early Christian Literature.* Edited by S. Döpp and W. Geerlings. New York: Crossroad, 2000.

Kannengiesser, Charles, ed. *Handbook of Patristic Exegesis: The Bible in Ancient Christianity.* 2 Volumes. Leiden: Brill, 2004.

Kelly, J. N. D. *Golden Mouth. The Story of John Chrysostom: Ascetic, Preacher, Bishop.* Ithaca, NY: Cornell University Press, 1995.

Kennedy, George A. *A New History of Classical Rhetoric.* Princeton: Princeton University Press, 1994.

Kerrigan, Alexander. *St. Cyril of Alexandria: Interpreter of the Old Testament.* Rome: Pontifical Biblical Institute, 1952.

Lange, N. de. *Origen and the Jews.* Cambridge: Cambridge University Press, 1976.

Lauro, Elizabeth Ann Dively. *The Soul and Spirit of Scripture within Origen's Exegesis.* Leiden: Brill, 2005.

Lubac, Henri de. *Medieval Exegesis: The Four Senses of Scripture.* Translated by Mark Sebanc. Grand Rapids: Eerdmans, 1998.

Manetti, Giovanni. *Theories of the Sign in Classical Antiquity.* Translated by C. Richardson. Bloomington: Indiana University Press, 1993.

Martens, Peter W. *Origen and Scripture: The Contours of the Exegetical Life.* Oxford: Oxford University Press, 2012.

McLeod, Frederick. *Theodore of Mopsuestia.* The Early Church Fathers. London: Routledge, 2009.

_____. "Theodore of Mopsuestia Revisited." *Theological Studies* 61 (2000): 447–80.

Miller, Patricia Cox. *Women in Early Christianity: Translations from Greek Texts.* Washington, DC: Catholic University of America Press, 2005.

Quasten, J. *Patrology.* 4 Volumes. Allen, TX: Christian Classics, 1995.

Rajak, Tessa. "Talking at Trypho: Christian Apologetic as Anti-Judaism in Justin's *Dialogue with Trypho the Jew.*" Pages 59–80 in *Apologetics in the Roman Empire: Pagans, Jews, and Christians.* Edited by M. J. Edwards, M. Edwards, S. Price, and C. Rowland. Oxford: Clarendon, 1999.

Rebenich, Stefan. *Jerome.* The Early Church Fathers. London and New York: Routledge, 2002.

Sheridan, Mark. *Language for God in Patristic Tradition: Wrestling with Biblical Anthropomorphism.* Downers Grove, IL: InterVarsity, 2015.

Simonetti, Manlio. *Biblical Interpretation in the Early Church: A Historical Introduction to Patristic Exegesis.* Translated by John A. Hughes. Edinburgh: T&T Clark, 1994.

Skarsaune, Oskar. *The Proof from Prophecy. Studies in Justin Martyr's Proof-Text Tradition: Text-Type, Provenance, Theological Profile.* Supplements to Vetus Testamentum 5. Leiden: Brill, 1987.

Sterling, Gregory E. "'The Jewish Philosophy': Reading Moses via Hellenistic Philosophy according to Philo." Pages 129–54 in *Reading Philo: A Handbook to Philo of Alexandria.* Edited by T. Seland. Grand Rapids: Eerdmans, 2014.

Stern, Jacob, trans. *Palaephatus: On Unbelievable Tales.* Wauconda, IL: Bolchazy-Carducci, 1996.

Thomson, Robert, trans. *Athanasius: Contra Gentes and De Incarnatione.* Oxford: Clarendon, 1971.

Toom, Tarmo. "Augustine's Hermeneutics: The Science of Divinely Given Signs." Pages 77–108 in *Patristic Theories of Biblical Interpretation: The Latin Fathers.* Edited by Tarmo Toom. Cambridge: Cambridge University Press, 2016.

Tredennick, Hugh, trans. *Aristotle: Metaphysics, Books 1–9.* Loeb Classical Library 271. Cambridge, MA: Harvard University Press, 1933.

Usher, M. D. *Homeric Stitchings: The Homeric Centos of the Empress Eudocia.* Lanham, MD: Rowman & Littlefield, 1998.

Wilken, Robert L. "The Homeric Cento in Irenaeus, '*Adversus haereses*' 1.9.4." *Vigiliae Christianae* 21 (1967): 25–33.

Name and Subject Index

Scripture Index

Ancient Authors and Works Index